# BULL PEN CHRONICLES

I-Witnessed Brouhaha of a Stony Mountain Game Warden

## STEPHEN H. PORTER

# DEDICATION

For Betsy, my brown-eyed tequila girl, my darlin' companion, graciously enduring my eccentric avocations of answering the calls of the wild.

Understand, you are the foundation of what I require more than anything; love, support, a warm home and loving family. You are always on my mind.

## "CHERISH IS THE WORD"

# WARNING SHOT!

**"As sure as stink on skunk, all ensuing scrawl transpired!"**

However, nothing can be perceived as the rock-hard truth. These loosely stitched adventures document a coverlet of bygone days I remember. The stories are authentic yet melded, gelded, blended, and distorted to tarnish no one. Names of the lawless have been severely ravaged to protect whatever innocence the shamefaced may possess. Personal behavioral traits are guardedly accurate to maintain the attributes of those playing the outdoor games. My writings are purposely written to entertain the innocent, bamboozle the illicit, torture the blameworthy and terrorize the fanatical. My oft delusionary memories of names and places, the mix-matching of events with truths and half-truths, and my premeditated embellishment obliterates all tracks of individuality while revealing the character of hunters and fishermen found anywhere.

Undoubtedly, some will seek themselves in this book; they may very well be. However, there is no mirror image of any one person, only reflections of those crossing paths with a wandering boy, hunter, and Colorado District Wildlife Manager, during the last half of the 20th century. If you think you see yourself or someone you know, consider it merely personal paranoia, although such illusions may shed light on who you or they are, once were, or could become.

That said, I would never let veracity get in the way of a good story!

"Every journey into the past is complicated by delusions, false memories, false namings of real events." **Adrienne Rich**

"That's the way the stick floats!"

Stephen H. Porter

# CONTENTS

Note to Reader x

1. FRONT SIGHT 1
2. Arakun Hunt 8
3. Ode to the Mexican – Aught Five 15
4. Ashes to Ashes, Dust to Dust??? 23
5. Bishop Tricks 27
6. A Fly Full Of Worm-Dirt 32
7. Cletus B. Black 35
8. Dog Bites 39
9. Fowl Play 41
10. Home Runs – Private Places For A Secretive Mind. 44
11. They Shoot Moose, Don't They? 57
12. Moose Drool 62
13. Grandma's Mantra 65
14. Unforgiven Trespasses 72
15. Lap Dog 78
16. Dogs and Their Best Friends 80
17. Beadhead Renegade 89
18. In A Rut 93
19. Beetle 96
20. Aschews 100
21. Two Ledge Tales 106
22. Two Balls In The Side Pocket 117
23. Reign On The Roaring Fork 121
24. There's A Little Pig In Everyone! 123
25. Field Oscar 129
26. Ridin' Herd On Dead Horse 134
27. Bearly Trapped 138
28. Chumbums 143
29. The Rogues Of Rosebud 148
30. Whether Or Not! 157
31. Goose Flats 159
32. Dorothy And The Wizard 161
33. Dancin' With The Devil In The Pale Moonlight 165

34. Piscatory Math                                        175
35. Two 'Moos' For Brother Vicar                          178
36. Restless Natives                                      184
37. Wilhelm– Telling Overtures of a Pilfering Nimrod      188
38. Clothes Lined                                         199
39. Foggy Mountain Breakdown                              202
40. Pounding Sand                                         208
41. Willy Peonya                                          211
42. Shaggy Maned Fungus Eater                             215
43. Baker's Dozen                                         218
44. Shepherd's Purse                                      227
45. Wassailor                                             229
46. One Percent                                           233
47. Tommie Foolery                                        240
48. Shorty's Wyakin                                       243
49. Lunch Take                                            246
50. Surefire Bet                                          248
51. Mexican Ridge Twenty Aught 06                         250
52. HindSight                                             255

About the Author                                          261
Acknowledgments                                           264

# AND THE WARDEN SAID, "I'LL CATCH YOU LATER!"

# NOTE TO READER

MAKE NO MISTAKE! The following tales are not written to tarnish the shining image of hunters and fishermen. They are a celebration of the success stories of wildlife officers working FOR the 90% good, those noble men and women who honor the outdoors and the wild by doing it right, AGAINST the 10% bad, those blameworthy miscreants who defile the sports and the wild by doing it wrong.

**SHP**

# FRONT SIGHT

*"Oh! that my young life were a lasting dream!*
EdgarAllan Poe "Dreams"

The force of nature energizing these writings began, naturally so, with an adventuresome boy wandering the northwest Ohio outback. Lured by persuasive cravings to probe the outdoor world, I reflexively began pursuing dreams yet dreamt, feelings yet felt, and knowledge yet discovered. I was, and still am, driven to answer nature's primal calls by seeking out and questioning HER infinite mysteries. NATURE is intricate deeply intertwined into my nature.

AND THERE I WAS! five years young in a mid-city neighborhood, 'cowboyed up' as Roy Rogers patrolling my home range for anything out of order. Spying an errant robin perched on a branch of a towering front yard maple, I gave ample warning before firing a string of caps from my pot metal 'six guns'. The red-breasted invader chirped and returned fire with a startlingly accurate 'potshot', depositing a white-washing load of crap onto the center of my forehead. As distressed young cowboys always do, I retreated to Mom, articulating a woeful tale as the black and white gooey glob tracked down the inside corner of a closed eye to the bottom of my nose. Mother, firmly wiping my face with a rank dish rag, smilingly answered without pause, "You probably deserved it." This was not the compassion I was seeking, and her words mysteriously haunt my thoughts to this very day!

My yearnings to explore the wilds intensified with successive moves: to a neighborhood bordering Ohio farmland; to a rural rental farmhouse; and a final move in the early 60's to an older, warmly comfortable countryside home on three acres. Journeys across croplands tracking weedy fence-lines, wading creeks and ditches, and investigating woodlands nurtured my innate yearning for adventure, freedom, independence and a recurring need to be, at times, alone and away. I was born under a wandering star

*"Not all those who wander are lost."*
**— J.R.R. Tolkien, The Fellowship of the Ring**

Entering my teens my voyaging stimulated an inherent impulse to hunt 'varmints' of all kinds. Hunting small game further intensified my allure to the wilds. I became a disciple of the Jack O'Conner era (I hunt with .270 Winchesters to this day) fervently studying stories of savvy outdoorsmen penning their adventures in stunning detail, sending my outdoor interests into an overpowering addiction. Reading Outdoor Life, Louis L'Amour, Gene Hill, Zane Grey etc. plus a preponderance of TV cowboy shows enticed a strong attraction to the mysticism of West, including the Native American Cultures. As a high school senior discovering certain colleges and universities offered degrees in wildlife biology, I chose the 'road less traveled' and 'jumped off' westward.

*"If you come to a fork in the road, take it."* Yogi Berra

Completing a year at Utah State University, I married my farm girl sweetheart, and, like two unguided missiles, we launched west with great expectations.

Two summers of rangeland inventory with the Forest Service in

Wyoming's Grey's River and another with the Utah Division of Wildlife in the Book Cliffs, I found myself in living heaven! Turned down for permanent employment with Utah for religious idiocrasies, I reluctantly accepted a position as a wildlife biologist with the U.S. Fish and Wildlife Service in North Carolina. Suffering through the unfamiliar southern culture less than a year, I zealously mailed dozens of applications to western states, finally landing a job as a Wildlife Conservation Officer in Colorado. Following a year of intensive classroom training and statewide field assignments, I asked for and was granted a district assignment in the remote, sparsely populated, mountainous wilds of North Park, Colorado. Armed with a ticket book, badge and six gun, I was instructed to strictly and fairly enforce wildlife law while, at the same time, cultivate a working relationship with the local populace.

Our move to this massive, high elevation sagebrush Park bordered by forest rimmed by granite peaks, was a no-brainer for me but undeniably a wary risk for my rural Ohio wife. However, our 'New Park' gradually provided the life stimulating riches of raising a family in this secluded mountain valley. Interweaving strong family bonds with good friends and ardent community relationships sanctioned discovering self, purpose, and a strong sense of place, affording unlimited personal and professional fortunes. We were rich!

Blazing warden trails throughout my slice of the 'Stony Mountains', ghosting ridges, creeks and lakes across untrammeled wilds, I contacted the unsuspecting and counted coupe on the outdoor bad. I worked tirelessly for the outdoor majority; those hunting and fishing conservationists wisely, ethically and legally utilizing nature's bounty. Words cannot express the internal passion of protecting Colorado's wildlife resource, a noble vocation indeed! I salute the worldwide corps of warden warriors relentlessly obsessed by the fiery drive to protect the wild.

Frequent journeys seemingly somewhere close to nowhere, I began scribing my adventures for personal satisfaction as memoirs for myself and family.

*"Better to write for yourself and have no public than to write for the public and have no self."* **Cyril Connolly**

However, as my career and personal hunting and fishing experience evolved, so did my purpose. Stalking both sides of the fence as a hunter/fisherman and a wildlife officer provided special insights for understanding the mental psyche of outdoor sportsmen. My focus expanded to the more complex issues of analyzing human outdoor (mis)behavior as well as documenting the diversified personal and societal values tendered by the outdoor sports. I soon realized my words may carry a message to all having an insatiable love for the furtive wild, whether or not they hunt or fish. By listening to endless stories told by the old-time game wardens, I understood the great loss of not documenting their roles in the evolution of Colorado's wildlife history. Thus, what began as writings for personal pleasure, evolved into essays to optimistically stimulate the thoughts of all cherishing the wild.

So many times, during my career as a wildlife law enforcement officer I was told I should write a book. Many friends thoroughly enjoyed the unceasing stories of my wildland escapades. The idea of a book always there, I began giving it serious thought upon retirement, only to find myself stumbling through a maze of scribbled notes, rough drafts, and formal manuscripts having no semblance of order, and overwhelmed by the complexity of the writing task at hand. After a very slow start, inspiration driven perseverance began paying dividends as I bundled drafts into chapters revealing the essence of men and women interacting with the wild. Waiting until the ripe age of 68 proffered the time and seasoned perspective necessary for analyzing my compositions, I finally experienced the overwhelming joy of writing with commitment and purpose.

My chronicles are passionately scripted as an endorsement for hunting, fishing and trapping across the North American Continent; my heartfelt endowment for the adventurous career sportsmen's license dollars provided me. My crosshairs are focused on the perpetuation of the outdoor sports as a meaningful, moral and ethical form of recreation serving, since early in the twentieth century, as the foundation for protecting our country's rich and diverse wildlife heritage. Expectantly, they may illuminate and promote the hunting and fishing majority as valuable members of society recognized not only as those harvesting game and fish, but also the tried and true conservationists actively sustaining our wildlife heritage. Whatever side of the law hunters and fishermen choose, their license fees, plus associated excises on fishing and hunting equipment, have provided funding for creating the most successful and sustainable plan for wildlife management in the world – the North American Model of Wildlife Conservation. North American hunters and fishermen, beginning in the 1860's, were among the first to crusade for wildlife protection. More importantly, they remain the steadfast leaders for sustainable conservation of all wildlife for all people (secured by Supreme Court Decisions of the Public Trust Doctrine, the pillar of North American Conservation, dictating wildlife belongs to the people to be managed in trust for the people by government agencies).

The time of these dissertations ticked during my watch as a Colorado State District Wildlife Manager ('game warden') stationed in what Native Americans called the 'Bull Pen' because of its historically large population of bison, especially the number of overwintering bulls.

Painting experiences into words will hopefully canvas your imagination with portraits of the varied faces worn by hunters and fishermen. Flavored throughout with humor – simmering the satirical agony and ecstasy of human behavior in the wild's gamey sauce – emphasizes nothing is so farfetched, so humorous, so human, as the conscience-comforting rationalizations of those entangled in the angst of their own misdeeds. My cache of memories are not an egotistical crowing of a herculean warden capturing felonious outdoor miscreants. The lead role is not the warden, but the galaxy of starring characters encountered; unique personalities glowing in their own eccentric charm. Exposing human beings exercising the natural phenomena of being human affords realistic glimpses into their very core. Spiced with my experiences as a hunter and fisherman, my writings may aid in defining the great personal satisfaction these sports offer. My messages are not only for the majority good, the ethical responsibly exercising their hunting and fishing privileges, but also for the bad and ugly occasionally or habitually doing it wrong: the man with too many fish who referred to me as an asshole pig; the man with an illegal elk bluff charging with clench fists calling me a cocky son of a bitchin' banty-rooster; the woman with illegal fish in her purse insinuating I did not have a legal father; the man wanting to go for his gun until I was able to talk him down...

Personal life's lessons are often ignored, rarely documented and ultimately forever lost. My experiences, never duplicated or taken away, are me; a man carrying a tremendous, ever-increasing reverence for the wild beasts. My successes, if any, come from patience and persistence rather than greatness. There are 'wardens' across the world whose endeavors greatly exceed my own. There is a book within every warden; as many stories as there are hunters and fishermen; outdoor adventures to be told, retold and embellished to entertain and captivate young and old alike.

I have always said:

*'there are a million stories in the naked woods.'*

The voyage was more than I could have ever imagined, the sum far exceeding its parts. It was the journey, not the destination, making it all worthwhile!

If what follows is as stimulating to the reader as it has been for the writer, I will be twice blessed. I cordially invite you to join me, Stephen H. Porter, as a hunter and fisherman and a wandering warden travelling his scripted passageways playing the wild game of stalking human and wild beasts. Every tale has a lurking message, waiting to be flushed and harvested to stimulate your thoughts. Good hunting!

So mother, you were right! My lifetime opportunities, experiences, goals, and achievements were, for the most part, hard-earned and well-deserved. Working under My God as His force of nature, I was given personal insights for crafting my destiny with sensible decisions and hard work. Fate, luck, and chance played their roles as Betsy and I designed our life's strategies. The freedom and independence of formulating our personal game plan and living its consequences is how we survived – a meaningful life the American way! Marrying the most wonderful girl in the entire world – one who accepted and fully supported me despite my many flaws – unremittingly continues to be the wisest decision of my life. Raising two fantastic children, Marc and Anne, in our Walden home, both successfully chasing down their own vision quests, further rewarded us with their spouses and five wonderful grandchildren. So, a decision as a young lad to hunt and fish led to a most honorable avocation of protecting and managing Colorado's rich wildlife resources supporting the personal wealth only a family can provide. I am a blessed man indeed!

The book defines the essence of my being; the most thought out, long term challenge of my life. My pleasure will come from those who read, enjoy, and comprehend its purpose, my fear will come from those who do not.

Understand,
**I HAD TO WRITE THESE CHRONICLES!**

# ARAKUN HUNT

Arakun (*aroughcoune; ahrak-coon-em*): Algonquin Native
American for raccoon meaning 'he who scratches, rubs, scrubs
with his hands'. Procyon (before the dog) lotor (washes):
scientific name for raccoon.

As a teenage lad, I thrived in rural Northwestern Ohio with my
parents and three sisters in an old, two-story countryside house
surrounded by fields of grain, hay, pastures, and woodlands laced with
creeks, brushy runs and fence rows. Large, traditional farmhouses with
siloed barns were economically tied to small agriculturally founded
villages. At 16, I was stalwart enough to handle the arduous labor
offered by my neighbor Gene Line, a vivacious farmer raising hogs,
cultivating crops, and custom baling hay and straw. Gene, and his
hardy father Marvin, infused a robust work ethic launching employment opportunities throughout my life.

Gene and compadres Bob McClelland, Jerry Beach, and 'Coon' Joe
Romick were my legendary childhood heroes; prosperous, hard
working men always finding time to play brutally competitive barn

basketball, follow local high school sports and relentlessly execute practical jokes on anyone and everyone. They were also hardcore members of the local raccoon hunting community. In those days hounding coons was a popular form of rural recreation for pest control and marketing the fur of these pervasively pesky critters. Raccoons, omnivorous carnivores consuming virtually any plant or animal material, fervently wreak havoc on croplands, stored grain, gardens and poultry. Often occupying outbuildings, marking them with an abundance of granular spiked fecal spoor, they relentlessly earn a reputation as troublesome vermin.

I vividly recall hearing through an open bedroom window the August night chitter-chatter of raccoons raiding the family's sweet corn patch days before picking. Prices for their thick winter pelts never covered costs of agriculture damages or the expenses of feeding the hunting hounds. Profits were made only by skilled trappers having the time to harvest large numbers when fur prices were high. However, sport hunting raccoons in those days provided adventuresome nocturnal pursuit of the ring-tailed masked bandits during fall and early winter.

Summertime in the 1960's offered the extremely popular 'off season' coon dog trials held in nearby Kenton, Ohio where hounds competed by racing a caged raccoon through water raceways and over land to ascertain the prestigious title of champion. It was a time for the coon hunting gentry, aka rednecks, to gather and exercise their passion for the chase, guns and hounds in a 'swappin' trader row, flea market atmosphere. For a teenage boy it was a spirited sporting paradise of pretty girls, hounds, and free flowing booze. In those days these trials were a big deal, characterizing a culturally significant community event well attended by bands of rustic sportsmen tightly wrapped in tradition, rural independence and true American pride. *Did I mention pretty girls?* Sadly coon hunting, once deeply woven into the cultural fabric of the Midwest, has all but disappeared.

Known throughout the neighborhood for my prowess in assassinating wayward woodchucks, farmers often contacted me to eradicate any and all pests – pigeons, starlings, sparrows, groundhogs, and raccoons. Some rewarded me with bricks of .22 ammo, although my inherent motivation was the hunting adventure, not economics. Gene, aware of my hunting obsession, flagged me down one fall afternoon during my routine four-mile after school run and invited me to their nighttime coon hunt. Thus, began my membership into the local coon hunting corps where I quickly became hooked by the out-and-out thrill of releasing hounds into the darkness, leisurely driving country roads with frequent stops to echolocate and interpret the hounds bawling barks. Every dog sang its own song, changing tune heralding whether hunting for scent, on scent, or treeing a raccoon. The pedigreed assortment of Black and Tans, Redbones, Blue Ticks and an occasional illicit crossbreed provided pompous swagger for their owners deciphering the drawling bays of their night-veiled hounds, boasting when their hound was first on scent or first to tree a ringtail. Torn ears and facial lacerations inflicted by fighting coons provided tangible evidence of their dog's mettle, offering bonus crowing rights. I soon realized coon hunting was as much about the hounds as it was about the raccoon.

Imagine the overwhelming pride when Gene presented me a female Blue Tick pup from a litter of his prize Bitch, Blue. Passionately, I named the pup 'Ole Bets' after my lovely high school fräulein and future wife, Betsy. *Not necessarily a wise decision!* Rapidly learning the expense of feeding the ravenous pup, I watched in amazement as Ole Bets grew into her feet and out of her puppy clumsiness, evolving into a slick-ticked coonhound extraordinaire by the time the hardwoods donned their brilliant fall foliage. My sisters failed to comprehend my declaration of Ole Bets' worth after she chased down and killed several feral barn cats. By her second season, my hound fully understood her purpose; competitively fast- tracking scent, hastily relocating lost spoor when a coon crossed a creek, and often fighting a coon before it was treed. Ole Bets developed into a 'one man' hound loyal to me alone, establishing a mutual bond known only to those owning a great hunting dog.

Most hunts began in Gene's backyard along a woodlot drainage ditch bordering an old cemetery above Eagle Creek. Once released, the hounds typically cut scent straightaway and treed a coon before reaching the stream. One dark November night, however, the hounds ran curiously silent; noiseless after our two jeeps made several square mile trips surrounding the creek. Finally, the pack howled 'striking scent' well upstream from the cemetery. Repeatedly changing directions and crossing the creek several times signaled they were being outsmarted by a wayward coon. Parking in the cemetery, Gene caught me completely off-guard by asking me to grab a lantern and intercept the dogs if they stayed in the creek bottom. He would pick me up at the old cement county bridge and, if the dogs crossed the road, would wait for me while the other jeep continued to the second bridge. *Holy Crap, I was headed into the night alone!* My grit at stake, I had no recourse but to pull up my big boy pants, light the lantern and proceed. To my advantage I was very familiar with the area; to my detriment I had never trekked single-handedly through the pitch of any night. My vivid imagination already enhancing this maiden nocturnal venture, the push of Gene's eyes and the pull of the bawling hounds propelled me onward. Haloed in the lantern's lambent light, I valiantly trudged into the mystifying opaqueness of the looming shush. Owl-like, I scanned ahead watching the lamp wash over the coldly sculpted headstones engraved with familiar names of local families, including those I hunted with this very night. Stalking the cemetery in daylight, I often pondered the measure of these lifeless souls and how long it would be before their existence would be entirely forgotten! Tonight however, my ordinarily familiar world was in eerie motion; tree-branching arms bearing leafless fingers massaging the shifting silhouettes of rigid in-line monuments standing like soldiers on the manicured ground. Weaving through the sod laden corpses, I futilely snubbed the breeze murmuring through the cemetery's custodial maples; haunting mantras reminded me I was scared shitless!

And there I was, having endured boot hill's stony wrath, I hesitated at the fence line above the creek listening to the howling hounds sprinting towards Gene's farmhouse. Wide-eyed, I focused on the home's yard light beaconing my salvation like a landlubberly lighthouse. Understand, lazing in the comfort of my bed, windows wide open on wonderfully breezy summer Ohio nights, I fancied translating the sounds of the countryside's night beasts: deliberating who the owl was bidding; what Katy really did; and who whipped poor Will. But not tonight! Any and all sounds sharply yanked my looming phobia!

The gazillion stars twinkling above the ghastly timbre of the creek bottom capped a gut-retching netherworld nemesis. My supercharged thoughts zapped me into sensory overload rendering incomprehensible implications of what the night was about to relinquish!

Nevertheless, I crossed the fence allowing gravity to pull me downhill into the unbeknownst of the eerie creek bottom. My fear-driven pace slowed as my eyes adjusted to the night, providing solace as I identified some well-known landmarks. Bee-lining with steadfast determination would be my ploy, outpacing whatever the darkness held. Coursing the creek to the cobblestone shallows of the farm-vehicle crossing, I waded across in my knee-high gum rubber Redball boots and fast-tracked up the narrow dirt road. On track to intercept the hounds near the farmhouse, all was well. I could do this! Astonishingly, Ole Bets bawled her brash song of hitting scent causing an abrupt directional change as the remaining hounds harmoniously signaled a close chase was on. I rejected the mind-wrenching fervor of penetrating the streamside copse by straight-lining to a harvested cornfield fencerow. Fortunately, the hounds treed the coon fifty yards away and, bushwhacking through thick brush, I found the dogs howling fervently at the base of a mighty Burr Oak; a 'contemplation' tree I had climbed many times to sway with its limber, upper limbs. Amidst the springing hounds, I was unable to 'shine' the ringtail in my lantern light. Knowing it was not a den tree, the beast had no possible means of escape. The familiar grinding hum of the jeep's engine consolingly announced the 'boys' arrival and their spotlights soon ignited the beast's fiery eyes high in the oak's main stem. The hunters leashed and strenuously secured the hounds well away from the oak, prohibiting a mob attack on the downed beast. I scrutinized the coon occasionally hiding its head from the blazing spotlights in a tree crotch attempting to disguise its presence. Gene handed me his .22 bolt action Marlin and the hunting corps zealously watched me lay a lead ball behind the raccoon's ear. All were in awe as the free-falling beast pinballed through the branches, hitting the ground with a dead-weight thud. Filled with the jubilant exaltation of success, I lifted the large buck by its hind legs running my fingers through its dense early winter pelt as the corps debated its market value. Showering me with praise the gang celebrated with the bonding male mumbo-jumbo of good hounds, my perseverance in staying with the dogs and my marksmanship in humanely bringing down the coon.

Unknowingly, I crossed one of many bridges to adulthood that night, a purposeful gift from my mentoring friend Gene. While much of what I experienced in the woods stayed in the woods, all remains within me to this day. Simple lessons learned, including abandoning one's lantern or shutting off a flashlight when crossing a cattle pasture, were taught by once observing my intellectually challenged school mate run for his life barely ahead of a stampeding angus bull. Lighted lantern haphazardly swinging, the frightened lad finally abandoned the 'Embury No.2 Air Pilot' and hand hurtled over a palm gouging, cloth ripping barbed wire fence.

Conflict resolution was instilled on yet another hunt when this same flabby fool provokingly picked a fight with me. After easily cleaning the chubby chump's clock sending him to the jeep in nose bleeding sobs, the boy's father surprisingly congratulated me, telling me to never pass a chance to whip his bullying son. Undaunted by defeat, this hapless stooge picked two additional fights on the school grounds, the last one resulting in his face-shredding demise by my newly purchased class ring. Totally humiliated in front of our class-mates, the bullying loser finally accepted his inability to conquer the smaller, but sturdier me.

Coon hunting initiated me to home brew and chewing tobacco. Long-cut Mail Pouch immediately launched me high into a dizzying mental cosmos before downing me in a projectile gut-retching rage. Home brew, while lending an important contribution to the coon hunting tradition, taught me my imbibing limitations after gulping the 'recipes' viciously spirited blend caused an inebriated rib and ego bruising fall from a mid-sized maple while dislodging a dead raccoon. And most importantly, I began appreciating my passion for hunting extended far beyond harvesting wild beasts. Learning the dusking haunts and habits of the ring-tail were stimulating enough, but it was the all-encompassing experience, the in-betweens, that propelled my innate hunting desire forward. The spiritual mysticism of night hunting across the Ohio countryside was heavily seasoned with ardent friendships, physical and emotional challenges, moral responsibilities and ethical decisions. The joys of personalizing and hunting with dogs; the satisfaction of taking care of and marketing fur; the emotional highs and lows of witnessing death - Nature's lesson of the circle of life; all the rituals, traditions, legacy and skills that heartily thicken the gamey sauce of this timeworn hunting sport elevated my voracious hunting crave to higher levels, influencing essential lifetime decisions yet to come.

Boyhood pride is an exceptionally strong emotion. Coon hunting, and the young-hearted men who mentored me, presented me high self-esteem and a sense of place and purpose, vitally important attributes as one travels life's challenging road. Although my years of coon hunting were numbered as school, sports, my girl and college consumed my life, those Dark Knight Adventures were one of many epoch cavaliers jousting me towards manhood. Make no mistake, it was a very good thing to take for the boy I was then, and the man I am now.

The cemetery now enshrines mine and my wife's mother and father, and many of her kin. It is also the final resting place of Gene Line and so many more acquaintances influencing my formative years, proving it takes a village to raise a child. Whenever I return to my boyhood Ohio 'wilderness' I visit the cemetery, standing on what I consider the most peaceful piece of sacred ground I ever walked. This burial ground, as otherworldly as it was on that bleak November night many years ago, remains even more so to this day; oh, but for so many different reasons. And, if I listen closely, my imagination offers the sound of Ole Bets bawling her way through the Eagle Creek bottoms.

*"The hunter that travels out into the woods is lost to the world, yet finds himself."*
Unknown

# ODE TO THE MEXICAN – AUGHT FIVE

Colorado smoke pole season, September Aught-Five,
On a mountain christened the Mexican.
Our time in the wild nurturing instinctive drives,
My tradition with Kirb, Cousin Tim and young Keenan.

Considerate wives letting husbands be boys,
For a week stalking wapiti and deer.
Camped on the mountain to play with our toys,
Testing skills honed over the years.

The hidden sights, the noiseless sounds,
Air tasting of smells of the wild.
Catlike stalks through timbered ground,
Sharpening senses and instincts long veiled.

Time by the sun, to hell with our watches,
Hobbling times fast horse in fair chase,
Of royal stags ghosting thru aspen patches.
The tranquil mountain unwinding our pace.

Kirb, Keenan and I in quest of mule deer,
Tim licensed for royal elk stag,
We head to the hills loaded with gear,
Sights fixated on filling our tag.

At the property fence, I fight the taught gate,
Spying a string of buck deer totaling seven,
Filing through tall sage in mid-afternoon heat,
In the lead a mind-boggling 7X7!

Four younger bucks trail three old and wise,
Mountain sculpted and aged to perfection.
Awestruck I judge the big three's size,
Winding through sage towards the aspen.

Glaring through scope, eyes blurry and aching,
My heart in my mouth, my stomach in knots,
Weak in the knees, my hands begin shaking.
A full week ahead to connect all the dots.

One last gaze before they are gone like a dream,
The mountain's magnificent seven.
Polished antlers in sunlight they gleam,
I focus intensely on the 7X7.

His antlers massive with long pointed tines,
Heavy brows on pearly burred bases.
My mind whispered loudly, 'Could this buck be mine?'
I ponder his most favored places.

The second buck splendidly grand as the first,
Carrying a rack of five points on a side.
The third a colossal three by three,
No brows but antlers high and wide.

My mind made up, the challenge spring creek clear,
I accept the mountain's bold dare.
The two biggest or nothing, no others need fear,
The wrath of the muzzleloader I bear.

Alone the first night, a North windstorm from hell,
El Diablo blowing his wrath to the heavens.
Amid falling branches and trees the bucks cast their spell,
I lie haunted by the 7X7!

Morning dawned quickly, just the mountain and me,
A rare chance to enjoy the time alone some.
Watching and hoping for another chance to see,
The two bucks holding my heart for ransom.

With great expectation, my senses like razors,
I stalk the Munk/Shawver line.
Hunting buck deer, I live for, I savor,
No sign of 'my' bucks beam and tine!

I guard Ory's spring til dusk paints the sky slate,
Four good bucks and a doe in for a swallow.
But no big boys today as I patiently wait,
Thru twilight I trek down thru the hollow.

Stalking the road past downfall and spring,
I marvel at the number of does towing fawn,
Slipping noiselessly through sage as if on wing,
Fading ghostlike into aspen they bound.

Supper ham and split pea, my own recipe,
I wait for Kirb and young Keenan.
They arrive quite late, Kirb pours a stout whiskey,
I narrate the story of the magnificent seven.

A necklace for Keenan of claw, bone, and beads,
A bear claw choker, I crafted with pleasure,
Commemorating his past hunting deeds,
A well-deserved gift for him to treasure.

Kirb's body still healing, down in the back,
His passion for the hunt fiercely burns.
His whiskey kicks in, he's quick in the sack,
Hushing our stories much too soon.

Day two finds young Keenan and I,
Hunting Munks' ridge at dawn.
Keenan stalks slowly, I shadow nearby,
Jumping a small buck and a doe with a fawn.

We meet at the gate and make a new plan,
A favored strategy to creep through the Hole.
The high trail for Keenan, the low trail I stand,
Big bucks or nothing our goal.

Watching young Keenan stealthily stalk,
My presences totally unknown.
A careful aim and a shot, down goes a buck,
Keenan videos it fall backwards and down!

Sneaking in from behind, Keenan admiring his prize,
I stealthily snake in and scare him,
Catching him off guard, he jumps in surprise.
Laughing, I ask, "What's all the noise, Pilgrim!"

I hike over the ridge, Kirb sound asleep in camp.
Hearing the news of his son's great buck,
He rises from hammock and rowdily chants,
"Is there no end to young Keenan's good luck?"

Kirb and I come across the young lad,
Dragging out his buck near the road.
Pictures snapped of proud hunter and dad,
Another Mexican Ridge story unfolds.

Monday passes by with elk in our way,
Keenan back to school at days end.
Cousin Tim arrives for four hunting days,
We meet on the mountain once again.

Mornings of stout coffee, juice, and whole grain,
New plans amidst bugling bulls as dawn edgily waits.
Kirb crawls out of bed groaning with pain,
Combing his hair asking, "Is my part straight?"

Lunch back at camp, our bellies quite full,
Tim and Kirb pass out in deep slumber.
I plan my next journey in the afternoon lull,
Hopefully wishing for a late day blunder!

Happy hour or two of chips and good whiskey,
As I prepare veg and charred meat.
Kirb begins evenings quite frisky,
But after supper and two drinks he's asleep.

Maker's Mark fuels our un-abridged tales,
In a camp often quite crass.
Kirb's brand of wisdom, often he wails,
"You're all out of your ass!"

Kirb tending fire as we argue the trivial and trite,
Defending good science, bad politics denounced,
When debating mule deer's' methods of flight,
I say STOTT, Kirb says BOINK, Tim says BOUNCE!

As darkness befalls, we hear the grand calls,
Of howling song dogs and bulls bugling,
Resonating their presence across timbered halls,
Harmonies comforting our sleep til morning.

Awakened by sounds of scurrying feet,
Rodent pirates stealing through darkness of night,
Searching for parcels of crumb and scrap meat.
Our food secured in boxes locked tight!

The week ambles on, days running as one,
Colorful stories around warm fire burning.
Discussing Nature's veiled unknowns,
Wild lessons we all are learning.

Deer browsing open sage and thick aspen glen,
Bedding on rocky ridge and limber pine rim.
We listen, we watch, making new plans,
Our quest for big stags looking grim.

To camp we return with adventures anew,
Pining tomes of mishaps and mistakes.
Big bucks and big bulls much to our rue,
They elude, they trick, they escape.

Stalking worn trails of livestock and game.
Searching rims, ridges, saddles, and ravines,
Unwavering efforts seemingly futile and vain,
Are bountifully replenished by the in-betweens.

Daily ventures to lairs we know quite well,
Visiting landmarks given our special names.
The Gerber trail, stump pond, old windmill,
Etched aspen bark recording harvested game.

The enchanted forest, Ory's spring, old reservoir,
The lay down fence, crow's nest, and timber blowdown,
Hidden bear dens, homestead cabins of yore,
Don this grand mountain we love and renown.

We talk of fresh spoor of seldom seen bear,
And visits to black, oily elk wallows.
Of sage grouse, marten, strange noises we hear,
Of wrens weaving through marsh shallows.

Towhees prowling thick grass and shrubs,
Nutcracker beaks piercing limber pinecones,
Woodpeckers beating out spiders and grubs.
Song sparrows singing familiar spring tones.

Dawn the last day sneaking through steep limber cover,
Four bucks browsing by challenge my soul.
Cowboy voices below, the enticement swiftly over,
I plan a lone stalk through the Hole.

A small buck disappears, a spike bull jumps from his bed,
Startled by a foot cracking branch.
Deer everywhere, above, below, and ahead,
I yearn for the big bucks' attendance.

They do not appear as my hunt's end is near,
I suffer through looming frustration.
Kirb silently stalks by, following like a bear,
I startle him into despair and laugh with jubilation!

The drive back to camp, tired and forlorn,
I ask Kirb "Where the hell are those big deer?"
Alas, on the ridge we hunted this morn,
Kirb spies and exclaims, "Right there!"

We stare not believing, as the buck turns away,
Shaking his head while coursing thick aspen.
I grab my rifle and sprint up the red clay,
Powered by adrenalin fueled hunting passion.

Making a wide circle, the 7X7 not seen.
I jump small bucks, a doe, and a fawn.
His tracks reveal an escape quick and clean,
I trek back to camp, expectations eternally gone.

The season over, reality bites with sting,
We sit in camp weary but never disheartened.
Us older men humbled, Keenan once again King,
Our fortitude challenged, skills tested and sharpened.

Life's secrets as a predator known to disclose,
Lessons of one's life and strong will.
For hunting is more than striking death blows,
Success measured by the quest, not the kill.

Motives for hunting camouflaged in these lines,
Unfolding our desire to harvest game.
The hunt extending beyond meat or tine,
Unwinding in Nature with good friends our aim.

I, celebrating fifty and seven years,
Nature nurtured by the mountain's wild soul.
My spirit runs high, I leave with great cheer,
Gratifyingly haunted by stags and their ghoul.

A hearty thanks to the Shawvers, true and dear friends,
Blessing our footprints on their mountain.
Devoted hunter/conservationists, this great Kansas clan,
Their selfless deeds for the wild well known.

**SHP**

# ASHES TO ASHES, DUST TO DUST???

There I was, early morning in late November checking ice thickness at Lake John. Sportsmen, having no bounds, were repeatedly calling for information on ice conditions, eager to take advantage of the typically excellent fishing at freeze up. With shuffling baby steps, I carefully walked twenty yards from the north shoreline and drilled through approximately four inches of crystal hard ice; enough for some but I require six to eight inches of ice before walking on any Bull Pen lake!

Big game seasons ended, the skulking hunting masses gone, I relished this late falling quiescence, a time when I could play the warden game on my own terms, rather than the game playing me. Wayfaring at my own pace, aimlessly checking big game migration patterns; following out off-road vehicle and human tracks; following leads of unsolved cases; checking coyote hunters and early winter fishermen; watching the living wild prepare for the imminent cold packing dead of winter; was a good time to take.

Today, a fresh blanket of polar white snow below a grey curtain of low banking clouds, conveyed the sinister tranquility of an abandoned church. My mind traced the real reason I was here; exercising the privileges of my small game hunting license to call in and harvest a coyote and to scope the migrating deer wintering on Sheep Ridge. Surly bucks, driven out of their hidden lairs by raging hormonal desires to breed, were fully exposed and easy to locate on the snow-covered ridges, aspen draws and benching sage hillsides. *Where were they only a few weeks ago?*

Pummeling through bumper deep snow on the lake's west side I glimpsed two familiar long-tailed silhouettes, heads cocked my way, loping off the ice into the shoreline sage. Tracing the snow-covered lake, I spied a mass of hair and antler spread across a patch of crimson colored ice fifty yards from the lake's edge. Parking my truck next to a snow plowing trail coming off the ridge, I found the bloodied tracks of a running deer accompanied by paw prints of several coyotes trekking the steep bank towards the lake. The snow snitched the age-old tale of predator vs prey; a wounded deer dragging a broken front leg pursued by a band of hungry song dogs. Survival of the fittest in living color!

Surveying the 'crime scene' from above the lake, the panorama scratched a thrilling mystery novel, graphically told by the snow's glacial whiteness scarred by hooves and paws and illustrated in bloody, gut-wrenching gore. The conclusion obvious, I could not resist reading the final chapter interpreted by the tracks. Nature's way is one of swiftness, her stories shared with those lucky enough to be present or close behind, leaving others to question and to wonder.

The buck's demise was penned as soon as he hit the frozen lake, immediately losing footing defined by the spread-legged skid marks etched across the ice. He went down twice, attacked from all sides in typical coyote pack fashion. A slight blood trail beginning with the first fall, ended in blood-shedding splatters and congealed pools at the second. In human terms death came inhumanely slow as he was shredded alive by the tearing, ripping fangs of a competitive pack of predators. Natures beautiful tale of survival does not recognize cruelty or tragedy, only the inherent defiance of achieving whatever it takes to survive. The evolving circle of life where, in this case, coyotes have timelessly sculpted deer and deer have sculpted coyotes into what both are today. Hair and hide scattered in all directions, entrails spread yards away in a jellying pile, the carcass remained intact save a missing front quarter. The hind quarters were stripped to the bone, large chunks ripped away, consumed and packed off demonstrated by bloodied trails and drag marks trailing away from the carcass. What this morning was a living mule deer buck had been reduced to a lifeless corpse, a large ration of its meat weighing heavily in the stomachs of a pack of coyotes!

Returning to my truck, I continued bucking deep snow and pulled into the south boat ramp. Noticing the outhouse door wedged open by drifted snow, I began shoveling and spotted a heavy cardboard tube, closed on both ends with metal caps, standing upright on the floor next to the toilet. Picking it up, I read the typed label identifying of a crematorium and the name and address of a man described as 'deceased'. A moment passed before I realized I was holding a cardboard urn possibly containing the ashes of a dead man! *SURREAL!* Apprehensively shaking the container, I found it mostly empty although a light cloud of dust drifted off one end. *"All we are is dust in the wind.... Kansas.*

The ashen residue of a man choosing to have his remains reduced by a fast burn rather than a slow cold rot in a grave, I pictured a bereaved family losing a loved patriarch and, at his request, spreading his ashes over his favored fishing hole. But then my twisted mind took the darker trail of a sour woman scorned exercising her marital wrath over the open seat of an outdoor thunder throne; his final internment the cold frozen bowels of an outhouse pyre! *Surely not ...?*

Facing the dilemma of what to do with the urn, I left it next to the toilet, gifting the next user a chance to ponder, as did I, the man's demise.

Post holing afoot to the ridge top above the deer, I concealed my outline against a large boulder. Two short blasts on my Circe Cottontail Rabbit distress call, a song dog charged out of nowhere, directly towards me. Stopping to ascertain the whereabouts of the 'troubled hare', the coyote absorbed my 55-grain bullet, wilting in its tracks only 25 steps from the end of my 22-250s smoking barrel. It was the first coyote I called in and no doubt the most exciting ten seconds of my hunting life. John Henry's hammer steeling through its core, I approached the heavily furred, white bellied beast, noted the freshly bloodstained muzzle, having met its end searching for a fresh rabbit dessert. I stared in gaping in awe at the curling cloud of steam leaving the beasts open chest wound, its yellow eyes lasering skyward taking it to wherever dead coyotes go. Exhilarated beyond words, I surveyed the gun blue clouds shrouding the massive frozen landscape. Arvins, Lord of the Hunter and the Hunted, wove my feelings into reflective thoughts: the prime pelt worn by the 'medicine wolf'; the buck's remains scattered over the troubled snow, and the ashen remains of an unknown man; three death scenarios reposed in Nature's open morgue, revealing Her predestined mortal promise of life, then death, to be recycled into life sustaining dust. *A grande scheme indeed!*

Then, the resonating silence was brusquely disturbed by the scratchy prattle of magpies gleaning the deer's remains, the cracking of settling ice on the lake and an unseen sputtering of a ranch tractor. Life goes on and, it is good!

*Requiescat In Pace – rest in peace*

# BISHOP TRICKS

And there I was! Mid-October 1970 found me, a junior majoring in Wildlife Biology at Utah State University, overwhelmed by the boundless adventures the wildly open west tendered this Ohio country boy. My latest, an offer to join my apartment manager in a traditional family deer camp, would not be refused despite realizing the invitation masked the starkly familiar ploy of religious conversion.

I hunted deer the previous year from horseback; a midnight ride into the rugged mountains east of Toole with my roommate. From a sunrise high ridge vantage, I watched countless hunters swarm the ridges below like ants on bread crusts. Deer running everywhere, I embarrassingly experienced a case of buck fever firing at a running buck no less than a quarter mile away. Later, witnessing one hunter wound a deer and another put it down, I was jaw struck watching them engage in a knock-down drag-out fist fight ultimately quelled by their hunting buddies. A dangerous site indeed; armed men acting like kids. This was only the beginning of my education on the behavior and attitudes of the rank and file of western hunters.

This day, arriving at camp after classes, my apprentice awkwardness was eased by the warm greetings of the camp members. Thoroughly absorbing the ambience of the orderly camp-- wood stove heated wall tents, meat poles, and a Dutch Oven Deer Stew simmering above glowing campfire coals -- I was living a dream! Heavy canvas wall tents hugging a huge campfire ring were picturesquely set in aspen blazing their fall colors. The head clansman boldly proclaimed he was a Bishop, a prominent Church position. The other camp members introduced themselves as elders holding assorted congregational titles

Evening involved soaking homemade bread in savory stew around a roaring fire, drinking Coke, listening to Scriptures from their 'Book', stories of worldly missions and past deer hunts. And, wait for it, when asked my religion, I habitually replied, "I am a devout Methodist." Inevitably, asked if I contemplated joining their Church, I curtly responded, "Not at this time." For a moment, all remained quiet as the flames strobed over the clans' sober faces.

Night's chill creeping into our bones, bedtime came early. Nestled in down on a comfortable cot, while the wood stove snapped, crackled and popped a cozy warmth, I restlessly anticipated tomorrow's adventures. Rudely roused too early by sounds of clanging pans, slamming stove doors and clouds of heavy wood smoke, I quickly slipped into long johns, jeans, heavy socks, boots, and a sweatshirt under a lined jean jacket. Exiting the tent, I was greeted by a star studded sky twinkling through a biting chill gnawing away my drowsy morning torpor. All was right in my world.

Wolfing down a greasy sausage, egg and hash brown breakfast, I was directed to hunt the ridge above camp while the others stalked to traditional hunting lairs. Posting in an aspen clump overlooking a brushy saddle, senses on full alert, I nervously shivered in optimistic anxiety. The morning quiet, amplified the rustling of stirring beasts, signaling there would be no shortage of deer. This hunting unit required harvesting only buck deer and I, like everyone else, had my sights set on a wall hanger. Protecting does and fawns successfully allowed the population to increase in size after a series of severe winters. As the sun's rays radiated through the quakies, two spotted fawns bounded my way before breaking to a stop, eyes, nose and ears intensely focused on **me.** *Wow!* An unseen deer snorted and began crunching through dry aspen leaves with the fawns in tow. A camp member appeared, promptly scolding me for not shooting one or both of the fawns. *What!* "Camp meat", he said, haughtily scoffing when I explained shooting them never crossed my mind. The dismayed hunter left me in a cloud of emotional confusion.

Stalking to a rocky outcrop overlooking a sagebrush draw, I detected several does and fawns crossing the adjacent ridge. When the last doe stopped to look back the resounding crack of a rifle instantaneously jolted me to my core. Detecting footsteps where I last saw the doe another hunter materialized, drew his pistol and fired one shot towards the ground. *What the hell?* Recognizing the Bishop, I walked down the hill and found the hunting saint standing over the dead doe grinning like a Cheshire Cat. Based on my earlier experience, I queried if the (illegal) doe was "camp meat'. The Bishop laughed asserting, "No, it is too risky to deal with a large animal this far from camp." Shrugging, the Bishop strolled away leaving me in yet another moral quandary. Astonishment turning to anger, I field dressed and hung the doe in the shade of a spruce tree before returning to camp. As hunters drifted in for lunch, I openly described my intentions of bringing out the illegal doe. No one offering help, the Bishop made it crystal clear I was on my own. All camp members obviously agitated, I realized I was no longer a welcome "candidate" and returned home! These self-righteous pillars of coveted religious doctrines were nothing but rogue poachers.

Deliberating the hornet's nest I provoked, I elected to take the chance of being stung by contacting a good friend whose wife drew a doe license in a nearby hunting unit. Concerned they may refuse involvement with an illegal deer, I was surprised by their instantaneous acceptance, explaining illegally transferring licenses was a routine practice in their hunting culture. *Imagine that!* Thus, without firing a shot, I became intertwined in illegal hunting activities rationalized away because, "Everyone does it!" Believing I was morally right, my conscience suffered the turmoil of knowing my friend was legally wrong.

Returning the following morning, my friend and I drug out the doe and tagged it with his wife's license (she was working and unable to join us). Would you believe on the drive back into town, on a sharp mountain curve, we encountered a strategically located game check station? A dark cloud enveloped me realizing my seemingly moral decision would end with a hefty fine and possible loss of my hunting privileges. Gathering my wits, I studied the check station crew actively inspecting and recording licenses, data and deer. The crisply uniformed wildlife officers were clearly searching out violations while the biologists collected teeth for aging. A naïve recruit to the league of wildlife miscreants, I resolved to judiciously accept full responsibility for the illegal deer as well as the illicit transfer of my friend's license.

*"Oh, what a tangled web we weave...when we first practice to deceive"*
*Walter Scott, Marmion.*

Our turn, a non-uniformed student volunteer waved us forward, inspected the doe and requested a hunting license. I self-consciously handed over the fraudulent permit. Questioned why the name on the license was 'Judy' I, in a flash of unabashed thoughtlessness, declared my name was **"Jud"**! Everyone laughed though not for the same reasons! The volunteer missed the license was clearly issued to a female. Amazed by the ease of my deceit, I continued crafting fictitious answers. Turning towards the wildlife officers obviously engaged with a violation involving several deer, the volunteer handed back the license and waved us on! Imagine the deceitful duo's cringing tension as we drove by the busy wardens. Suffering the guilt-ridden shame of breaking wildlife law, while my companion joyfully celebrated my spontaneous deviance, I could not muster a smile.

And so it was, one evening cherishing the elders of the Smith and Young gang and, the very next day, loathing them. These scripture quoting zealots defied their pious proclamations with deeds of irresponsible hunting behavior guided by no moral compass. I was initially haunted whether I should have sacrificed the Bishop for the common good? ¿quién sabe? **WHO KNOWS?** Given the circumstances of friendship, my evolving outdoor ethic and hunting inexperience, I would probably not. However, I instigated my new rule of hunting and fishing only with the people I know and respect, making it known upfront I would report any and all violations encountered.

*"Fools multiply when wise men are silent."* Nelson Mandela

There were many more incidents of flagrant outdoor misbehavior during my formative years, all providing valuable lessons for my pending career and hunting life: a school mate sneaking out a small fawn inside the carcass of his legal doe; the same colleague firing at and hopefully missing a bull elk in thick cover during deer season; a road hunting friend poaching pheasants from his truck window in and out of the city limits. Another incident occurred during archery season when the same friend involved with the afore-mentioned illegal deer, arrowed a domestic sheep 'testing' the proficiency of his arrows to kill. Undoubtedly, these events not only fueled my fire for becoming a crusader for the hunting and fishing sports but also provided my life purpose; a vision quest to intensely pursue a wildlife biology degree for a career as a wildlife officer to bring a semblance of order to the chaotic games people play in the wilds.

*That's the way the stick floats!*

# A FLY FULL OF WORM-DIRT

April 1979. My brain clogged after failed negotiations with rancher Twitch Guyberg to build a permanent elk proof fence around his haystacks, I needed a break. At that time the Division of Wildlife furnished the fencing materials if the rancher agreed to provide the labor for constructing the twelve foot high gated enclosures. Twitch wanted the fence materials alright, but only if the State also provided the labor. The previous long and bitter winter demanded wardens work 24/7 for three months addressing elk damages on the inestimable haystacks circling the Bull Pen. Still, after the end of the damage season, thousands of dollars were paid to ranchers for hay damage reimbursement. Permanent high wire fencing solved the problem but Twitch and I were deadlocked, meaning the winter elk damage to his stacked hay would continue. A lose/lose situation for all, I left Twitch's ranch house frustrated and angry.

So there I was, in dire need of a brain flushing hunt for angling delinquents, I parked my vehicle above the Roaring Fork, the stunningly warm, spring morning already refreshing my troubled mind. A car was parked at the public fishing access (leased by the State from the very same Twitch Guyberg) in front of the large sign outlining the regulations: <u>fishing waters restricted to the use of flies and lures only</u>.

These regulations, effective at protecting the resource from overuse and corresponding overharvest, were habitually abused by those master baiters of the fishing world.

Hiding my truck in a gravel pit, I stalked below the bluff overlooking the stream and detected a fisherman weaving through the willows. A glimpse through my binoculars revealed a man carrying the proverbial Styrofoam "can of worms." *Hoka Hey!* Following a cow trail into the willows, I spied the worm soaking piscator catch and creel a brown trout, re-bait his hook with a squirming garden hackle and continue angling.

Deploying a favored tactic of 'now you see me, now you don't', I stepped into full view making sure the worm dunker detected me before I quickly disappeared back into the willows. I planned to weigh the man's performance as tangible evidence of his blatant disregard of the law.

The events that followed were solid Warden Gold; the bullion of human antics that make a warden's vocation priceless. Rounding a large willow, I startled the fisherman busily forcing the worm laden mass of the bait box into the open-zippered crotch of his pants. The sheer sight of the hangdog man with the ball of peaty worm-dirt hanging out of his trousers was a Polaroid moment indeed.

When the fisherman looked up, I blurted, "Your zippers open!" Both focusing on the squirming, night crawling wad suspended from the fisherman's open fly, I smilingly inquired if he was aware of the bait restrictions on the Roaring Fork. Imagine the audacity of this humiliated dupe shaking his head no! Requesting identification, I watched this peculiar looking man fling the worm wad into the willows. His oversized, slightly cocked head housed black beady eyes overlooking reading glasses perched on a long porcine nose. His large hogs-head chest and the 'tool shed' belly were supported by grossly short, chubby legs. Stubby arms bearing small sausage fingered hands mimicked a famous cartoon caricature; *Alas, Porky Pig was a fisherman.*

The fishing license identified one Verm Dibbler, now shamefacedly staring downwards in guilt ridden silence. Thinking the show had ended, I explained I would be issuing a citation for using bait. Verm, instantaneously grabbed his chest with clasped hands, dropped to one knee and painfully squealed through face wrenching contortions that he was having a heart attack. Terrified, I braced Verm's shoulders slowly easing him onto one side to prevent him from rolling into Roaring Fork. Picture the pitiful sight of this squatty man lying in a fetal position, gasping like a grounded carp and possibly dying. Thinking the worse, I shouted I would race to my truck and radio for an ambulance. Spontaneously jumping up like a jack-in-the-box, Verm declared he was OK, reiterating his chronic congestive heart failure would ultimately be his demise.

Caught between angry and entertained, I remained suspicious. Had this man pulled off an Academy Award winning heart-stopping sham or was he indeed ill. Not taking any chances I insisted on calling for an ambulance. Verm, adamantly maintaining he was alright, switched gears and, crocodile tears running down his face, began describing his wife as a vicious witchy woman who would beat him into a pulp upon discovering his citation for, of all things, fishing with worms. I contemplated a nuptial bond so easily shattered by the simple misuse of a garden hackle. Standing before me was a pathetic espoused man with one wife too many. Taking the reins, I sternly advised Verm to pull up his big boy pants and quit crying. *There is no crying in fishing!* Sobbing, Verm cried, "For God's sake what is going to happen to me?" I assured Verm illegally fishing with bait was not the crime of the century; there is no death penalty for the illegal use of worms!

Walking through marsh grass towards my vehicle, a snipe flushed at Verm's feet and literally scared the bejesus out of what was left of his disheveled psyche. While I scratched the tic, the podgy porker asked how he could keep this incident from his wife. After detailing the option of paying the fine on the spot Verm, grinnin' like a possum licking a sardine can, opened his wallet and counted away the wrath of his predicament. Firmly grasping my hand, he graciously thanked me for his salvation. As he waddled away, I mused witnessing Verm's miraculous myocardial infarction recovery, suitable for publication in the most technical of medical journals.

*"Th, th, th, th, that's all folks!"*

# CLETUS B. BLACK

*One impulse from a vernal wood*
*May teach you more of man,*
*Of moral and evil good,*
*Than all the sages can.*
-William Wordsworth, "The Tables Turned," 1798

I was introduced to Cletus B. Black by compatriot, Sir Don Gore. Drinking fine whiskey in Black's cozy motor home parked in Sir Don's back yard was an annual fall hunting ritual. I particularly enjoyed watching Don and Cletus pretend they liked each other; each bearing a mutual tolerance bound by the civil bonds of family. Cletus was a macho male chauvinist making annual 'Teddy Roosevelt' jaunts westward to hunt deer, elk and antelope. An avid Land of Lincoln nimrod, Cletus incessantly gloated over his hunting achievements despite, as I soon learned, a large abyss in his hunting demeanor and skills. The secret of his success was relentless persistence; an extreme hunting drive overpowering his outdoor incompetence. Cletus traveled with his sweet loyal wife, Muffin, in an incredibly comfortable motor home. To his credit, he loved wild meat and was a master butcher who, along with Muffin, meticulously boned the entire carcass, sliced the prime cuts into medium sized steaks and ground the remaining scraps into hamburger. After soaking all meat in vinegar overnight, the steaks were run thru a tenderizer. The meat was double wrapped and quick frozen in a large chest freezer carried on the rear of the RV. Familiar with the waste occurring with so many hunters, I was quite impressed with Cletus' system of meat processing. Cletus typically returned home with a freezer full of prime antelope, deer and occasionally elk meat, bigheadedly maintaining his hometown image as the Great White Hunter.

Sir Don, in a slick move of literally passing the buck, coerced me to be Cletus' Wyoming deer hunting guide. My district bordering Wyoming, I half-heartedly accepted, fully aware I had been set up. Because age and health were overtaking his physical abilities, Cletus made perfectly clear he preferred road hunting over trekking the outback. Not wanting to babysit Cletus across rough terrain anyway, I planned reacquainting myself with the maze of unmapped, back country two-tracks bordering the Colorado/Wyoming state line. Contacting unsuspecting hunters seldom seeing a warden from either state was always a productive endeavor.

And there we were, bouncing across the myriad of logging and jeep roads made by timber hacks, sheep herders, hunters and cattleman over the last century. Cletus frequently asked if we were in Colorado or Wyoming and I would smilingly reply, "Damned if I know", mimicking the topographical landmark drainage we were winding through, Damfino Park, meaning nothing to Cletus but quite entertaining to me. Never asking for further clarification, Cletus apparently figured we were driving in eternal circles; we were indeed! Fortunately, deer were abundant making our road hunting quests rewarding as we weaved across the imaginary state line. When a buck deer materialized on the Colorado side, Cletus would pout sourly for being outlawed to fill his Wyoming license so close to the state line. Fully aware of my zero tolerance for field misbehavior, Cletus was annually rewarded with a legal Wyoming buck while riding shotgun with this Colorado warden.

Hunting will ultimately define a person's character and, after several years listening to Cletus crowingly squawk his hunting transgressions, I branded him a boastful shooter rather than a sporting huntsman. Killing game was Cletus' full measure of success and returning home with anything less than a full freezer meant his hunt was a total waste of time. In the presence of game Cletus often suffered an overwhelming surge of buck ague, transforming into an adrenaline-laced, feverish madman losing nearly all cognitive and motor skills. Making matters worse, he was a horrendous marksman on his best day. If his first shot scored, he was as amazed as anyone. I once observed Cletus miss a standing broadside shot at a five-point bull elk followed by jacking all remaining shells onto the ground as the stag disappeared in the aspens. On another occasion, I screamed "quit shooting" at two fleeing bucks after his first shot dropped one dead in its tracks. Only when I led the enraged man to the dead buck did he realize I saved him from shooting one too many deer. Trembling with the wild willies, his face bearing a big pile of guilt shit, the poor man painfully comprehended he was hidebound by a lack of hunting prowess; a man who could not stay out of his own way.

On another hunt, I invited my young son Marc to ride with Cletus and I as an introduction to big game hunting. Marc, sitting high on a wooden box between Cletus and I, puffed up like a spring tick, provided an extra set of youthful eyes often pin-pointing game before we did. On this hunt I enjoyed Marc's first swear words while cruising through the BlackHall Mountain clear-cuts. When Marc pointed out the antlered heads of three bucks strolling through new growth lodgepole, I instructed Cletus to exit the vehicle, kneel off road and wait until the deer walked into the open. The unsuspecting deer were on course to exit the pines less than forty yards out; a picture-perfect ambuscade! Marc, wide-eyed and intensely focused on the deer, listened as Cletus quickly exited the pickup, noisily jacked a shell into the chamber and, unbelievably, loudly slammed the pickup door! Watching the alarmed deer turn and vanish into the pines, Marc whispered, *"Dumb Ass."* The dumbfounded Cletus uttered not a word, moping for more than an hour.

Cletus' hunting face mirrored the self-centered man he was. Overlooking many of hunting's intangibles, the in-betweens highlighting the entirety of one's quest to harvest game, I pondered whether he actually enjoyed hunting; riding shotgun wearing an ever sour, gut-punched grimace as if laboring a grueling job. However, once a carcass was hanging, Cletus fervently skinned, quartered, boned and processed the meat.

Overall, I enjoyed the down time spent with Cletus B. Black. It was a nourishing pause prior to the chaotic big game seasons allowing time to expand my pastime of analyzing hunter behavior. Never lasting more than three days, I celebrated the hunter's success with Sir Don, quietly sipping aged bourbon as Cletus belted out manly deeds of stamina, unlawful behavior and success. Never missing a chance to emphasize the illegality of Cletus' misdeeds, I would grimly smile as he articulated nonsensical rationalizations for breaking wildlife law. I regarded his illicit verbalizations the conceited palavering of an old school nimrod frustrated because he could no longer function as the great hunter he allegedly once was. The man's ego driven drive to fill his larder displaced any sense of a moral, ethical or legal conscience.

Before returning to Illinois, Cletus always rewarded me a firm handshake and a bottle of Maker's Mark, a 'bone' treasured by any warden law dog. Aging eventually disabled Cletus ending his trips westward and, as all hunters do, he gradually faded away.


*"Where ignorance is bliss, tis folly to be wise."*
Thomas Grey (1742)

# DOG BITES

The very nature of a warden's vocation presents seemingly endless dog tales, beginning with their own loyal pets to the highly unpredictable encounters with dogs of all breeds travelling with outdoor recreationists. This tragic story is one of them.

May, 1987. Summoned to Lake John to investigate a complaint involving a pit bull running at large and threatening a nearby camp, I located the alleged offender chained to a stake in a camp belonging to a thickly maned and profoundly tattooed biker type. The sleeping pit bull sensing danger (dogs despise uniformed officers), stood, eyes glaring into mine and snarled a lip curling guttural growl. Calming the dog, Hairball uttered, "Don't worry, he will not bite." *Yeah Right!* Taking several self-defensive steps backwards, I explained I was responding to a report accusing his unleashed dog of disturbing fishermen. Infuriated, he rowdily began ripping my hindquarters for meddling in matters I had no authority to address. *WRONG!*

Before I could counter, a yapping miniature poodle, belonging to the very woman who called in the complaint, pranced into Hairball's campsite, and charged the pit bull, nipping its back legs. *NOT GOOD!* In a blink, the pit bull seized the diminutive poodle by its neck, squeezed out its last whimper with several shakes and thrust it onto the ground like a rag doll. Yes, the curly haired poodle was dead. Staring in total disbelief, Hairball turned to me and angrily declared, "That dog should have been on a leash!" And yes, it got worse. The now extremely panic-stricken woman owning the poodle, shedding tears like a leaky pipe, bawled I was to blame for her dog's murder (her words)! At the same time, the pit bull owner belligerently demanded I write her a ticket for not having the deceased poodle leashed.

Gazing at the lifeless corpse, blood oozing from tooth puncture wounds and encircled by cottony tufts of hair, it was obvious both dog owners were not happy with the way it all ended. Having no dog in this fight, my initial thoughts were to waive writing citations, sensing both had suffered enough, justice had been duly served. However, both dog owners in my face uncompromisingly demanding charges be filed, it was crystal clear I was the bad guy no matter which road I took. When the law's an ass, someone has to kick it! Right? I, an equal opportunity warden prick, scratched out tics to both!

*Letting sleeping dogs lie, in this case, was simply impossible!*

# FOWL PLAY

Weary after working hunting seasons four months straight, Thanksgiving in the 70's and 80's became vitally important for my overall well-being. It was an equally treasured holiday for my wife Betsy, son Marc and daughter Anne, as our getaway to 'civilization', making an annual trip to Brush, Colorado to celebrate with Wildlife Officer Larry Budde, his wife Anne and sons David and Brian. Larry and I trained together in Denver and were very good friends. Anne, present when my daughter was born, developed an equally close friendship with Betsy. Thanksgiving Day began at dawn with Betsy and Anne preparing a free ranging turkey and a buffet of potatoes, gravy, salads, vegetables and desserts washed down with champagne. Afterwards, I would lie on the living room floor and enter a tryptophan induced napping stupor lasting for hours. The girls, young Brian in tow, would spend the following days power shopping for Christmas gifts in Greeley and Fort Collins, while us 'boys' took to the fields, ponds and river bottoms pursuing waterfowl, pheasants, quail, squirrels and rabbits. It was a very good occasion for all.

As wildlife officers, Larry and I became quite proficient as a team hunting down miscreants working big game hunters in the Bull Pen or small game and waterfowl hunters in the eastern plains, taking great pleasure piecing together the complicated puzzles often crafted by deviant hunting scofflaws. And so it was, before daylight Thanksgiving Day in 1978, Larry called out to work a case with fellow officers, found me hunting as a lone wolf on the seep ponds below Pruitt Reservoir. Tossing out a light decoy spread veiling myself in a shoreline thicket, I watched, listened and waited for shooting light. Protected from a bitter wind by the dam, the silhouettes of low flying mallards barely clearing the weir came into view, circling overhead softly 'cacking' a greeting before noisily splashing down into my decoys. Legal shooting time fifteen minutes out, it was a picture-perfect morning for harvesting a brace of back shot drake mallards. Giving time for enough light for species and sex identification, I soon retrieved two fat drake mallards from my decoys. Was it possible I would be abnormally early for the holiday feast?

Imagine the bane when two duck hunters rudely invaded 'my' hidey-hole (there was no reason for them to set up so close to me) on adjoining open water. The two intruders, standing unconcealed in the cattails, would certainly be in direct competition with my hunting gambit. Ducks, easily detecting the fully exposed pair, instinctively climbed and flared triggering long-range shots, interrupting my opportunities for harvest over the decoys. Deciding to leave with two in the bag, I began packing up when one of the 'trespassers' approached and asked if I would join them, expressing my decoys on 'their' water would greatly enhance success for all. And then, as it almost always happens, my magnetic ability to attract outdoor miscreants occurred once again when the hunters explained their intentions to harvest two daily bag limits due to yesterday's poor luck and todays' perfect conditions (very cold, windy, and the reservoir freezing up) would easily grant (illegally) bagging an extra limit. And, wait for it, he proclaimed they wanted only drake mallards, would take the first limit to their vehicle allowing the picked carcasses time to cool, fooling the thermometers of even the most seasoned wardens! *SHUTUP!* The evil hunting men do in my face, I faced the dilemma of leaving or continuing to hunt as a working warden. Good wardenmanship, with a rare opportunity to capture first degree duck poachers while hunting with them, demanded I remain.

And so it began, Deke and his companion Sprig firing 12 gauge heavy loads at any and all ducks, no matter the distance, before any had a chance to decoy into range of my 20 gauge. The marsh devils, retrieving only drake mallards, quickly bagged their limit. While Sprig cautiously carried ten drakes to their vehicle, Deke suspiciously questioned why I was not shooting and offered me a drake mallard. I refused his gift explaining my 20-gauge dictated waiting until the ducks decoyed closer and I would patiently wait until they finished and harvest my own. In warden mode, I was very aggravated but uncertain when to act. Both were killing and wounding hen and drake mallards but retrieving only drakes from the cattail morass. Deke earlier called out Sprig for combing the marsh for downed hens, ordering him to leave them. Good shots, wilting most ducks into the cattails, they also wounded others, flying away to suffer a lingering death elsewhere. Arrogantly proud, as outlaws are, I decided to end their criminal behavior sooner rather than later, halting their carnage of wounding and wasting ducks.

Suddenly a man appeared! It was Larry, in full uniform, sloshing through the marshy muck, no doubt concerned why I was late (as usual) for Thanksgiving dinner. Warden gold! Larry joined me giving the two hunters' time to ponder, and intently listened to my tale of the two poachers working on their second limit. The highly suspicious poaching pair stood in awe when Larry stated we would aid searching for their downed hen mallards. After retrieving several hens Larry and I escorted Deke and Sprig to their vehicle. All proverbial birds in hand, Sprig crapping down both legs in mouth gaping apprehension, Deke declared entrapment! We sent the hapless pair home after scratching out fat tics for their hunting misdemeanors. Sprig honorably paid his fine through the mail. Deke, however, chose going to court and, in front of 'poacher friendly' judge, declared he had been framed. To my utter dismay, the judge dismissed the charges based on continuing the case would require the 'warden' to make another long, costly trip from the mountains, an unnecessary burden on the justice system. *Yeah, right!*

"*Justice without force is powerless; force without justice is tyrannical.*"Blaise Pascal

# HOME RUNS – PRIVATE PLACES FOR A SECRETIVE MIND.

One mid-summer Friday evening (TGIF!) I, in an 'end- of- week trance', wound through the Fort's heavy traffic concocting tasks of mowin', fixin', shoppin' and, as always, wishin' I was fishin'. A mind fragmented by a grueling week snarled in the office, I was in dire need of a mentally mending weekend. Now an 'administrator', a self-inflicted wound of climbing the professional ladder requiring a move from 'my' mountain to an inner-city office tendered major challenges. Oh, to be back in the field! Drifting homeward in the stop and go traffic, my imagination wildly floated into the melody of moving waters, harmonizing with the luring mantra of those temptress Sirens incessantly testing my determined resolve to wade the milieu of a favored river. Dazing at a stoplight's red glow, images of a late afternoon river dimpled with egg laying caddis fluttered through my thoughts; my hand-woven elk hair cork bobbing in and out of sight over nipping trout... **HONK, HONK, HONK!!!** ...the car behind rudely blew away the illusory 'hatch' like a brisk canyon wind. But, like a favored song, the hallucinations returned at the next light, a self-defense mechanism I practiced to perfection. Quick as a minnow, my Saturday routines were swapped with a plan of fly-fishing a savored place; furling line over familiar pools, riffles, seams, pockets, and backwaters. So let it be done! I presented the getaway plan to my wife Betsy over a margarita in a quiet restaurant, a Friday evening tradition since moving to the Fort. Contracted enslavement to a stack of domestic tasks, my wife graciously approved a leave of absence citing good behavior. Somehow, she knew without understanding the mental strengths my fishing weaknesses provide. But sure as stink on skunk, I did not escape without the incomprehensible proverbial inquiry,

"What time will you be home?" *Time?*

"Well uh., after dark", I replied knowing my caring companion, bless her heart, would hold firm to any agenda I truthfully couldn't vow. Frightfully envisioning multitudes of near death experiences, I could potentially encounter -lions, tigers, bears, murderers, falls, drownings, car accidents- anytime I ventured alone into the wilds, she would fret in overdrive until I returned! *"Babe, I love you!"* Remorsefully conceding, "There are no clocks on the river. I promise to call immediately, once I receive a cell phone signal."

So, at O-dark-thirty the following morning I faded from the bright city lights into the lamp black obscurity of the highlands, washing down a greased bagel with a go-cup of strong Columbian. In 45 minutes, I crossed the 'line', marveling the dawn's grandeur radiantly beaming volcanic eruptions of flaming reds and molten oranges through wispy clouds in the rearview mirror. Furred and feathered life forms in pine and sage whizz past a windshield splattered by a plethora of insect carcasses: a coyote mousing a meadow; mule deer jumping the highway fence, elk fading into pine and a diversity of raptors soaring the ridge top thermals. Of course, a bounty of antelope polka-dotted the high plains; bucks vigilantly surveying their kingdom from high vantages and does with fawns in tow hugging the verdant meadows. Continuing south from Fort Sanders, the high plains gem, I sang with Seger, Springsteen, Cash and Walker. Switch-backing Woods Creek and through Fox Park in the Medicine Bow Range, I pondered the fate of Jacques La Ramie, the French-Canadian free trapper who vanished trapping the river carrying his namesake. Some blamed the Arapaho, but then again, they were always blamed. Crossing the 'line' again, I received an Emperor's welcome from the towering peaks of a distant Wilderness; lordly pinnacles standing guard over 'North Park' where, for twenty plus years, I lived, played, worked and raised a family as its wildlife protector. Reluctantly abandoning this high elevation sagen jewel set in mountain granite to fulfill a career, I returned today as a coveting visitor adrift in a whirlwind of bygone memories; resplendent sensations of returning 'home' to the remote expanse the Native Americans once called the Bull Pen; the headwaters of the legendary North Platte River. Turning northwest I smiled crossing 'my' river, finding it running full and slightly off color from yesterday's rain. Exiting the highway, near the 'line', I opened the first of two wire gates, consciously scanning the ground for fresh human spoor. To my pleasure, the sandy red gravel was undisturbed. So many times, I opened and closed these barbed hand hackers tracking rod and gun carrying nimrods. On my watch, I took great pride playing 'river keeper', checking bank fishermen and the argosy of rafts floating through the deep river canyon; a sentinel on hidden overlooks earnestly anticipating the beastly pleasures, human and otherwise, this river wild offered. During my formative years scratching tics to the inattentive came relatively easy. But as word spread there was a 'new sheriff in town' the public mass began accepting the responsibilities of licensing themselves on both sides of the line. I knew I was gaining ground when outfitters requested a license agency closer to the river access points. However, if there were fishermen, there would be tics to scratch. *But that was yesterday, and yesterday's gone.* Today a fisherman grinding over the eroded two-track through borderland sage to the veiled river canyon, I smiled again finding no camps or vehicles at the trailhead. *Sweet!* No longer necessary to hide a vehicle I parked, loaded my pack and begin the fifteen-minute hike down the narrow draw leading to the river. Halfway, I celebrated a hen blue grouse guarding her brood chasing grasshoppers through the sage. One eye on me, she herded the chicks into thick willow, disappearing in camo-feather disguise. One can only imagine how ravenous Native Americans or early explorers relished encountering this relatively easy, lip smacking prey. Literally! Continuing through a finger of aspen I spy the faded, rusty **'FLY AND LURE ONLY'** sign nailed beyond reach to deter removal by the disobedient; quite pleasing to the man hanging it there years before. Crossing a tree shaded freshet alive by the grace of summer rains, I listened to the river's music before seeing it. Rounding a rocky outcrop, THERE SHE IS! The rewards begin by simply being here I pause, taking in the serenity of the fluid quicksilver winding through steep canyon walls of rocky sage, aspen and pine. Absorbing the mesmerizing tonic of moving water, I studied its serpentine banks outlined by gravel and willows scoured annually by springtime ice razoring through the canyon. The diversity of vegetation sustains a superfluity of animal life – creatures great and small – biologically linked to Her waters; a place where life's placidity overwhelms the savagery of death. Today, contentedly separated from civilization, I will play the role of predator, armed with experience, to thoroughly enjoy all the river wild has to offer. Knowing only me and my God understand why I love this place, I am overwhelmed with pleasure.

Once commissioned to work both sides of the 'line', today I am likewise licensed to fish the same, trekking between Teepee Creek and (of all names) Porter Creek! These are my home waters, the perpetually transforming river I know so well but will never fully understand, the place I am unremittingly schooled on everything wild, normally accompanied only by my shadow. No longer essential to ghost willow and pine, or take cover in rocky bluff, I overtly swagger down to the riverbank, my spirit overwhelmed by the sensations of wilderness freedom and independence. Spotting a bright white container labeled "Night Snakes" lying next to two beer cans and a forked stick stuck into the shoreline mud, I am reminded 'my' waters are trespassed by others, including riverbank skels habitually scenting their posts, advertising their illicit presence. Cussing, I tuck the littering spoor into my pack, hoping the river rogues will someday suffer the wrath of a skulking warden. *Maybe even today?*

Relic exoskeletons of the pre-runoff 'Bunyan' bug hatch, so well described by Norman McLean, cover the shoreline rocks, their crusty capacious shells a surreal reminder of an earlier emergence. Late for the dawning nymph 'drift', the smoky clouds of amorous tricos wafting above the river advises tying on a Banker's Hour dry. This seasonal amatory display underscored by nuzzling trout in a backwater pool provided entertainment as I rigged my pole and line. The canyon walls microwaving my face and arms, I applied a thick coat of sunscreen before hiding my lunch laden pack into the willowy shade. Amazingly, these waters were void of mosquitoes! Other than the frequent deerfly drill or a creepy crawling tic, one need not worry about bugs. The cloudless morn quietly still, I anticipated Aeolus' decision to whisper quiet zephyrs or roar line knotting blasts. Canyon winds were not a matter of if, but when, and how strong. Stubbornly resisting tying on a Stimulator with a bead-head something dropper, I knot a #18 Renegade, my favored morning searching pattern. *(Best fly in the west!)* Laced with optimism, I invaded the mayfly clouds, my inner voice murmuring 'probably – maybe – hopefully' the river will soon come alive. Landing one before breaking off a scrappy rainbow, the rises are silenced. Slogging into the muddy backwater, I carelessly stumbled over unseen obstacles searching familiar trout lairs. Finding the mid-stream riffles and pocket waters quiet, I waded upstream to an island. A lightning bolt of anticipation surged down my spine upon spying a pod of bank- hugging browns nosing the surface film of a frothy backwater pool. Greedily intent on hooking them all, I quartered below the pod and delivered the Renegade above the closest downstream trout. The ravenously competing maxi- pod proffered several fleshy browns before spooking the rest. Life's complexity sometimes straightforwardly simple, it became fish-eye clear there would be no shutout in today's game. The slightly discolored water complemented my piscatorial skills, making me feel more proficient than I really am: an open-air drama typically short-lived and fictional.

Gratified, I cross to a shoreline trail paralleling a large span of beaver pond still water, my eyes fixated on frequent rises in the riffles above the glassy flat. The ancient beaver lodge, active since making my first tracks, often served as an ambuscade for river rats floating by in rubber rafts. Many stimulating, sweet and sour discussions transpired here, some ending with sharing my warden stylus. Splashing along the shoreline wavelets I am stopped in my tracks by a distinctive line of very fresh, pigeon-toed pad and claw impressions of a medium size black bear. Aware the beast was near (they always are) I slow my pace, senses on full alert, wondering if the bruin's private eyes were watching ME! Spoor the rule and sightings the exception enhances the marvelous mysteries of Ursus, I amazingly perceived a shadowy movement across the river before spying the coal black beast lounging at the base of a large ponderosa pine. As I continued fishing, the bear and I cautiously eyed each before it suddenly vanished into its timbered domain.

Netting a hefty foot-long rainbow from the riffles above the pond, my inner voice crowed to an over-inflated ego, "Man, I'm good!" Releasing the trout while planning a stalk on one of three feeding near the far bank, my peripheral vision perceived a formidable rise form in front of the beaver lodge. False casting, I balk when another fish surfaced even closer. And then another! Skillfully dead drifting the Renegade several times over the feeding lanes; **NOTHING!** Tying on a Trico spinner; **Nada!** Predictably, the rises ceased. I replicated this scenario almost every visit because I once successfully landed a giant hook-jawed brown on a #22 spent Trico! Aware these broad shouldered river rogues spook easily and are rarely caught, memory driven temptation prevails in spite of knowing these gold plated slabs will rudely ignore or, even worse, visibly refuse my dry fly. In the rare event of a hookup they consistently broke off after a line tightening run into the depths of the beaver runs; a dry fly in these still waters rarely restoreth my soul. So, this compulsive visionary finally yields and I reverse strategy; *"When small caliber fire fails, resort to grenades!"* Walking the river bank earlier, I remember flushing lots of hoppers. Now, blessed by an intensifying breeze, not one of Ernest Schwiebert's *Grasshopper Winds* mind you, but enough for a fraudulent fish sting, I knot on a size 8 'Dave's' replication and haphazardly splash it into the middle of the wind worried water. **BLAM!** I am rewarded instantly by the primal pull of personal achievement when a bulky brown launched, bass-like from the murky depths. But it was not until the second liftoff did I fully realize the vaulting fish was still attached to my line. Who says browns don't jump? The bruiser, holding all the aces and wildcards, torpedoed upstream stripping line into fast water before turning inside out, slack-lining back, and finally anchoring in deep water. Just as a professional moment stroked my self-esteem, I tripped forward, counter with an awkward step rearward and, without pause, back slapped into the water with the grace of a falling redwood. Tippet and moxie snapped, I cautiously search for witnesses. Castor

Flats now solemnly quiet, I submissively sit on the bank regaining composure wondering if my adrenalin flow matched that of the beastly salmonid now wearing my hand-tied lip jewelry. But wait! A preponderance of trout sipping spent mayflies dot the rock laden pools above! Daunted and without bearing I lapse into a state of euphoric madness, carelessly flinging a mayfly spinner with harried imprecision and poor technique, resulting in inevitable leader knots, back snapping flies and vegetative hook- ups. Firing bullets rather than drifting feathers, I gathered my dampened soul and trudged upstream to dry my clothes and salvage my self-discipline. Shedding my waders, I reclined sunward against the bank investing time to 'read' a favored deep-water pool fashioned by a boulder dam funneling several chords of white-water scouring a swirling abyss before blending into a span of ever calming currents. Experience prescribed rigging a high floating Stimulator with a red Copper John dropper, a deadly duo of hair and wire introduced to me by a good friend now living in Yellowstone country. Standing, I donned my dank waders and began fishing the calmer water before casting dead center over the boulder dam. Watching the Stimulator dash into the run, I detected a fish flash quickly swamping the Stimulator. Valiantly announcing **RAINBOW** to the deafly alive surroundings, the river heralds my mistaken identity with an eighteen-inch, buffalo- humped **BROWN TROUT!** Humbly wrong but haughtily happy, I clipped the line above the deeply hooked dropper in the trout's toothy jaw before reviving and releasing the beast into the pool's fading depths. Like everything in life, fishing's lessons arise from mistakes, misjudgments, miscalculations, misinterpretations and, of course, success. The pool greatly disturbed; I move on.

Energized, I wade into a stretch of fast water bubbling over and through sculpted mid-sized boulders forming a maze of opaque pocket water, V-necked runs and dancing riffles. Known to hold a preponderance of voracious, smaller sized trout, it provoked a neurotic effervescing mix inspiring even the finest fishermen. Picking the pocket water like a thief, I short-lined into an intoxicating tempo of furling line over the nervous rivulets. Sliding over greasy boulders my squinting eyes traced the bobbing Stimulator. Strikes missed and fish lost came fast and furious, but I managed to net a half dozen, eight to fourteen-inch browns and rainbows. Leaving the fast water, I cast to a well-known bankside run below the mouth of Teepee Creek. On the first float, a silvery flash guzzles my Stimulator propelling a robust rainbow skyward before making several rod bending runs. Floundering towards the bank I firmly stripped in line while towing the salmonid slab into the grassy shallows. The female cut-bow resembled an over-inflated football, a beautiful mix of milky white-edged pectorals, contrasting dark and light wormy green vermiculations across her broad back, and wide lines of iridescent flash on both sides. The bold blood-red slashes beneath her cheeks reveal her cutthroat ties. Reviving her underwater with gentle hands, I pondered whether this trout will be here next year and, even more, will I. Today life is good, real good! Taking a mid-stream seat on a sun-drenched, goose crap laden flat rock 'throne', I finished a bottle of warm water. Sun weary and hungry I wondered why I failed packing lunch into my vest. Sauntering downstream, I began calculating numbers, sizes and species caught and, instantaneously scold my conscience for blemishing such a grand day with statistics. Today's measure was a sum of the misses, losses, catches multiplied by the soul soothing in-betweens tendered by the river wilderness. Triumph extended far beyond the tangibility of hands-on fish!

Nearing my gear, I detected the gravelly grind of waders. Two men materialized, their spin cast rods snitching the all too familiar ploys of lawless bait fishermen. A squirming water drenched crawler below a lead weight dangles from the rod of one preparing to cast. *Angling miscreants outwardly violate the very fly and lure and size regulations significantly upgrading this spectacularly fragile wild trout fishery!* Outraged and without credentials, my badge of courage surfaces out of genuine concern for the river and its fish. As a warden, poachers were challenging prey in my vocational quest to protect the wild. But today, as a fisherman, these piscatory rapscallions really pissed me off!

Totally engrossed drowning garden hackles, both failed to detect my presence. Stalking people, a skill I perfected into an art form, this heedless pair would not have sensed a charging bull moose! From behind, I brashly queried, "What, in the wide, wide world of sports are you guys doing?" Caught completely off guard, both nearly soiled their waders. In a state of capture myopathy, one cut the line with his front teeth and threw the baited hook into the river. The man facing me stared blankly at the squirming, garden hackle held between his thumb and forefinger. Savoring the moment, I bedeviled the worm dunkers trance asking if they noticed the bald eagle sitting in the tree across the river. Thinking they were off the hook, so to speak, one asked, "What eagle?" Pointing out the national treasure perched in plain sight in a dead standing pine across the river, I declared, "the one watching you illegally fish with bait!" As the impaled worm twisted its dowsing death, one lied, "We're not using bait." I chuckled hyena-like afore emphatically divulging I would be turning them in! And I did! Quickly packing up, I fast-tracked the steep trail and contacted the sheriff's dispatch on my cell phone. Providing detailed physical descriptions of the fish poachers, their vehicle and its license plate number, I made it crystal clear I would testify in court as a witness to their blatant misdeeds. The dispatcher, knowing from past experience my tenacity as a wildlife officer, reminded me of the difficulty of contacting wayward wardens but would pass the information on to officers on either side of the line. *Been there done that!* Patiently waiting 45 minutes, dispatch called back stating she was unable to contact any wardens but would continue trying. *DAMN!* Returning to the river, I crossed paths with the winded offenders hiking the steep trail to their vehicle. When asked if I turned them in, I smilingly said nothing. Outraged and verbally belligerent, the scumbags took biting chunks out of my rear end, continuing their lewd blasphemy until well out of sight. Suddenly all became eerily quiet and, fearing the scoundrels may vandalize my truck, I breathed in a sigh of relief hearing their vehicle leave the parking area. The master baiters had wound my spring tight and I needed time to uncoil. The wilderness halcyon tendered me a vital opportunity to bask in the late afternoon warmth, to repose and anni-hilate my well-earned lunch, and to saturate my mind with the seclu-sion found only in the wild. The soothing sensations of aloneness, having nothing to do with loneliness, renovated and relaxed my inner life-force. An hour later, a warmly gentle rain awoke me from a spirit cleansing nap. Fishing through several ephemeral showers and sitting out a downpour under pine I filled my lungs with the earthy scent of sage and pine. A merganser family appeared, as they always do, intermittently diving for their next meal. *Have you ever witnessed, from above, the underwater flight of a merganser 'soaring' through the river's undercurrents in harrowing pursuit of small fish?*

Increasing Caddis clouds skimming the water's surface caught my eye, the braided currents interrupted by trout snapping up the tent winged Trichopterans. Brown winged, green bodied caddis pelted my face like shrapnel, crawling behind my glasses, down my neck and all over my clothing. Infused within the superfluity of insects and trout, I intuitively began fishing with the river. An indispensable friendship indeed! Elk Hair Caddis the evening's match, the feeding intensified with the dusking light, offering hits on nearly every cast. Ticks of time erased, my 'off the clock' repose endured. Fishing is not killing time, it is living it; an amnesia state of mind where your spirit blends with your senses while playing the fishing game. Casting spells of magic curls with my graphite wand, watching my fly dip and jog the riffling opaque until the impending darkness began shadowing doubt on its whereabouts. Fishing in the blind to resonating rises, striking out on most, I scored a few ten-inch browns. Suddenly, without warning, this biological marvel of fish and insect abruptly halted. *Who threw the switch?* The unexplainable end of any hatch characterizes the river's mystical incarnate charm. Surrendering to nightfall, I returned to my pack, broke down the rod and changed into my hiking gear. Trekking upwards, I perceived the quiet restlessness of the river one last time before quickening my pace through the invisibly familiar forest. At the summit I discover a most pleasant surprise leaning against the pole fence bordering the parking area. ALAS, the man of the Snowy Range, a cherished personal and professional Red Shirt – an Akicita , the Lakota Sioux word for the shirt wearers, the respected warriors serving as watchman (police) for the hunts, camps and traveling bands; a befitting title for any warden. Wyoming Officer Biff Burton greeted me with a wide Autumn grin bragging, "I got 'em!" Biff continues, "They were quite unhappy saying you threatened them." "Words can be quite menacing, silence even more," I chortled. Biff laughed adding they requested a court appearance until told their snitch was a game warden. Avoiding a trip to Saratoga to post bond, both paid their fines on the spot. Besides the illegal bait, they possessed three undersized trout and only one had a fishing license. A wardens' coupe indeed!

"So how was the fishing?" Burton asked, like any warden would. "Fair," I answered, like any fisherman would. We both smiled. I offered Burton a cold beer and, taking great pleasure in the tingling chill over parched throats, we revived stories of times past. Then, contentedly watching the officer's truck bounce homeward to a late supper and tolerant wife, I savored the moment before initiating my re-entry into the material world. No city lights dousing the night, I was over-whelmed by the bajillion stars saturating the big sky. Reminiscences wisped through my mind; recalling camping here with my teenage son Marc and daughter Annie, longing to do it again; gazing into a dancing fire with true friends, remembering the look on one's face (a whirling dervish earlier proclaiming no campfire could possibly melt glass) watching his beer bottle shrivel into a molten liquid glob!; drinking swigs of coffee laced with Old Overholt with aging friend Bill Porter-field, after a day of good fishing. On his last trip into the canyon, Old Bill sadly declared he was no longer physically able to climb the steep hill. Bill, my treasured fly tying and fly-fishing mentor, long gone under, is heartily missed.

I identify with this section of river like no other, because of trout. I experienced wonders most will never, because of trout. I grew profes-sionally here, because of trout. I cultivated solid friendships here, because of trout. I am a better conservationist, biologist and naturalist, because of trout. My heart, soul and spirit have been eternally enriched, because of trout. Because of trout, I acknowledge my imper-fections, making me a better man. Nothing can replace these adven-tures; my being would have a tremendous void without them. Many of my life's lessons are instilled in the river's ebb and flows, her riffles and runs, her shallows and depths. Nature, innately woven throughout my nature, nurtured my entire life. The wild ecstasy of this river, my kindred spirit, taught me to fish with a fly, and oh so much more! Understand, wildness is intricately entwined into my overall well-being. I believe we are all innately tied to Nature and should befriend at least one river, a mountain or, for that matter, any wild place. A well-known river or mountain melds deep within your soul as one discovers solutions to life's questions while persistently leading to countless uncertainties. Repeatedly visiting a river as a fisherman, or a mountain as a hunter, playing a predatory role in Nature's life and death games, instills a richer understanding of one's self. But take note, I will never declare to be an expert on this river because of fishing; HER ever-changing conditions require constant adjustment of knowledge, expertise and judgement, forever maintaining my amateur status as a student. SHE is simply more complicated than I can reason. But I treasure the challenges of playing the fishing game on **'My Home Runs',** attempting to decrypt the ever-changing river rules. A slugfest of pop flies, balks, hits, runs and errors, the river today was exceedingly generous, proffering gifts far exceeding catching trout.

The reader may question whether all events happened during a single river trip. Maybe, but what is most important, it all happened. Time blending like spring currents, I muse how my normally one-dimensional mind easily forgetting yesterday, could replay with extreme accuracy aged relics of past hunting and fishing events extending all the way to my youth. My mind somehow caches outdoor adventures where they can be effortlessly retrieved, urging my quick return and, hopefully, vitalizing my spirit when I can no longer.

I jealously guard 'my' river as a confidential secret shared only with a chosen few bonded friends deemed trustworthy river wards. Some, reprimanding me for taking far too long bringing them here, must understand this is my way of maintaining the river's relatively unspoiled tranquility. No longer wearing a badge, I understand my responsibilities of remaining one of the many river keepers, paying close attention to its conservation and management, and playing my role in maintaining order within the fishing ranks. Today I stepped up to the plate to ensure those defiling the river were subjected to the wrath of an equally protecting warden. Not a job for one lone ranger, the river requires a corps of government personnel and private individuals working for the common good.

Driving home replenished but exhausted, I am now eager to fulfill tomorrow's promises. Switching on the radio, the weatherman announced, "if you liked today, tomorrow will be its mirror image!"

Once again, those seductive Sirens began singing alluring fishing odes, commanding a prompt return. Hitting pavement, I phone my worried wife who lovingly wishes me Godspeed. *Oh, what a lucky man, I am.*

> *"For the moment at least, we fall into that class of fishermen who fancy themselves to be poet/philosophers, and from that vantage point we manage to pull off one of the neatest tricks in all of sport: the fewer fish we catch the more superior we feel. -----"*
> — John Gierach, Sex, Death, and Fly-Fishing

# THEY SHOOT MOOSE, DON'T THEY?

Transplanting moose into the Bull Pen, a career long aspiration of Wildlife Officer Sir Don Gore, became a reality in the late 1970's. Sir Don, Wildlife Officer John Wagner and I eagerly played integral roles in the historic moose 'reintroductions' working closely with biologists on the initial habitat evaluations, formal public and government agency input, meetings with local ranchers and building fenced holding pens on the 'Big Bottoms' of the Illinois River. We provided critical on ground support for the 1978 release of the moose from Utah (Uintah Mountains) and the 1979 capture and release of the moose from Wyoming (Jackson Hole). Taking place during the winter months, these labor-intensive endeavors required coordination of equipment and manpower of state and federal agencies. Well planned and well executed, bringing moose into Colorado served as an exemplary template for the biological, social and economic issues involved in modern day wildlife management.

Facing resistance from local ranchers concerning private land fence and forage damage, compromises were made on population strategies paving the way for what has become one of Colorado's most successful wildlife management stories. High level community support for moose was ultimately reflected by legislative recognition under the leadership of Senator Dave Wattenburg, officially declaring Jackson County as the Moose Viewing Capital of Colorado in 1995. The Moose Viewing Center located west of Cameron Pass on the Colorado State Forest is a tremendously popular stop for the multitudes of all interested in the history and biology of moose. Moose continue expanding their range and numbers across Colorado and are an immensely popular addition to the state's diverse and abundant populations of wildlife. *"Hell, I was there!"*

The term reintroduction was initially criticized as there were no records of sustainable populations occurring in Colorado, only documented sightings of individual moose dating back to the 1850's; likely transient animals wandering in from Wyoming or Utah.

And so it was, moose thrived and expanded throughout the Bull Pen, increasing to population levels allowing limited harvest. Hunting moose, a primary goal of the moose management plan, was identified as an essential component for maintaining moose numbers within defined habitat parameters. Hunting presently provides unique recreational opportunities and table fare for those lucky enough to draw a license. Hunting license dollars brought moose into Colorado, provides monies for management, and offers hunters and nonhunters alike exceptional wildlife adventures.

From the beginning, states with sustainable moose populations (Utah, Wyoming, Idaho and Montana) warned of the imminent problems associated with hunters, primarily those hunting elk, unlawfully shooting moose. Prior to the transplant, on October 18, 1976, a cow moose observed early morning the opening day of elk season on Independence Mountain was killed by an elk hunter in a matter of hours. Beginning with the transplant until now, Colorado wildlife officers across the state regrettably spend considerable time investigating wounded, spoiled carcasses or skeletons of illegally killed moose. The art and science of professionally handling illegal kills, salvaging meat, investigating kill sites and tracking down shooters is an unfortunate yet predictable warden responsibility. There is nothing more loathsome than staring at a spoiled moose carcass with no clues whatsoever who killed it. Most reports occur during the big game seasons when the hunting masses invade Colorado's mountains. Locating kill sites involves detecting the stagnant odor of a rotting carcass and/or the sights and sounds of crows, jays and magpies, or the spoking trails of coyotes and/or bear radiating into kill sights (especially when there is snow). Field techniques exercised to root out what the forest and willow drainages offer when giving up their dead involves collecting and recording evidence (spent casings, bullets retrieved from carcasses using a metal detector), photographing and following out boot and vehicle tracks, and questioning hunters, hopefully leading to one or more suspects. The first illegal moose I salvaged occurred high on the South Fork of the Michigan River drainage accompanied by Wildlife Officers Howard Spear and John Wagner. The carcass, spoiled and rancid, caused a retching Wagner to leave, me suffering intermittent dry heaves, and Spear, without hesitation, field dressing the beast with no bodily repercussions at all. My second illegal kill I field dressed alone on the Illinois River drainage, late at night with a flashlight in my mouth; a most challenging task indeed.

Moose cases are characteristically unique, often taking on a life of their own. Some accounts are anonymous, possibly from those responsible or not wanting to become involved. Others are conscience driven admissions from those turning themselves in. Illegal kills reported by law abiding, ethical hunters policing their own ranks represent the heroes of the hunting world and are considered the most effective overall deterrent in the prevention of wildlife crimes.

Normally, most shooters rapidly distance themselves from their misdeeds, leaving the entire area immediately. Bullets, even arrows, are often retrieved but offer little unless additional information leads the wardens to a shooter. Make no mistake, moose shooters turning themselves in receive much lighter treatment than those aggressively tracked down. All however, depending upon the circumstances, are guilty of varying degrees of irresponsibility, carelessness, disregard for safety or wildlife law, incompetence, and poor hunting skills. Some have no business hunting at all.

I immediately began spending time analyzing the psyche of those illegally killing moose. Each incident as intriguing as the shooters themselves, the details often provided insight on the ways and means of preventing future mistakes. The most popular excuses involve misidentification during the heat of the hunting moment (buck fever), shooting without identifying one's target and, of course, the party hunting syndrome of believing one can shoot any animal perceived as an elk if the proper licenses are available. Many captured shooters admit previously hunting moose and/or recently observing moose in the same area they mistakenly killed one. By far the lowest percentage of illegal kills involve blatant poaching for meat or antlers, occurring primarily before or after big game seasons when there are fewer people around (a large, heavy moose carcass is extremely difficult to bring out of the woods undetected). To this day, in spite of the continuing agency efforts in public education and law enforcement, illegal killing remains a primary moose management obstacle; a dark cloud for hunters and the hunting sport. Recognizing only a small minority of hunters are engaged in the poaching of moose, it is the majority hunting good who suffer most from illegal kills; numbers are added into the total annual moose harvest models resulting in fewer moose licenses available to the hunting public.

However, given a shred of evidence, wardens have made amazing, seemingly unachievable cases against those on the run. So often a name or vehicle description can bind the dangling frayed threads of 'nothing' into a woven cord providing sufficient information to wrap up a case.

I solved one case with Regional Fish Biologist Steve Puttman based on incessantly gathering intelligence from elk camps located in the vicinity of a recent illegal calf moose kill. Beginning with a vehicle description, a physical description of the man, an approximate address (Arvada, CO) from a camp who had spoken with him, matching boot tracks at the kill site, an abandoned camp, and driver's license information from the Sheriff's Office, we ferreted out the man and called his residence. His wife answered stating yes, he had been elk hunting but returned and was currently in bed because he was feeling very poorly. She summoned him to the phone and he immediately came clean revealing a great deal of embarrassment and remorse. He voluntarily made a trip to Sage Hen the following day cooperating fully with a detailed statement of his mistake and graciously accepting his fine of $1370!

Another relatively uncomplicated case involved a young Minnesota man hunting with and turned in by a trusted ranch foreman for killing three moose – a cow with two calves! First, picture Biologist Steve Steinert driving down a steep, mud frozen, snow covered two-track, steering mostly sidewards with an overload of three moose stacked cab high in his pickup bed. Next, picture the young, forlorn poacher explaining to Wildlife Officer Kirk Snyder and I he thought he was filling the elk licenses of his entire hunting party in spite of their being only two cow licenses available; stating he simply forgot party hunting was illegal in Colorado; singing the all too familiar 'land of 10,000 lakes' ballad killing others' game was legal in Minnesota. *Right!* And finally, picture him phoning his wife from our Sage Hen office, sorrowfully explaining they had to cancel their purchase of a new vehicle so he could cover the fines of his hunting misdeeds. Incredibly, his father graciously paid the entire $4100 fine, in cash, on the spot! Needless to say, these hunters never hunted the privately owned, game abounding ranch again.

*Go on, take the money and run!* ......Steve Miller Band

Captured moose shooters, like many others involved in Bull Pen wildlife crimes, are routinely seated alone in the agency's Sage Hen office, an intimidating warden room we wardens referred to as the 'Wiggle Room' – a place to squirm while contemplating their demise. It is here or at the kill sites where the (un)worthiest testimonials are bequeathed, with some skillful warden coaxing, in a poacher's own words. Case in point:

# MOOSE DROOL

October 1985. And there we were, Wildlife Officer Keith Kahler and I responding to a call concerning a wounded moose in the Illinois River timber cuts. Three concerned elk hunters, camped near the site where moose were initially transplanted, directed us to a salvageable, dead, yearling bull moose. Field dressing it, we discovered a jacketed bullet indicating the moose had been shot through its shoulder by a high-powered rifle. Because of the timely efforts of these three responsible men, we were able to donate the highly palatable meat to the needy. Finding no additional evidence and having no leads, we could only wait, hoping for additional information.

Unbelievingly, the following morning I was contacted by a Mr. Red Vixen at our Sage Hen Headquarters. Mr. Vixen, his head-cocking sneer already revealing a conceited ego, unremorsefully crowed 'accidentally' killing a moose in the very location we field dressed the bull the day before! Vixen's haughty behavior already overriding his integrity, I recognized the beginning of yet another thought-provoking account of man and beast.

His written account (verbatim);

*"I started hunting about 10:15 am on 10-14-1985 and saw elk tracks in some over cut timber about 4 blocks from where I parked my car. I then*

*proceeded to an open park where I sat and waited. Right across the park was about 100 yrds. were Lodge pole pine trees, not to thick at first then 30 farther they were very black. I saw 5 or 6 bodies of animals moving casually along the trees. I studied them for about 15 minutes to determine what they were. Because of their color and movement and because of the light conditions, I decided they were elk, not horses, deer or cattle. Then I shot one time as to place my shot in the lower chest cavity behind the front leg as all I saw was a three-foot section of the shoulder and part of the front leg. I knew I hit the animal and when I went over to clean it, found that it was a moose. I did not realize there was moose in that area as I have never hunted there before."*

Recognizing Vixen's lack of shame in revealing what I considered highly irresponsible behavior, I readily accepted his invitation to revisit the kill site. His written statement revealing a severe lack of hunting skills, Vixen continued offering incriminating insights on how and why he inadvertently killed the moose. On our way, he described finding the wounded bull alive but unable to stand, and he elected to leave it alone. The middle-aged Vixen also disclosed he had hunted moose in other states.

Vixen's final proclamations remains with me to this very day:

*"I turn into an animal while hunting. Hunting is a jungle type fighting situation causing me to intensely drool, especially when field dressing game animals."*

At the kill site he pointed out the location he shot from, approximating 50 yards. Asking why he shot the moose without first verifying sex (antlers!) and species, his answer detailed because he believed the animal was an elk and knowing his hunting partner was 150 yards away with an antlerless elk license, it did not matter if he shot a bull or a cow. *WRONG!* Questioning why he hunted without a rifle scope or binoculars, Vixen replied his eyesight was excellent, he desired neither! *SERIOUSLY!*

So, given these senselessness circumstances, what does a warden say? I began by articulating shooting the moose was not an accident, but a series of blatant violations of the moral, ethical, levelheaded and legal codes of modern-day hunting. I admonished his failure to obey Colorado's party hunting laws. Unscathed, Vixen countered he was aware party hunting is illegal, but since everyone does it, why does it matter? Firing back, I asserted it mattered because it would have prevented the demise of a young bull moose. If not for the concerned elk hunters taking time to report it, the bull would have spoiled turning his misdemeanors into a charge of felony waste of big game! Leaving the wounded bull to suffer an untimely death portrays the irresponsible, inhumane behavior of one having no business hunting at all. I let him know I considered his confessions the straightforward words of a conscienceless poacher.

To his unappreciative displeasure, I charged him only for killing the moose, ignoring other costly charges as a reward for turning himself in. Believing coming to my office and justifying his conduct elevated his status as a hunter, Vixen viewed my 'deal' unjust and demanded a court appearance. Although found guilty, his fine was reduced from $1100.00 to $498.00 by a lenient judge, allowing a $600 discount for truthfully confessing his misdeeds; completely discounting the details outlined in my case report, Vixen's written statement, and the charges I graciously ignored.

*"No good deed goes unpunished!" Oscar Wilde*

Leaving the courtroom, Vixen alleged the judge should have dismissed the entire case, making him wonder why he came to me in the first place. In retrospect, so did I!

You be the judge!

*"Justice? -- You get justice in the next world. In this one you have the law."*
*William Gaddis*

# GRANDMA'S MANTRA

D aylight's fore glow silhouetting the east range, I gulped down my customary juice and bran curiously watching Betsy exercise her morning ritual of breakfast bribery; offering their two young'uns a world of treasures if they ate OR being grounded indefinitely if they did not. Marc, our elder son, sat in glazed silence enjoying his morning stupor while his ever-restless sister, Annie, mothered her *living* dolls. Issuing a verbal warning to the kids and a good luck kiss for my wife, I roared north out of Sage Hen. It was mid-July and hot, at least in Bull Pen standards. Today's design was to work a sagebrush lake during the morning's dawning cool and then head west to the comfortable high elevation pleasantness of the forest. Mosquitoes buzzed rampant throughout the sagebrush bottomlands this time of year and one can only evade their piercing torment by working the early morning hours. By mid-morning, awakened by the sun's warming rays, they swarmed in dense clouds seeking a blood meal from anything having a heartbeat.

Turning into Cowdrey Lake, and following a faint two track, I eased my vehicle along a fence line leading to a vantage offering a birds-eye view of the southwest corner of the lake. Fishermen accessed the opposite side of the lake by driving through the Loban 'Apaloosa' Ranch after paying a fee to ranch manager Tom Hackleman, one of the Bull Pen's seasoned, authentic cowboys. For some, this off the main road 'hideaway' tendered an extra sense of security that, with the good fishing, enticed them into violating fishing law.

I scratched many tics covertly spying on this lake. The grapevine, telegraphing babble essential for warden success, whispered incessant gossip of multitudes of illegal trout hidden in the most unimaginable places: secret compartments built below camper floors; sunken coolers in the irrigation ditches; five gallon gas cans; wheel wells and hub caps; as well as several recent reports of iced down bags of illegal trout hanging down one hole of the two-holer outhouse (poaching scumwads with crappy tastes)! Incredibly, I once found myself casing the crapper hoping, if nothing else, to appease or at least amuse those fishermen present. And I did. Hiding trout, an inherent art form for many a miscreant, could only be countered by a warden's ability to seek them out. Admittedly, I never 'smelled' out the intriguing report of the fishy outhouse.

My assigned district covered more than 800 square miles of mountain forest and rolling sage encompassing untold numbers of trout laden lakes and miles of streams. Most of the time, like any warden, I travelled as a Lone Ranger stalking the wilds. My work could be described as inefficient and unmanageable, but a necessary force for maintaining a semblance of law and order while 'flying the flag' for the wild. Cowdrey Lake, always in need of warden charge, was heavily stocked with hatchery-raised, 8 to 12-inch rainbows I dubbed 'wind up' trout because of the ease of catching them when first stocked. The lake, not experiencing a winterkill for several years, carried a high percentage of the previous year's trout which regained their wild roots and grew significantly in length and weight on the natural forage provided by the lakes productive waters.

Bank fishing, often difficult due to the tangling mats of moss and algae blooming along the shoreline, was exceptional on the Loban Ranch side because the prevailing west winds kept the waters weed-free a good distance from the bank. My routine was concealing my truck behind a willow choked irrigation ditch to secretly scrutinize the lake's first shift of early fishermen. Scoping a lone boat on the water, I found one of two fishermen was actually glassing me! My veiled lairs were often discovered by the vigilantly aware and it was not unusual to see fishermen searching for wardens through their own optics. Once detected, some 'Paul Revered' my presence to other fishermen, a kind of honor amongst thieves. Initially, this angered me, but I soon recognized such tattling to be a valuable enforcement tool. Those searching out my presence or absence are critical players in the warden game, providing a semblance of uneasiness seasoning the paranoia of errant fishermen watching for, discussing and cussing the antics of a covert warden. *"To him who is in fear, everything rustles."* Sophocles. Once detected, I simply waved and watched them hastily set down their optics pretending not to have seen me. Today, however, I had a new tactic from my bag of tricks.

While the boatmen continued watching , I exited my pickup, opened the truck's utility box, pulled out a set of fencing pliers and a hammer, and proceeded to 'fix' thirty yards of fence; pounding posts and twisting wire for ten minutes before driving down the fence line and disappearing into a draw bordered by a willowy ditch. Enjoying a brood of sage grouse walking the ditch bank, I angled my vehicle towards the opposite shoreline, and peered through the willows. Through the window mounted spotting scope, 'Big Eye.' My fencing ruse successful, the boatmen were once again fishing intently. The cool temperatures allowed turning the scope to its full 60 power providing an undistorted view of all fishermen soon to be washed by the rising morning sun. Thinking out loud I mumbled, *"the Big Eye doesn't lie."* The sun, peeking over the Medicine Bow Range, promised another warm and dry day essential for the Bull Pen's haymakers busily harvesting their single crop of highly popular native grass hay. I adjusted the glaring rearview mirror to reflect on the east range and its towering granite peaks. The morning radiating her warming smile across my back, I gazed through the scope through one open eye.

Several campers were parked across the lake but only one 'early bird' was outside; an elderly woman busily tending SEVEN fishing poles set in red rod holders, the gleaming monofilament lines tautly extending into the lake's waters. She was skillfully handling bites, baiting hooks, casting and reeling lines, landing and stringing trout. Trout were biting frantically and her theatrics of tending to the frenzy was most entertaining. On one occasion this dramatic dowager expressed her frustration of missing a bite by waving a clenched fist at the lake. The show was on.

Expecting someone to exit the campers at any time, I watched her catch and keep ten trout, two over her limit of eight. Not knowing how many trout she caught before my arrival, I chose ending the old frump's fun early as she was only adding to her fine with each additional trout. She was also in violation of fishing with at least five more poles than allowed by law.

Anxious to scratch the tic and head to the high country, I hastily drove through the ranch, opening and closing several stinging barbed wire gates while shooing away the ranch's stunning appaloosas. Topping the hill overlooking the campers I could see the old lady landing yet another trout. Hearing my vehicle, she looked over her shoulder freezing solid while playing a fierce tug of war with the fish. I walked over and broke her icy glare by stating it would be best if she threw that one back. Amazingly, she did. Wearing a light blue 'pioneer' bonnet with a ruffled rim in front, an ankle length blue patterned calico granny dress and black knee-high rubber boots, the spry little lady resembled a cast member of Wagon Train. Her countless years displayed a stooped back, wrinkled face, steel grey hair tightly pulled back into a bun, and root-like veined hands. A bronzed face contrasted boldly with sparkling crystal blue eyes flashing the vitality rarely seen in most a fraction of her age. Here was a very old woman, life fire roaring, enjoying every precious moment of her new age. Smiling cordially, I asked how she was doing. Predictably, she admitted catching a few. *A few too many!* I inquired about the seven poles and she said all but two belonged to her relatives in the camper. Walking over to the stringer I counted eleven trout out loud asking how many belonged to her. Answering she was not sure but several belonged to her <u>husband</u>; she was obviously familiar playing the warden game.

Asking to see a fishing and driver's license, I followed her to the camper and as she raked through her purse, I could see a pair of sleepy eyes peering over bed covers. A young child asked, "Grandma, have you caught any fish?" Maude answered, "Fishing was very good but seems to be getting worse." Handing me her fishing license she politely refused to show a driver's license chortling, "I am not driving." Not pushing it, I reviewed her fishing license amazingly discovering this woman, Maude Gran Damme, was not just old, she was an ancient, aged to perfection, collectible antique; her vintage going back to the late 1800's. Her eighty-eight years nearly three times my current age!

A withered looking man, later identified as L.B. Damme, stepped out of the camper and I, thinking he was Maude's husband, asked to see his fishing license. L.B. arrogantly replied, "What the hell for? Mom is the only one fishing!" Realizing my mistake, I politely told the man I needed to see his father's license setting off yet another explosion from L.B.'s bucket mouth, "What in the hell are you talking about? My father died years ago!" Wow! Old Methuselah had apparently met his maker and, according to Maude, was still catching trout. The son, having no clue of what was happening, instinctively went to his mother's aid, chastising me for harassing his elderly mom. Maude swelled with pride as her son admonished my charming nature. Knowing my 'fun' would decline with the awakening of the others, I motioned Maude over to the poles hoping to break up the mother/son tag team. Keeping her busy, I requested she reel in the lines, sternly stating I previously observed her catch eleven trout and would have to issue her a citation for three fish over the limit. Without a word she reeled in the seven lines, short-stepped backwards up the bank and sat down on the tailgate of their pickup. Her son continued his tongue lashings demanding to know what his mother had done to warrant such vile treatment. Hoping for Maude's response, I watched her head rise slowly and through a cinnamon sweet smile clearly snarl, in the quivering undertones of a pious old lady, "Blow it out your ass you little prick!" Shaking a crooked finger she followed with, "one day you will regret this you son-of-a-bitch." This seemingly sweet little old lady had hastily transformed into the Cowdrey Lake Bitch. Her words evoked similar reactions from everyone as L.B. tapped out a Woody Woodpecker laugh while I quietly chuckled behind a closed mouthed grin. Teething on my butt cheeks, Maude accused me of illicitly allowing her to break the law by not stopping her from over-bagging on trout. I courteously replied I ended her misdeeds early to lessen her impending troubles.

Normally, such an outburst would seal the demise of any ensnared poacher, but this golden girl was different. Uncharacteristically, my mind debated on whether to 'hang paper' or simply end the contact with a biting warning. Her son, detecting the seven rods and the stringer of trout, reloaded and fired another verbal barrage of meaningless blanks questioning the warden's ability to prove who caught the fish. *Now that's the ticket!* Like quail shooting out of a thicket, my following words flushed away any chance of leniency. It was crystal clear a warning would serve no justice to either Maude or L.B., both displaying a blatant disregard for the law and lawman. In their eyes, I was wrong, ticket or not. Hastily scratching out the tic, I cited Maude for three illegal trout while L.B. continued snapping like a heel biting hound. Recapping not citing her for the extra rods, my words fell on ignorant, deaf ears. With a cordial smile I handed her the ticket, confiscated three of the smaller trout and wished them both a good day.

Returning to my truck, the pair continued wailing about the unfairness of the fishing world and its rogue wardens. L.B stated they would contact a lawyer and have my job after appearing in court. Unpredictably, while opening and shutting gates, I found my normally flint hard enforcement demeanor being chipped away by lingering strikes of remorse. Scoping the old lady from the lake's public side, I observed her sitting on the bank with the rest of her group obviously looking back at me. My melting soul was instantly quick-frozen as the old warhorse stood up, waved to make sure she had my attention and arrogantly flipped me the bird! *Now that was a grandmother that would make anyone proud!*

In all my years as a wildlife enforcement officer, I questioned only a handful of my citations. But the old veteran fish pilferer Maude Gran Damme will always hold a special place in my heart. I will never forget that little old lady sitting on the back of the 'Conestoga's' tailgate. A lily needing no gild, her hard-earned, beauty worn with dignity, advertised her seniority rights in aged splendor symbolizing the old way; the fast disappearing generation of independent and rawhide tough pioneer stock that settled our nation. God bless you Maude Gran Damme, wherever you are.

*Esto perpetua. – may you live forever*

# UNFORGIVEN TRESPASSES

During my watch, ranch property boundaries tightened significantly as landowners began taking advantage of the financial benefits of hunting and fishing. By limiting access to lands harboring healthy big game populations, landowners experienced a surge in hunter trespass. After local law enforcement clarified their response to trespass complaints demanded the landowner or his manager file formal charges, property-owners became indignantly proficient at capturing the secreting wraiths literally red handed, with game in hand. In turn, wardens discovered rapid response often resulted in weighty wildlife violations exceeding the trespass charge itself.

Now, imagine an isolated ranch hidden in a stunning valley of willowy hay meadows, divided by a narrow creek, bordered in gnarly ridges of aspen, sage, and pine, and guarded by the heavily forested Buffalo Peak. Paint in a timeworn log barn, a timbered loft above its horse stalls, associated pole corrals, a one-story ranch house, a log guest cabin, and a large Quonset shop. Brushing in mother cows with calves, sturdy draft horses, and a blue heeler dog should complete your mental mural of a traditional working Rocky Mountain cattle ranch. Buffalo Peak, Buffalo Ridge, Buffalo Creek and the number of ancient buffalo skulls found on the property over the years historically defines the Ranch's namesake. The Buffalo Ranch, then managed by Steve Story, wife Linda, daughter Marla and son Bart, was blessed with a family laboring tirelessly for an absentee landowner, as if the property were their own. Stalwart stockmen, cowboys in every sense of the word, their knowledge of cattle and horse flesh was second to none. I bootlegged their expertise to better comprehend the local Stockgrowers demands for resolving their big game conflicts. For this Ohio greenhorn, I was fortunate both personally and professionally to befriend the Story family.

Next, enliven the ranch and the surrounding public and private lands with an abundant big game population tendering first-rate hunting opportunities during the late summer and fall hunting seasons. Avid hunters themselves, the Story's enlisted a select corps of hard-core sportsmen to harvest big game, especially elk, creating tightly bonded, long term friendships exemplifying the timeless legacy of modern-day hunting cultures.

The ranch, bordered by remotely accessible public lands to the south, islands of public and private lands to the east and west, tendered irresistible temptations for the scheming as well as the opportunistic hunting public. The Buffalo Ranch was a trespassing magnet! During the big game hunting seasons, the Story's' were haunted by consistent, blatant trespass violations from all sides of the property. Poaching intruders, willing to cross forbidden boundaries, openly entered onto and pirated game off the property. Understand, wardens routinely encounter and address private land trespass throughout the Bull Pen, but not one measured up to the number of miscreants invading the Buffalo Ranch during my watch.


**DOUBLE TAKES!** Capturing wildlife outlaws' multiple times is greatly increased by their innate tenacity to violate law unrestricted by a legal or moral compass. The story of one man, Iza Gatecrasher, exemplifies the mindset of such an outlaw. Poaching without capture placing him well ahead of the warden game, my success bagging Iza began one elk season and ended a year later.

**Take One.** 1981 Elk season. Finding no one around a public land elk camp, Wildlife Officer Larry Budde and I combed the area and discovered a skinned, quartered, and untagged bull elk hidden in thick aspen. Hours later, four hunters arrived carrying unfilled bull elk licenses. Denying knowledge of the untagged bull, their stories abruptly changed when separated, all acknowledging the bull was killed 'somewhere' by camp member Iza Gatecrasher. They did not (illegally) tag the bull because they wanted to continue hunting, further disclosing Iza did not tag the bull because he was licensed to kill a cow elk. *Hoka Hey!* The strong scent of party hunting in the air, Iza unexpectedly drove into camp with a freshly killed cow elk, properly tagged with his license! The gut-wrenching spectacle of two wardens outwardly worn on his grimacing face, Iza wilted like a frosted wildflower when interviewed, making clear he alone killed the bull illegally with no involvement of his hunting companions. When asked where he killed both elk, he faltered, stating they were killed near Buffalo Peak. Larry and I scratched Iza's tic, confiscated the bull and drove away with five demoralized hunters glaring into my rearview mirror. The red flags hoisted, warden intuition whispered there were additional stories, some untold and others yet written, needing time for future warden scrutiny.

**Take Two.** 1982 elk season. Fast forward a year (and one week) later. Diligently burning the candle at both ends working big game seasons, I needed a break! Thirsting for a taste of good whiskey, my radio abnormally quiet, I stole into the Buffalo Ranch around lunchtime. After inspecting the customary barnful of legally tagged elk hanging in the drive-in hay loft, I entered the ranch's Quonset, temporarily converted into a bunkhouse and gathering place for the visiting hunters. Steve, Linda and all their hunters greeted me with a Red Solo cup of iced Wild Turkey while we all traded hunting tales and my adventures of capturing miscreants. It did not take long before they began cursing trespassers, several intruders evading capture during their morning hunt. Planning to hunt a large expanse of heavy timber, I heartily agreed to join them to stretch my legs and clear my mind. Always in warden mode, I cunningly volunteered to walk the property fence line, a familiar secretive entrance for the hunting bad.

Despite yearning a brief break from the season's reality, my magnetism for attracting trouble was about to draw me into another adventure. Taking a stand along the fence, a truck carrying several hunters flashed through the heavy aspen fifty yards below. All quiet, I stalked the fence, crested a small knob, and spotted a flash of hunter orange moving towards the ranch property. Brightly clad in fluorescent orange myself, I attempted hiding in plain sight and watched a rifle bearing man walk up to the fence, scan all directions, apparently gazing right over me! In a flash, he crawled under the bottom wire and ghosted into the private property. Eager to enter the property without detection, little did he know he was within fifty yards of his warden maker. *Hoka Hey!*

As I cautiously moved along the fence to maintain sight of the intruder, he suddenly hid behind a tree, undoubtedly glimpsing a member of Buffalo Ranch hunting party. Literally tiptoeing back to the fence, he all but soiled his camo denims when I heartily greeted the scalawag with a smiling, **"HELLO!"** In a state of mutual recognition, would you believe I was eye to eye with Iza Gatecrasher! His ashen face blending with the aspen bark behind, Iza undoubtedly was facing his worst nightmare! *What are the odds?* Requesting his license, I asked if he had written permission to hunt the Buffalo Ranch, knowing he did not. Handing me his unfilled cow license, Iza lied saying he had verbal permission but could not remember the ranch manager's name. Iza's past was about to outrun him.

Crapping razor blades, Iza was tensely anxious to 'get out of Dodge'. Placing his license in my field notebook, I turned him loose affirming I would contact him later, smilingly watching him scamper downhill like a fleeing rabbit. In a matter of minutes, a barrage of earsplitting rifle shots echoed throughout the forest, sniping me into full alert! *Buffalo Ranch hunters?* Topping another knob, I observed a dead cow elk, a floundering spike bull and a hunter killing another wounded cow. *DAMN!* All this taking place with the background music of Iza fast driving the two-track below, honking his horn and yelling GAME WARDEN! Noticing a second hunter walking up to the dead cow, I now had three downed elk and two unfamiliar hunters illegally hunting Buffalo Ranch property! Announcing my presence with another lively **"HELLO"**, the wide-eyed pair were visibly spell-bound by the sight of a uniformed warden axing what they initially perceived as particularly good hunting luck. Their licenses identified Iza's brother in crime Ima and his criminal compadre, Willy Howl. Ima, licensed for a bull elk, had killed a cow, and wounded the spike. Poor Willy, also licensed for a bull, had killed a cow. And poor ole Iza, unknowingly just had his illegally killed cow stolen away by a game warden in the right place at their wrong time. With a sly grin, much to their chagrin, I directed the hang dog pair to kill the wounded spike bull, field dress all three elk, and rudely suggested recruiting Iza to help drag the elk down to the road.

After retrieving my vehicle, I met all three poachers along the road and loaded their illegal bounty into my pickup. Scratching hefty tics to Ima and Willy for the trespass and three illegal elk, they chose to mail in their fines. Iza, however, facing a suspension of his hunting license privileges based on his previous year's transgressions, requested a court appearance hoping for leniency. To his dismay, an intolerant judge found him guilty and Iza's hunting and fishing privileges were later suspended for three years!

Days later, another wasted spike bull was found on Buffalo Ranch property, no doubt collateral damage of the Gatecrashers misdeeds. A vivid illustration of how illegal trespass and party hunting promotes the carnage of waste, wounding loss, and unsportsmanlike overkill.

The tale of Iza and his gang does not end here. Steve Story, often dissatisfied with the pain inflicted by my tics, would frequently request a rendezvous at the ranch's barn with some of the more blatant intruders. A tall, lanky, soft spoken, square jawed black hat cowboy, Steve was a dominating figure any given day. However, standing in front of captured intruders in the barn's shadowy courtroom, he transformed into an ass chewing magistrate. So, there they were, Iza, Ima and Willy, the very day of their capture, openly facing their cowboy judge, backed by a jury of Steve's family, hunter friends, and a warden; shamefacedly about to receive a fire and brimstone ass ripping sermon beyond their wildest imagination. Reprimands inflicting more pain than any tic I scratched, Steve not only brazed their rear ends but also scarred their minds with a searing oratory barnstorming the seriousness of violating private property ownership. Placing them in his shoes, Steve hammered the impact of their transgressions by querying what they would do if unknown thieves invaded their property. Leaving with charred asses, dented minds, an empty wallet, no elk and facing the loss of their hunting privileges, they remained silent, not a word spoken until Steve demanded their comments, listening attentively while each intruder remorsefully confessed their impulsive apologies.

And so, like flies on cow crap, the ranch continued buzzing with trespassers. Countless tics were scratched, many worthy tales also scribed in these chronicles.

This I know, those entering the Buffalo Ranch as trespassers, after suffering the wrath of Steve Story, left in a very disturbed frame of mind.


*"Oh, what a tangled web we weave...when first we practice to deceive."*
Walter Scott, Marmion

# LAP DOG

June 1984. And there I was, pulling off the gravel road as the small, irregularly shaped reservoir came into sight. My truck veiled in low-hanging branches, I mounted the Big Eye to the window and searched the shoreline. Slack-Weiss Reservoir, heavily stocked with catchable rainbow trout, was a hodge-podge for illicit behavior of all kinds. From this vantage, I detected violations of wildlife law, illegal drug use and sales, spousal abuse as well as discovering stolen vehicles and those having outstanding arrest warrants. In 1978, witnessing blatant hard drug abuse, I led local law enforcement authorities into a $20,000 methamphetamine drug bust! Rarely disappointed, I anxiously anticipated today's adventures.

The morning warming fast, I welcomed the shimmering aspen shade and slight breeze. Scanning the reservoir, I observed only one person sitting on the far side of the reservoir. Zooming in, I focused on a man sitting behind two fishing poles propped on forked sticks petting a black dog in his lap. No one else around, I elected checking his fishing license and trekking the forest cool of Arapaho Lakes. Taking one last peak, imagine my amazement when the black dog materialized into a woman's head, vigorously working over the fruit of her companion's loins. In a blink, she stood donning only shorts and tennis shoes, grabbed her man's hand and, while he pulled up his shorts, both scurried up the bank into a camper. Polite wardensmanship dictated giving the fiery couple time to turn down the heat. Driving to their side of the lake, I walked over to the poles confirming both lines extended into the water and finding one jerking wildly revealing a "FISH ON"! Standing by the poles, I could not see the camper. Forty-five minutes later, I knocked on the camper door announcing I was a wildlife officer checking fishing licenses. Finding the spent pair asleep, a disheveled man eventually opened the door and handed me his license identifying one Headly Bone. Bone openly confessed both poles were his and he had not purchased the required stamp permitting fishing with two poles. THAT WAS EASY! When informed the poles were out of the camper's view and had not been checked for almost an hour (illegal), Bone stubbornly insisted they were always within his sight. However, he instantaneously wilted when I baited my line explaining there was a hooked fish on one of his. Bone's lap mate exited the camper and raucously protested the disruptive nuisance of my presence. When asked for her ID she presented a driver's license identifying one B.J. Hooker, undoubtedly one of the ugliest women I ever encountered; the rarity of a driver's license photo enhancing the unsightliness of the person standing before me! While Bone reeled in the rainbow, B.J. cursed a diatribe of vulgarities targeting rogue 'cops' perpetually harassing the innocent. Advising I arrived when they were sitting on the bank, the foul-mouthed 'lap woman' silently cowered back into her doghouse, no doubt pondering what all I witnessed. Considering it mischievously impolite to cite Bone for his 'unattended rod' (RIGHT?) I scratched a tic for the two pole violations.

*There are a million stories in the naked woods!*

# DOGS AND THEIR BEST FRIENDS

*"If you pick up a starving dog, and make him prosperous, he will not bite you. This is the principal difference between a dog and a man."*
The tragedy of Pudd'nhead Wilson. Mark Twain

Self defensively, Wildlife Officers adapt to the highly variable dog behavior encountered during their myriad of field contacts. My canine education began instantaneously when assigned to the Bull Pen. During the 70's a preponderance of runaway dogs roamed the streets of Sage Hen. Painful yelps of hounds 'hung up' in coupled fervor on Main Street, dog fights, relentless barking and road kills crushed into lifeless corpses all around town were commonplace. My first week, walking the two blocks from home to the courthouse to meet the sheriff, I was fiercely pursued by a snarling, tooth baring mutt; a near death experience triggering a world class 100-yard dash I never again achieved. On another occasion I was pummeled by a fence jumping Saint Bernard while riding my bike to share a whiskey with compadre Sir Don Gore and his wife Tolly Ann. Scraping away gravel ground into my bloody raw elbows and forearms, I realized I had been bitten. Sir Don's neighbor, witnessing the entire event, pledged his dog would never bite! *Yeah, Right!* Yup, a trip to Doc France, who cleaned and bandaged the wound assuring rabies was nothing to worry about. Well, the dog did not die and obviously either did I, so the story continues.

Thus, began my initiation into an endless accumulation of dog and dog owner adventures tracking my entire career. I was present when officer Sig 'Slick' Palm drew his revolver on a viciously advancing dog described by his owner as friendly. Sig spontaneously blurted, "Want your dog dead?" and the dog was hastily kenneled by its panic-stricken master. Several area ranchers declared their cattle dogs 'shovel trained', meaning it was safe to get out of your truck only if carrying a shovel! Impending threats of dog attacks repeatedly reinforced by nips, torn pant legs and skin breaking bites, resulted in the evolution of strategic 'ninja' foot maneuvers to protect myself from malicious dog behavior.

Another canine calamity developed when accessing Mexican Ridge required driving through a private ranch and opening an unwieldy, very taut barb-wired gate. The ranch was guarded by a true junk yard dog spending most of its time roaming the nearby bone pile and machinery graveyard. Words cannot explain the intense fear suffered while rapidly opening and closing this loosely wired, barbed gate to elude the savagely advancing canine brute. This pit bull mix, renowned for killing badgers and dumping their carcasses on his owner's front door (badgers are top the food chain beasts fearing nothing), chased down and bit the UPS and gas men's rear ends so many times neither would exit their truck until the owner secured the dog.

Another seemingly harmless situation took place when I was greeted by a tail wagging lap dog while conversing with a family camping along Pinkham Creek. Rubbing the mutt's head in full view of mother and father it suddenly nipped my hand causing me to roll it across the campsite with a hard kick. Discovering the bite had not broken my skin, their son exited their tent and declared, "You shouldn't pet our dog because it has ringworm!"

As a sideline hobby, I began scrutinizing the relationships between dogs and their masters, learning as much about the man or woman as their beast. This is especially true with hunting dogs, due to the countless hours devoted to training their dog(s) to scent, point, flush and retrieve wild game, thus creating enduring innately bonded kinships. I am thoroughly convinced many dogs take on the personality traits of their owner: disciplined masters having controlled dogs; disorderly masters have unmanageable dogs; if a dog is obese, their master may need more exercise; a snooty master generates a snobby dog; laid back masters generates a dog blithe, etc. Understand the canine calamity when Fido's IQ is reduced to that of his incompetent master; or the tragedy of those masters futilely attempting to train a dog whose mental capacity falls short of Disney's Goofy. Conversely, I **once** hunted with a thick-witted ignoramus where it became crystal clear even his dog perceived him as an asshole.

On a South Dakota pheasant hunt, I chased down, leashed and verbally disciplined an uncontrollable black lab flushing birds well out of gun range. Glaring through its hollow eyes I saw the identical mindless stare worn by his aimlessly wandering master. There is nothing more disturbing than hunting with uncontrollable dogs, wondering whether to discipline the dog or his owner. The behavior of this dog and his master sent them on a one-way trip to pheasantlessville, never invited to hunt with our group again.

Of course, even the most disciplined dogs have their moments. I witnessed a highly trained German Shorthair search, scent and retrieve a downed quail in heavy cattails under the practiced commands of his master. The pointer, not seeing the bird go down, was directed across a mucky slough and easily scented and picked up the bird. Hard mouthing the quail to the edge of the slough it sat down, blatantly ignoring his master's commands. Reading the dog's mind, I expressed concern it was going to eat the quail triggering the owner to arrogantly declare his field trial champion dog never consumed game birds! Imagine my enjoyment watching him eat crow as the dog swallowed the entire quail in one huge *GULP!* Similarly, our hunting group enjoyed when another misbehaved hunting dog, after swimming the South Platte River on a grueling, long-distance retrieve of a downed duck, audaciously refuse to swim back. Totally snubbing the increasing resonance of his master's raucous commands, the entertained hunting party watched the dog pick, proficiently spit out feathers and consume, except for its head, feet and wings, the entire carcass!

Much to the dismay of their masters, some dogs are simply not programmed to hunt. Imagine Sierra, an overanxious female springer spaniel fading out of sight far ahead of our hunting line despite dragging two heavy rubber balls tethered to her harness through heavy cover. With great effort, her vocally animated, highly distraught master Mongo, chased her down and jailed the lowly fugitive into her kennel for the remainder of our hunting adventures.

Pursuing game with well-trained and obedient (most of the time) dogs with longtime friends generates extraordinary experiences far exceeding harvesting birds. Good hunting dogs able to scent and retrieve harvested upland game in heavy cover, some otherwise never found, are indispensable components of our hunts. Add their unique individual personalities and communicative techniques (tail wagging, eye contact, facial expressions, dominant or remissive behavior etc.) to their master's diverse vocalizations, whistle blowing, and personal antics, crafts a spectator sport, indeed! After several initial pheasant hunts, my young grandson asked if one of my compadres dogs was named 'goddammit'! For over six decades, I trailed countless hounds, labs, pointers, setters and mutts of all kinds, in incalculable hunting scenarios. My dogs, Betsy a blue tic Coon Hound and Smokey, a Black Lab, both long passed, afforded treasured memories that will follow me to my grave.

Dogs remain strongly intertwined into the tightly stitched fabric of our hunting gang referred as 'The Corps of Discordance'. Our voyages are well documented in a Journal passionately scribing a twenty-five-year cache of stalking the vast South Dakota prairies. We continue celebrating our legacy of men and their best friends hunting as a team until age will no longer allow! The 'Corps', their names, aliases and their dogs:

Rick Kahn (aka P.Rick) and Pointing Labs Julie (Stink), and Holly.

Tom Remington (akaWinchester) and English Setters Troon, Tess, Tucker, (the long-legged 'elephant fu..er'), Dickens and his latest pup Nel.

Ken Kehmeier (aka CantHitShitMeier) and Black Labs Rugger (the snorting pig) and Roux (the fast tongue licker).

Gary Miller (aka Ofer) and English Setters Cassie (the lazarus dog) and Annie.

John Smeltzer (aka Mongo) with Yellow Labs Kysa and Piper.

Bob Brown (aka Skidmarks) our South Dakota guide, no dogs but a quirky, quick witted critic of Corps members and their dogs.

Me,(aka Stan / Hobbit / Dwarf), also a dogless Corps member, eagerly trailed and gratefully exploited these skilled dogs at their owners' expense. Color me extremely indebted.

Three additional comrades and their dogs I hunted with extensively include: Larry Budde with his Black Lab Sadie; Cousin Tim with his Brittany Darby and German shorthairs Baron, Axel, Molly, Gretchen, Britta and Annie; and Kirk Snyder with his black lab Sable. Thanks for the memories!

This enumeration of men and their dogs is scribed not only to stimulate my memory of trailing them across endless miles of woodlands, streams and fields, but to emphasize the incredible number and diversity of hunting dogs inspiring our lives for over a half century. I grieved the heart-rending ceremonies of Ken and John spreading their dog's ashes over the sacred ground of past South Dakota hunts. I shared the agony of watching my friends' troubled hearts mushroom into ague fits after their dogs collapsed in total exhaustion in the field: a grieving Gary Miller carrying his presumably lifeless dog Annie back to our vehicles and the immense delight when she miraculously came back to life. The extreme vocal agony of a spinning Ken Kehmeier watching his presumably dying dog Rugger convulsing in wrenching seizures and, likewise, recovering unharmed. Yet another experience occurred when a South Dakota guide's dog passed out due heat exhaustion and was skillfully brought back to life by icing down his stomach and balls! All these events induced by the dogs' intensive, instinctive drive to hunt.

Now, it is well known wildlife officers and dogs go together like brook trout and beaver ponds. A lab (or other variable breeds) riding shotgun or in the back of a warden's truck remains the tradition of many Colorado wardens. Also, it has been said during one's lifetime, a man or woman will be blessed by one uniquely special dog. My good fortune came as a raven black lab registered as 'Smoke on Owl Mountain', whose canine IQ unremittingly surpassed mine. Riding in my vehicle and/or trekking together over the vast Bull Pen land-scapes, crafted a man/dog comradeship I will never again experi-ence. Smokey's 'soul' purpose was pleasing me and if I clearly expressed what I wanted, he would do it. If I failed, Smokey taught himself to sit and glare into my eyes apparently asking, 'please just let me know what it is you want'! During one training session, easing the pup into a flock of adult male sage grouse 'bombers' for a taste of scent before they flushed, I repeatedly called him back shouting undecipherable ever-changing commands. On cue, Smokey turned back and sat facing me with a head-cocking stare. Once I settled down, I coaxed him into the flock and watched him instinc-tively turn on his nose, scent, track and flush the birds. Surprisingly, without my direction, he tracked down and flushed several singles. It was then I realized Smokey was not the only one in training; his compliance depending entirely upon my ability to interconnect. By the third year, having educated each other well, we grew into a smooth-running team. Of course, Smokey had his moments; pissing on the untidy judge's pet infused, grubby wool pants on his way to the courthouse on a cold winter day; his unbreakable habit of crapping a butt load on the neighbor's yard; wolfing down fishermen's trout on stringers and creels along shorelines. But my time invested was consistently rewarded by untold adventures. And on one October day, Smokey verified the super canine he was to more than just his master:

## SMOKED DUCK – A PERSONAL FOWL

October 1989. There we were, parked next to a tent camp on the North Delaney Butte Lake, the Big Eye focused on three duck hunters hunkered along the shoreline sage. Hunting over a sizeable decoy spread, they were on good ground. Shielding my side door Bighorn Sheep emblem behind their vehicle, Smokey was already attentively focused on the hunters despite the 150 yards separating us. I admired the noble appearance of my bullish black lab through my sideview mirror; his black polished coat, blocky head, upright ears, tightly closed muzzle, fixated eyes and nervous sway making me a proud warden indeed! Could he really comprehend the activities of the three men focused in my scope? As it turned out, he did!

Late morning, the hunters began bagging decoys. Zooming in the Big Eye, I watched intently as they sorted and bagged ten harvested ducks. Then, displaying a behavioral characteristic of an outdoor outlaw, one intensely searched the shoreline before burying a carcass into a shallow shoreline grave. *Hoka Hey!* At that time Colorado hunting law decreed a point system where waterfowl species in relative short supply were assigned higher number values than those species more abundant. A daily bag limit for each hunter was reached when the point value of the last duck harvested reached or exceeded 100 points. A hunter was required to track the order of the birds he harvested, meaning if the first bird taken was worth 100 points, he or she was finished hunting for the day. Once a duck was harvested the hunter needed to identify the species and add it to his or her allotted 100 points. The point system offered the advantage of allowing a hunter to identify a duck once in hand rather than the difficulty of identifying a flying duck overhead. Responsible hunters' skilled at in-flight waterfowl identification, could avoid high point ducks and increase their overall daily bag limit in the spirit of conserving those waterfowl species in short supply.

With gear loaded on their backs, the threesome trudged my way, stopping momentarily for a short discussion after spotting me. At their campsite, they rudely ignored my presence until I greeted them with a cheerful 'Hello' and requested their hunting licenses. All three produced licenses, properly signed duck stamps, and plugged shotguns but faltered when asked to sort their ducks in the order they were shot. Admitting they were somewhat aware of the point system, they also confessed not being very proficient at duck identification. Staring into their hollow eyes, it was apparent they failed miserably managing their individual birds. So, I began sorting the ducks by species explaining the point value of each duck; three redheads (100 points each), five teal (35 points each), one shoveler (35 points), one widgeon (35 points).

One hunter (the grave digger), Barry Pochard, claimed the shoveler, two teal and one redhead (205 points) stating the redhead was the last one he harvested, obviously hopeful his mind computed math was correct. *Nope! 35+35+35 = 105 making the redhead illegal!* He also said one of the redheads was given to them by a man in a canoe. *Imagine that!* Firing my loaded question regarding the buried carcass, Pochard haughtily denied leaving a duck behind. *Release the hounds!* Lowering my tailgate, Smokey bolted into the sage and straight arrowed to the hunters' killing field. *WOW!* I (bluffingly) informed the awestruck hunters if my dog finds the bird before Pochard admitted his misdeeds, they will suffer more trouble than hiding one illegal duck. Steadfastly denying any wrongdoing, Pochard elected gambling Smokey would not find the buried bird.

As Smokey expertly zigzagged, nose to the ground, through their hunting area, we all watched in amazement when he scratched out and picked up the buried bird and immediately brought it to me. I swear to this day Smokey wore a shrewd smirk on his muzzle as he awarded me his prize. Surprisingly, it was not a duck at all, but an eared grebe, a totally protected waterbird species. Pochard, decisively affirmed his 'grave' misdeed, admitting he thought the bird was a coot - legal to harvest but not exceptionally good table fare! Hiding my amazement while enjoying Pochard's, I scratched out the tic for wasting the grebe and possession of one of the teal. Thoroughly explaining the point system and providing each hunter with a duck identification manual, I divided the remaining ducks between the other two hunters, giving them benefit of my doubts as to the species, number and order they had been harvested.

**Yo-o Rinty!**

# BEADHEAD RENEGADE

*"He that has the eyes to see and ears to hear may convince himself that no mortal can keep a secret. If his lips are silent, he chatters with his fingertips: betrayal oozes out of him at every pore."*
Sigmund Freud

L ate elk season and the rankled ranks of the 'last men hunting' were tired, frustrated and desperate. Elk, driven into remotely unknown or privately sanctioned hidey holes, linger until blown out by a major blast of cold, snowy weather. Indian Summer, such a rare Bull Pen gift, does not an elk season make. But such was the high-pressure lows of the 1981 elk hunt.

For hard core desperados, the withering season cultivates time to sew their illicit wild oats; trespassing, trading licenses, and opportunistically killing any and all elk for any available tags; a time when unlawfully killing elk takes a higher priority over the sporting harvest of filling one's own license. For reaping wardens, it affords cunning prospects for gathering the juicy spoor of pristine wildlife crimes.

So there I was, headed west to Red Canyon for an early morning venture into a remote hunting camp. Predictably, a call from the Sheriff's Office turned me south to address a trespass complaint involving a cow elk killed on private land. The reporting party, a Lone Star nimrod hunting the Buffalo Ranch, contacted the shooter and his companion dragging out the elk. Appraising their illegal trespass, he was aggressively threatened with multiple ultimatums to "try and do something about it." The infamous never to be ignored 'triple dog dare' initiated what would become the demise of two private land pirates. Wisely backing off, the witness asked ranch manager Steve Story to contact the Sheriff's Office and request a warden rendezvous at the kill site. Upon arriving, I found the wild-spy patiently waiting and quite distraught by the trespassers' demeanor, truly believing they were going to assault him. Walking uphill to the gut pile I penciled the details of what 'parts' remained and what were taken. Following the drag mark to where the elk had been loaded, I sketched tire tracks and boot imprints boldly outlined in the moist soil along a grassy meadow. As poachers frequently leave spoor, there lay a day-old gas receipt from the Rosebud Store scribing a name absent from the list of successful cow elk applicants for this unit but on the list in an adjacent unit. *Hoka Hey!* Ah, the bounty of fresh scent snitched by a perceptive witness delivering a detailed vehicle description, license plate number and physical descriptions of the two trespassers. I shared this information with my compadres hoping one would cross paths with the wandering shysters. Sure as stink on skunk, Supervisor Don Benson radioed the following morning he was holding the miscreants at the Rosebud Store. There, I spoke with Benson and Regional Manager Walter Graul who warned the hunters became very agitated when confronted with yesterday's trespass complaint. Administrator Graul remarked, "cracking them would be all but impossible." *Wait until they get a load of me!* Greeting the hunters with my signature smile, I cordially made small talk while reviewing their licenses. A license with a tag missing belonged to one Curly Dubhead, matching the name on the gas receipt found the previous day. Although Curly remained steadfast and rock solid, his partner exhibited a bad case of the heebie-jeebies. Asking where he killed his elk, Curly rudely replied it was none of my business. Benson mentioned visiting their camp on Illinois

Creek several days earlier cautioning the prevalence of moose in the area and to be careful not mistaking them for elk. Stating the need to check Curly's elk, both hunters growled obscenities for interruption of their hunting time. Hoping the drive would cool them down proved futile as Curly immediately began ripping the wardens' hind quarters for utilizing 'Gestapo' tactics to reprimand the innocent for the misdeeds of others. Curly was clearly passing my open-air test of guilt analysis.

Inspection of the elk carcass hanging from their camp's meat pole confirmed the cuts mirrored those at the gut pile. The boot tracks of both men outlined in the soot darkened dirt around the campfire matched those at the kill site as did the vehicle tire tracks. Knowing the end of this trail, I cut to the quick and proclaimed the elk illegal, not only because it was killed in the wrong unit, but also on private land where neither hunter had permission. Curly arrogantly reaffirmed the elk had been legally harvested on the public lands of Snyder Creek and, slack-jawing even his scheming sidekick, boldly announced he would escort the wardens to the gut pile! *Ah, another warden/poacher "magical mystery tour!"* Recognizing the golden opportunity of driving another nail into Curly's coffin, I cheerfully stated, "Let's go!" The newly energized game thieves snappily hopped into their pickup and, in a matter of minutes, we were all staring at the blood crusted visceral remnants of a coyote and magpie riddled gut pile possibly dating back to the days of Jim Bridger. *Dumb ass!* Holding back a shock gobble, I scolded the ninnyhammer for the dim-witted audacity of leading us to what could not possibly be the innards of his cow elk. Curly haughtily exclaimed, "Prove it!" Flipping the gut plate with the toe of my boot exposed the reproductive plumbing of a **BULL** elk! *TIMES UP!* Shaken but not stirred, Curly smothered Benson, Graul and I with names ranker than a day-old moose carcass, revealing the strangely familiar irrational behavior of a cornered miscreant. Rather than facing the oxymoron of gaining intelligence from two idiots, I escorted Curly to my pickup. Opening the passenger side door, Curly blatantly refused to hop into the bad guy's seat. Cutting to the bone with the knifing reminder of an eyewitness, seasoned wardensmanship guided me to back off and allow the rampant rogue time to reflect. I was at the top of my game; tracking down and harvesting wild culprits was my happy place.

Tangled in the thickets of this woods copse' lair, Curly began recognizing the truth was outrunning his lies. *"The heat is on."* Donned in heavy hunting clothing, brain 'squirming like a toad', his icy demeanor slowly thawed. Removal of his down-filled hunting cap revealed a hairline on full force follicle retreat. I watched in awe as tiny, evenly spaced oily droplets oozed a guilt-ridden pattern above Curly's forehead. Closer scrutiny revealed each globule emerged from a minute red prick containing a single hair; an obvious hair transplant. His cultivated crop of sprouting fibers reflected a beaded pattern shining like raindrops on a freshly waxed car hood. Curly's rigid demeanor drooped into one of a broken, shoe-staring man. Roused by my silence, Curly docilely confessed.

Interestingly, stopping at the Rosebud store for a Mountain Dew and candy bar, I was approached by a camera laden news team from Denver, asking for a taped interview explaining problems associated with hunter trespass on private lands. *Wagh*!


*"Another one bites the dust"*

# IN A RUT

There I was! Enjoying, at arm's length, a white-breasted nuthatch creeping upside down the trunk of an ancient Juniper tree picking off ants. If I only had my camera! I was sitting comfortably in the deer bed duff at the base of the tree overlooking the North Platte River's bountiful wilds. The rousing water below, bordered in a blend of willow, river grass, sandy banks and pine, warbled its blissful song winding its way into Wyoming. My early morning arrival was rewarded with scratching tics to two separate groups of river rafters; a man and a woman illegally fishing with worms, and later to an unlicensed angler who rashly ripped my hind quarters for not accepting his Wyoming fishing license. Morning river traffic heavy, I remained 'flying the colors' to spread word of a warden presence. Patiently, I waited for and intercepted angling rafters and bank fishermen from this bankside wilderness office. A heavy morning shower, refreshing the mountain air into an aromatic shrubland, juniper scent to die for, delayed maneuvering my 4X4 vehicle up the rocky rough, deeply rutted, now temporarily wet road. Even dry, the steeply narrow track allowed only experienced drivers' safe passage from the ridge above. Shanks' mare, also challenging, was indeed the safest access.

Now late afternoon, I considered moving on when voices suddenly announced I was no longer alone. Soon, four long- haired 'hippies' carrying a cooler clumsily stumbled by my hidden lair on their way to the river. They were the real deal – stringy hair, headbands, tie-dye pullover sleeveless shirts, sandals, jean cutoff jeans – not standard outdoorsmen attire. Ghosting to another hideaway overlooking a large fire ring, I watched the flower children gather wood while singing the familiar lyrics of songs I was quite fond of. Previously experiencing problems with scoundrels destroying the regulatory 'fly and lure' signs as well as burning the expensively carved Forest Service signs for firewood, I wondered if these could be my boys! Igniting a huge 'white man's' fire, the longhairs packed their bowls and began smoking weed chased with Tall Boy Buds. Oddly they packed no fishing gear! Feeding their heads, they raucously began prancing Indian style, arms spread wide, war whooping indecipherable chants around the fire ring. An amusing sight indeed! Their dancing ritual ended; one scrawny, disheveled hairball unexpectedly staggered away into the evening gloom.

Despite their illegally induced mind expansion, I decided against intruding upon the merrymaking of these otherwise harmless peacemakers and backtracked to my truck hidden in an off-road aspen draw. High centering my vehicle on the steep road after dark not in my game plan, I white knuckled upwards, vigilantly focused on evading its deep ruts. Maintaining traction and momentum, I weirdly sensed straddling an unknown, out of place object. Curious, after negotiating the roads nastiest section, I stopped, set the emergency brake and carefully side-stepped downhill. Would you believe I discovered the missing hippie tightly wedged in one of the road's crevices? *DAMN!* My tires had passed within inches of the man's body! The mud-covered hairball, embedded on his side, was visibly breathing but his unblinking blue eyes were staring into a world only known to him. Shaking him hard, the weed packing beer slogger showed no signs of consciousness. Unable to dislodge him, I walked down to his comrades and asked for assistance. Without questioning my sudden appearance, the high-flying dopers scrambled up the hill, grabbed their mindless compadre by an arm and a leg, yanked him out, and propped his limp body against an off-road serviceberry bush. One bitch-slapped the stoner's face several times, triggering a woeful moan followed by the joyful declaration from his buddies he was OK! **OOKKAAYY?** Before leaving, I directed the slap happy free spirit to stay with the semi-conscious pothead and the other two to retrieve their cooler, extinguish their fire, and help their comrade back to camp. Never hearing otherwise, I assumed the day tripper survived.

*Do you hear the music???*

# BEETLE

**P**EOPLE! WHO DA THUNK IT? While it was the enigmatic lure of this remotely wild, mountain valley initially guiding me to the Bull Pen, I had no idea the strong social bonds developed with its people would hold my family there for over two decades! My attraction was immediate, beginning with a July 1972 training assignment to work with Wildlife Officer John Ellenberger. Driving across the state line into Jackson County from Laramie, Wyoming, the starkly bold panoramic view of the Zirkels unexplainably appeared elusively familiar. At my training's end (1973), Ellenberger's district now vacant, I applied for and was granted the Bull Pen as my first district assignment. Now, over two decades since departing, I can honestly say the unique cultural charisma of the Bull Pen's populace makes it like no other place, to live, work and play!

While introducing myself to the community as their newly recruited 'game warden', I found most (not all) friendly and eager to discuss their many and varied opinions of wildlife management and law enforcement. Some conversations disclosed names of known wildlife law violators and one name, Beetle, consistently surfaced. Some whispered specific incidents, while others unjustly accused him as a diversionary tactic to mask their own misdeeds. Many, however, regarded Beetle a harmless, wayfaring outdoorsman, a boundless man of the woods who was simply born a century too late. Whatever he was, Beetle captivated my psyche from our very first contact. Every rural western town has one or more 'Beetle'; mischievous individuals with an abundance of free time to pilfer the wild's common. Like pesky squirrels in a bird feeder, they persistently challenge a warden's mettle defining the need for active wildlife law enforcement.

A military veteran on a medical disability, Beetle relentlessly hunted, fished and trapped the Bull Pen's dells and tors. Described by some as relatively unstable due to a tour of duty in the ostracized Vietnam war, I wondered who would not be? An alleged pot smoker, Beetle frequented the local bars but oddly did not imbibe any form of liquor, thriving on the establishments' social atmosphere as a reputable friend of all. Carrying mental scars of war, the Bull Pen wilds proffered a happy place where he roamed independently, at ease and alive. I branded Beetle as a first- and second-degree poacher, his deliberate misdeeds either preplanned or opportunistic. Over time, he was captured catching more than his legal limit of trout; shooting a cow elk on a bull elk license; spotlighting deer out of season; hiding illegally obtained wildlife in a 'secret' compartment of his truck. Wearing the hunting and fishing face of a coyote, Beetle helped himself to whatever the wild's buffet offered. But as our paths repeatedly crossed, I developed a curious respect for this nonconforming individualist marching to his own music. Beetle possessed a strong sense of personal values governed by a deep-rooted reverence for the wilds. His philosophical, emotionally charged intellect and charm defined him like no other; a peculiar man relentlessly jerking my favored pastime of analyzing people I encountered. For a long time, it was quite a rodeo. The law horse would buck Beetle off and he would immediately climb back on; I would scratch a tic or bark a warning and Beetle would pleasantly accept his medicine and cordially apologize, knowing we would meet again. If Beetle was in the Bull Pen's wilds, he most assuredly could be doing something wrong. Warden fruit waiting to be picked, but once harvested, would ripen again, and again, and again.

Beetle preyed primarily as a lone wolf, stalking solitarily in quick hitting forays veiled in deep woods or under the cloak of darkness,

experiencing the thrill of getting away undetected. However, he sometimes traveled with a pack of wide-ranging rogues led by a podgy,
shaved head man we wardens nicknamed Mr. Clean. These roughly
hewn, brazen poachers intimidated into submission all who questioned their nefarious behavior. Still their names constantly floated to
the top of the poaching cesspool. Wildlife Officer John Wagner and I
went out of our way to curtly converse with the pack's members, firing
loaded questions of how's the fishing, did you get your elk or I see you
drew a cow license; bulleted inquiries mushrooming trepidation
throughout their suspicious minds.

For a time, Beetle ran a popular greasy- spoon restaurant in Sage
Hen and rumors circulated his main courses suspiciously carried a
'gamey' tang. I found the menu quite savory, especially the Mexican
selections, but perchance spiked with a wild essence to both the palate
and nose. After an undercover wildlife investigator declared his
smothered burrito was laced with deer meat and sending a sample to
the lab, I arranged a one on one Beetle / warden confessional. Beetle, in
his special way, graciously denied wild game spiced his menu and
respectfully escorted me to the restaurant's basement where he was
processing a legally tagged buck deer. Revealing the expertly cut,
wrapped and neatly organized game meat in a large freezer was his
way of demonstrating it was for his consumption only. After the lab
pronounced the meat as 'primarily' pork, like Thoreau's "trout in the
milk", the allegations remained circumstantial, I let it go. Shortly there-
after, the restaurant closed its doors, never to again reopen.

I capitalized on Beetle's persistent outdoor presence by investing
time visiting his favored haunts and harvesting the grapevines yield of
his latest misdeeds. Beetle's vulnerability constantly scorched by near
misses, verbal warnings and capture, he began suffering the wrath of
the warden devil, openly questioning my uncanny ability to locate him
and probing point blank who was ratting him out. Piercing his
conscience with the sharp tip of paranoia, I shammed most of our
encounters were coincidental and related to his relentless violation of
wildlife laws. Rationalizing poaching satisfied an innate need for
putting wild meat on his table, he conversely admitted knowing it was
wrong.

Subsequently, Beetle proclaimed his repeated captures were prophetic warnings to change his ways. Recently assuming responsibility for raising his son from a failed marriage, his illicit behavior was now queried by the already troubled lad. I did not see this coming; an outdoor scoundrel staring into the mirror, not liking what he saw, soliciting my insights on personal family issues. Furthermore, our conversations turned to discussions of wildlife management and clarification of specific wildlife laws. Incredibly, Beetle progressed into my sounding board for evaluating current wildlife issues!

Reports of Beetle's misdeeds eventually ceased. Curiously , the warden grapevine sprouted a fresh informant bearing fruit of illegalities that would have otherwise gone undetected. Never certain, I assumed the informant was Beetle but neither I nor he revealed any confidential interchange during our frequent personal contacts. Secrecy, an essential seasoning injected into the meat of successful wardensmanship, generates credible cases while wildly stimulating the delirium of miscreants haunted by their snitches

Our final contact came long after Beetle left the Bull Pen when I received a handwritten letter scribing his poor health and a formal apology for his past wildlife transgressions. Emphasizing our relationship was one of his greatest lifetime memories, he hoped I felt the same. My attempts contacting him went unanswered and I never heard from him again. During my watch, Beetle evolved from a hardcore poacher to a practicing huntsman conservationist. Friendship is a virtue earned over time and, even though it sometimes bites you in the ass, is a necessary human force allowing a warden to keep on, keepin' on. Old friendships always the best, our bond was solidly anchored in mutual respect, trust and a philosophical love for the wild. Indeed, a curiously rare progression of the camaraderie between a warden and a poacher.

*"The immensity of man's power to destroy imposes a responsibility to preserve."* U.S. Congressman John F. Lacey, 1901

# ASCHEWS

1978. Independence Day weekend concluded as the lengthiest day of unyielding reprimands from a frazzled public of my entire career. If I was there, I was wrong!

Scoldings, tongue lashings, ass rippings…, call them what you like, wildlife officers are relentlessly confronted with raucous rebukes from outdoor recreationists. Receiving more than my share, I called them aschews, most arising from confrontations with hunters and fishermen. However, several extremely hostile encounters occurred at irrigation head gates defending Division of Wildlife water rights against infuriated landowners accusing me of stealing their water; a handheld shovel becoming my first line of defense. Understand, de-escalating aggressive situations requires tolerance, fortitude, a compelling war face, carefully chosen words and tones, plus a toolbox of defensive techniques and weapons to quell threats accelerating to potential bodily harm.

Naturally, name nicking wildlife officers goes hand in hand with aschews. Scoundrels and outdoor clowns have long proffered their devious cleverness to dub wardens mocking monikers: Bush Pig; Pine Fuzz; Crick Dick; Duck Dick; Brush Cop; Fish Cop are some of the more common. I was once called the Sphincter Police, a puzzling name from the warped mind of an inebriated scoundrel. My inaugural aschew and complementary alias occurred my first summer as an officer at a wildlife check station on the Colorado/Wyoming state line. Working with three newly minted Wildlife Officers, Howard Spear, Ken Miller, and John Wagner under the watchful eyes of the old guard, Supervisor Don Benson and Officers Sir Don Gore, Johnny Hobbs, and Sig Palm, we newbies, green as spring buffalo crap, were eager to prove ourselves worthy. One of our first clients was a Nebraska man and his pre-teen son hauling a pickup load of firewood. Like wolves on a snowbound moose, my comrades surrounded the pickup while I smilingly greeted the driver and asked if they had been fishing. Father, beer on his breath and discernably angry, declared they had not. Questioning the fishing poles in the pickup bed, Father acknowledged fishing in Wyoming, and therefore none of our business. Officer Palm, pointing out the state line sign, indicated he was in Colorado and currently under our jurisdiction. Even I, a rookie, sensed Father was a huckleberry ripe for picking. When asked about a red cooler barely visible under the load of firewood, Father launched from the pickup like a raging rodeo bull. Kicking out several empty beer cans, he squared into my face, thumped my chest with his fist and delivered a world class ass ripping, setting the gold standard for those following me throughout my career. My fortitude shaken and temper stirred, I regained a semblance of composure and asserted we needed to inspect the cooler. Father screamed, "Not without a warrant!" Clarifying that would take time, Father defiantly tossed out some firewood, pulled out the heavy cooler and flung its entire contents, 32 iced down trout, across the pavement and hollered, "You asshole pig!" Unprofessionally, I shouted, "You fish poaching son of a bitch!" fueling Father's blazing rage. Taking control, Supervisor Benson escorted Father away while I scratched out the $345 tic. After sending the disgruntled Father and his speechless son down the road, I tactfully apologized to Benson for my incompetent behavior. His encouraging reply was, "The man was lucky we didn't arrest and haul him to Sage Hen," followed by the stern warning, "You better learn to control your temper before it bites you in the ass!" Clearing the air, Officer Miller slapped my back and shouted, "Congratulations A.P.!" a nickname worn on my sleeve until I was later dubbed a "cocky, son of a bitchin' banty rooster!" Banty Rooster, blending well with my diminutive stature and enforcement swagger, stuck the rest of my career.

But I wander. Returning to that legendary Fourth of July weekend, I departed Sage Hen mid-morning in good humor after a pleasantly relaxed, chatty family breakfast. Primed for a demanding day interacting with a colossal holiday public, I must admit my loathe for working long holiday weekends!

Finding the lower elevation lakes overwhelmingly jam-packed, I slowly circled each exposing an enforcement presence, and vacated the looming heat driving towards the mountain cool of Big Creek Lake. It too was in wild disarray; overflowing campsites, noisy dirt bikes, illegal fireworks, unsupervised kids, nude swimmers, boats crowding bank fishermen etc. Parking off road on the lake's east side, I was instantly lambasted by a weighty man on a dirt bike for occupying a public parking place. Apologizing, I relinquished the spot and parked further up the road. Walking through the campground, I encountered a chap enraged by the irritating roar of motorbikes racing through campground. When he asked if it was legal to stretch a rope across the road to slow them down, I brusquely warned him to not even think about it. He countered all 'forest rangers' were useless expenditures of public funds. Radioing Forest Service personnel to handle the problem, I moved to the northeast boat ramp to chat with an elderly man fretfully untangling his young grandsons fishing line, an unmanageable bird's nest beyond repair. Looking my way, he turned to his wife and voiced, "it's the f...g game warden," as if grandson and I were deaf. Noting a fishing line in the water, I asked the crusty curmudgeon for his license and he rudely asserted he was not fishing. The boy, too young to need a license, I said no more while grandfather reprimanded me for everything from the poor fishing to never being around when needed. Imagine my delight when, smack in the middle of his fault-finding diatribe, an osprey hawk-fished a hefty rainbow ten yards offshore, its timing picture-perfect. Smiling, I left gramps and stalked the ridge above the lake's east bank, spotting a young man and his girlfriend fishing the shoreline. Asking for licenses, the man politely admitted not having one while his girlfriend, pole in hand, attempting to dislodge her lure from the lakes rocky bottom, curtly asserted she was not fishing. Offering my deal of the day I scratched out one tic to the apologetic man, while tolerating a tooth biting aschew from his girl for ruining their trip over a meaningless technicality.

Enough! I abandoned the recreating mass and trekked the remote stream between the Upper and Lower Lake. Approaching the Upper Lake, I sat against a pine above two middle-aged couples fishing below. Giving them ample time to exercise their fishing privileges, I began searching the shoreline for other fishermen. Quick as snake tongue, one of the women had inconspicuously left the group and was dropping her drawers in the timber right below me! Too late to divulge my presence, I turned away doing my best impression of a tree. *DAMN IT!* Hearing a shriek, I watched her bolt back to her comrades and Paul Revere my presence. Walking out of the pines, I awkwardly requested their fishing licenses. Watching three dig out licenses, guess who did not. Hindsight, so to speak, told me I should have avoided this contact entirely, comprehending I was opening a Pandora's Box of warden turmoil. Checking three valid licenses, the chastened woman expectedly declared she had not been fishing. Realizing a fast getaway was vital, I quickly explained I had observed her fishing with the pole lying on the bank. Giving notice she would be receiving a citation ignited the entire Yuras family: Tara, Rip, Rem and, of course, the unlicensed Torchy! Flanked on all sides, verbally hamstrung by a pack of mad wolves growling profanity laden threats, I self defensively retreated into the pines to scratch out Torchy's ticket. Writing a summons to court allowing her to howl her woes to a judge, I handed her the tic while she resumed vociferously attacking my rear cul-de-sac, calling me a perverted Peeping Tom. *My name is Steve!* Rem, her husband, caterwauled that their son was a prominent attorney who would have my job by publicly disclosing me as a distorted deviate. Promptly escaping, I scrambled to the east side of the lake to recuperate. No one around, I lingered thirty minutes and foolishly elected hiking the main trail to my pickup. Regrettably, I intercepted the wolf pack resting on a log halfway back to the lower lake. Rekindling their familial furor, I quick stepped through the horde, appreciating their collective vulgarity until out of hearing range.

A week later, the Yuras pack predictably cluttered my growing personnel file with yet another written complaint addressed to my agency's Director. Filtering the letter through my regional manager, my boss, to me for a written explanation, and back up the ladder for the Director's signature, a tactful reply was sent to the complainants defending my actions followed by Torchy, without giving any testimony, entering a guilty plea in county court.

In great need of wilderness therapy, I drove the rough road south and parked near a North Fork beaver pond. Donning a day pack, I hiked into Forester Creek and ate lunch. Studying a map, I decided to bushwhack rather than main trail into Blue Lake, cutting off a mile or more to my destination. Smart? Nope! My shortcut turned into two strenuous hours of slogging through willow choked marshlands, beaver ponds, and tramping over heavy timber downfall. Nevertheless, disturbing an adult osprey leading me to a yet discovered nest site with two chicks and flushing a preponderance of rapidly declining Boreal Toads made the trip professionally and personally worthwhile. Reaching the Hill Creek Trail accessing Blue Lake soaked in sweat, bug dope and sunscreen, I pondered whether I was attracting or displacing any nearby bears. No one at the lake, I stripped down and dove in, instantaneously losing air in both lungs and breathlessly splashing back to shore. The combination of glacial water and the light breeze across my body literally sent me into the initial stage of hypothermia. Warming in shoreline grass, absorbing the sounds of wilderness silence, I grasped there is nothing more spiritually exhilarating than the primal sensations invoked by Nature's wilds. Nothing!

No time to hike into Twin Lakes, I traveled the well-used trails towards my pickup and crossed paths with a chap carrying a fishing pole and a small cast iron skillet. *Imagine that!* Disclosing he was from Missouri and had hunted elk here in the past, I asked to see his fishing license and he said he did not have one but was not planning on fishing anyway. *Yeah, right!* As I stared at the pole and skillet, he realized the absurdity of his answer and countered he assumed licenses were not required in wilderness areas. When asked if he purchased an elk license when hunting here, he noticeably grasped where I was coming from and became silent. Leaving him in a noticeable quandary,

I warned him to watch his back. No one, licensed or not, would trek four miles into a lake teeming with trout and not fish. After waiting fifteen minutes, I ghosted into Blue Lake. *Once a warden, always a prick!* Watching the 'Cave State' boy landing several trout, I was amused by his incessant search for an incoming warden. FISH ON! Startling him by walking in from behind, he griped expecting to see me again, followed by a formidable aschew greatly infused with the words a..hole, and ending with the wail, "I finally found time to get away and along comes a f....ing game warden!" I answered, "Yeah, I get that a lot!" Advising he would be receiving a citation so infuriated the lad he flung his pole skyward while roto-rooting my backside in his unintelligible southern drawl. In the midst of the aschew, I explained he could pay the $68 fine here or face bonding in Sage Hen. Frantically pulling a wallet from his belt pack and counting out the fine, the deliriously mad Missourian, Shome Panhead, conveyed the mental capacity of his skillet. Calming him by explaining fishing without a license was not the crime of the century and clarifying he would not be charged for the illegal trout, I told him to enjoy dinner. Daylight burning, I rapidly main trailed to my pickup contemplating the odds of Panhead running into a wandering warden who, like him, had also retreated into wilderness to avoid the public mass. Driving past Big Creek Lake's boat ramp, I waved to the elderly gentleman still fishing with his grandson, returned his spiteful glare with a warden smile and happily headed home to tattle today's tales to an attentive family while savoring a delicious, microwaved home cooked dinner!

*Hit me with your best shot. Fire away!*

# TWO LEDGE TALES

S himmering in its pine clad hideaway, Two Ledge Reservoir is one
link in a chain of 'outlaw' lakes resting at the foot of Arapaho
Ridge. Cliff, Disappointment, Deep, Alder, Long, Kathleen, Brook,
Bundy, Flat, Finger and Beaver are its bandito sisters, as are several
nameless kettle ponds; liquid treasures cherished by all knowing them.
Rainbow trout stocked annually by the Division of Wildlife with aerial
'shots' of fingerlings, provided relatively small populations of good
sized, difficult to catch trout. Periodic fish 'winter kills' caused by thick
ice and heavy snows depleting the lakes' oxygen levels result in wide
variations of yearly angler success. These concealed tarns, interwoven
into spider-webbed strands of discreet foot and game trails, are
trekked by adventurers wandering off beaten paths. A myriad of
county-maintained logging roads and narrow jeep trails provide
motorized access above and below these secreted lakes to primitive
camp sites scattered throughout the area. Additional recreational
opportunities are provided by the three beaver choked 'brookie'
streams forming the main fork of Arapaho Creek and two nearby
reservoirs (Seymour and Slack-Weiss), heavily stocked with catchable
trout, rendering the basin a 'Redneck' hangout in contrast to wilderness areas accessible only by foot or horseback.

Sustaining a diverse and abundant wildlife population, the area tenders those with discerning eyes recurrent memorable wildlife adventures. An abundant black bear population often delivers shockingly unique entertainment for the camping public and surrounding private land mountain homes. Since the late 70s transplant, moose are a common sight, delighting all crossing their paths. Elk, deer, pine marten, coyote, mink, birds, squirrels, gulls, waterfowl and pelicans add to the diversity of wild creatures inhabiting the peaks, ridges, valleys and waters once homeland to the Native American Arapaho-the Nakasinena or Blue Sky Men; mostly forgotten, nameless souls I ponder to this day. For the venturesome, this magnificent arena provides unlimited recreational opportunities for escaping the monotony of modern life. *Everybody's working for the weekends!*

Disguised in dense timber, the Arapaho Basin lakes and streams lull the minds of outdoor outlaws into believing they are exempt from warden wrath; supplying wily wardens relentless contests of hide and seek throughout the serene copsewood. The forest sublime, occasionally disturbed by human voices or the clanging of vehicles crossing the loud cattle guard on the main road below, was my paradise for scratchin' tics; a covert haven for a covert warden.

Two Ledge, accessible by a mile of rough jeep road and a short walk over an unmarked trail, or a rough cross-country hike from a logging road above, is lightly fished because of its small number of medium sized to large, very difficult to catch, rainbow trout. Set under two diamond sheer bluffs, this veiled jewel provides the security sought by not only the public good, but also it's bad and ugly.

Personally, I enjoyed fishing here as a calming retreat, often bringing family and friends to camp, fish, picnic and drink good whiskey over a summer campfire. Although common to make warden hay when visiting the lake as a tourist, I revealed my identity only to blatant misconduct. By investing my time and expertise with a fly, the lake may selfishly surrender one or two of its grand salmonids. Only once did I catch five or six, keeping two large pink-fleshed, broadshouldered beasts for supper. On one trip, fishing the shallows to the top of my waders while compadre Kirk Snyder fished bankside, I excitedly described the 'hogs' rooting out caddis larvae in the mossy depths in front of me. Kirk, in his customary demeanor, sarcastically criticized my incessant chortling when, as if on cue, 'Moby Dick' rocketed high out of the water, landing with a water whacking belly smacker! As the 'whale's' wake waned, a jaw hanging Kirk realized Moby was indeed on the end of his line towing his wannabe fly, the infamous Pistol Pete (the closest thing to a fly used in Kirk's homeland, Trinidad, Colorado) into the lake's sinister depths. Then, quick as a burp, the lunker was gone in line snapping disaster as we gaped in a bug-eyed stupor.

On yet another excursion, I hiked my Ohio Brother-In-Law Roger and his two high school buddies into Two Ledge, set up a tidy camp and fire-cooked a supper of elk loin smothered in butter sautéed mushrooms and fresh sweet corn. Like wolves on freshly killed moose, the lads ravenously devoured what they claimed was the best damned supper they'd ever tasted. That evening, the boys stared in utter disbelief when I tossed the cap of a brand-new bottle of Wild Turkey into the campfire. Leaning against a sappy pine, I took great pleasure sipping straight whiskey over ice watching the lads blissfully dance to their own music, attesting their youthful manhood to the starry dome of the forest quiet. The whiskey spirits overtaking theirs, two expired into the pine needle duff. The last man standing, howling with the song dogs, stumbled a sweeping, unfocused arc into the tent's open door, collapsing face down onto his sleeping bag. Intoxicatingly mesmerized by the strobing fire casting a calming glow across the lake and into the pines, I absorbed a serenity occasionally disturbed by the snores, groans and farts of my fallen comrades. Sleeping under the stars, I suffered the rude awakening of a pesky deer mouse scampering up my sleeping bag and over my face; a diminutive force that could awaken the dead.

Camp life stirred late the next morning as a warm sun cresting the high ridge defrosted the boys while their livers filtered the evening's fun. After several pots of sheep herders' boiled coffee, a greased breakfast of bacon cooked eggs and campfire charred butter bread, the lads were soon laughing and joking about women, beer, and women. This golden trip plates their minds to this day as memories never to be forgotten; those all too often stolen away by the 'real worlds' demanding routines

During the summer months, I often received a call from Wildlife Officer Sir Don Gore, who proudly declared himself a professional trapper and not a law enforcement officer, requesting assistance in what he referred as 'warden work'. Sir Don, needing a tic or two scratched to maintain our boss' happiness, knew I would eagerly oblige capturing those defiling wildlife law. Besides, I found great relief in conversing with the white bear; his rousing stories of times past defined the old way, forever gone, of managing Colorado's wild. Sir Don would drop me near Cliff Lake to 'run the gauntlet' and wait patiently for my radio call on where to meet as I inevitably walked out captured miscreants to fulfill his law enforcement responsibilities. Whether working with Sir Don or as a lone wolf, Two Ledge reliably endowed a plethora of adventures and tics to scratch.

## ALYSSUM

*'There's a million stories in the naked woods!'*

June 1988. Any discourse on Two Ledge would be incomplete without mentioning Alyssum, the Sterling Lakeside Temptress illegally angling with salmon eggs (the lake was under a fly and lure only restriction) one luminous June afternoon. Stalking the shoreline, Wildlife Officer Kirk Snyder and I observed Alyssum and a young man camped on the opposite side of the lake. Focusing the Big Eye I verified both were fishing and we elected to make contact and move on. But wait, there's more! There she was, stunningly seated on a boulder framed in furtive lake and pine, the afternoon light washing her cheerful face bordered by lustrous, long brown hair while her boyfriend began snapping pictures. In a blink the young lass cast off her rag wool sweater energetically exposing her mate's Kodachrome with suggestive postures forever imprinting the wild imaginations of the two rudely watching wardens! Sweet as bee's breath, fresh as morning dew, she modeled a lengthy routine of fanciful poses. Whispering the Big Eye's revelations in tempting detail, I was brusquely interrupted when Kirk sternly barked, *"Give me the damn spotting scope!"*

However, the devil in the details, the ensuing specifics will forever remain unwritten; an act of warden chivalry safeguarding this wild mountain flower's integrity, acknowledging only Alyssum reflected the sun very well! Electing to prematurely end the photo shoot, we contacted the pair who, lines tightly stretched into the lake, predictably denied they were fishing. Making it clear we arrived over an hour ago and observed both fishing with bait, Alyssum's face visibly revealed her mind was tracking her previously alluring performance! Tics scratched to both for not having fishing licenses, we ignored the charge of illegally using bait believing wilderness justice had been duly served.

*"Here's Looking At You, Kid" Humphrey Bogart Casa Blanca 1942*

## FIRE WEED

August 1980. There I was, whiffing the pungent scent of marijuana long before stalking behind a young woman sitting yoga style in the thick green willows along the Two Ledge shoreline. Uncomfortably close, I elected crouching on one knee to spy. Observing her rod propped upwards on a rock, line tightly extended into the lake and a styrofoam worm container at her side, she was more than likely violating the 'fly and lure only' restrictions. Smoking weed, she was clearly zoned into the lake's tranquility. A voice from across the lake announced her White Knight boyfriend, later identified as one Zig Zagner, casting a lure walking the shoreline towards her. Watching her 'feed her head' I ascertained Allison was indeed in Wonderland; her carnal smile and unfocused eyes reflected the orgasmic pleasure of drug induced gratification. Finishing the joint, she reeled in a water-soaked worm, re-baited another giant garden hackle, and skillfully cast a long line into the lake. Listening to the Dormouse, Allison rolled and lit a fresh doobie as I prepared to penetrate her wilderness fog; her next flashback would be the unreality of having her roach clipped in the serenity of a favored forest lair.

As I prepared 'chasing rabbits', a third fisherman emerged out of nowhere and joined Allison. Both noticeably startled, Allison's presence undoubtedly thwarted the man from detecting me. While they small talked I cleared my throat and joined them. Glancing over her shoulder Allison displayed the expertise of a well-practiced toker, fluently burning through the taught fishing line with the joint before slipping her smoking hand into her purse, no doubt thinking she had obliterated all proof she was fishing. *Damn, she was good!* Checking the befuddled man's license and praising him for not fishing with bait, I purposely nudged Allison's worm container and asked for her license. I delightfully listened to her declaration of 'not fishing' and only 'enjoying the serenity of the lake.' Detailing her previous fishing activity, I listened to Allison, now feeling ten feet tall, snappily scold my audacity of secretly spying on the naively unaware. Suddenly, a curl of smoke wafted from her purse igniting a Kleenex and triggering the immediate expulsion of her hand. Shaking a singed hand, she spontaneously emptied her purse onto the ground revealing the smoldering illegal tinder, a bag of weed and miscellaneous illegal drug paraphernalia. Allison again ripped my behind for ruining what had been a mentally unwinding day. Zig, stoned as a Biblical adulteress, arrived to save his distressed damsel, buttressing her verbal flogging by dishonoring the credentials of my mother and illicit enforcement techniques. I swept away Zig's wind by pointing to the smoldering roach lying amid the rest of the contraband. A tic was scratched, the marijuana and paraphernalia confiscated, and a treaty signed with the covenants that paying the ticket would nullify any drug charges. Allison's White Knight's 'logic and proportion fell softly dead' when Zig began talking backwards, asking if they paid their fine would I return their bag of pot? My fiery stare abruptly extinguished the outlandish inquiry.

Switchbacking down the fender bending two-track, I wondered which one of the weed wacked twosome could possibly toke their vehicle safely down this road and back to Denver.

*"When you smoke the herb, it reveals you to yourself."* Bob Marley

## MAN ON THE RUN

And there I was, shrouded in low growth fir and buffaloberry above Two Ledge. I saw neither man nor beast but intuitively sensed a presence. Perhaps a muted sound or peripheral movement rang my alarm and, quick as a fly, I heard the unmistakable click of a closing reel bail and the soft grind of line winding onto a spool. A disorderly breeze wafted across the lake's surface breaking the sun's reflection into a million dancing gems. Echo-locating the sound, I quietly toe-stepped over the pine duff, avoiding fallen limbs and loose rocks, and soon glimpsed through hanging pine boughs, a man tending a fishing rod propped on a forked branch stuck into the shoreline mud. Through binoculars I observed he was wearing a black muscle man half shirt and blue jeans with rolled cuffs covering heavy, black Vibram hiking boots. His man's sculpted six pack waist, like a turtle's under shell, V-d upward and outward into a bulging mass of chest and upper arms. A thick stumpy neck supported a hefty head crowned by long, wavy locks held in check by a red-clothed head band. A light mustache overhanging the corners of his mouth accentuated white teeth and his bright crystal blue eyes lasered through dark cavernous sockets rimmed under a heavy unibrow. The man's Herculean appearance disguised his less than average height. From my vantage, this powerful resemblance of Charles Bronson was a uniquely atypical angler. Sitting down, the fisherman grabbed his beer and leaned against the steep bank. *A short-necked gargoyle swigging a long neck Bud.* The man was edgy, continually searching and listening in all directions, obviously feeling sensations someone was watching him. *Someone was!* I began contemplating the cause of this man's anxiety.

*To him who is in fear, everything rustles.* Sophocles

Scanning the shoreline with the 10X40s, my eyes locked on the steel blue outline of a long-barreled wheel gun on a heavy oil cloth next to the man. *Lock and Load Warden!* Changing strategy, I patiently watched until he moved away from the gun. Silently ghosting a game trail bearing fresh moose spoor to a position above him, I reveled not agitating his vigilance. Suddenly a Stellar Jay screaked the displeasure of having its territory invaded, startling us both. I watched him slowly scan his surroundings for whatever alarmed the jaybird. Using the confusion to announce my presence, I cleared my throat and cheerfully announced, "Game warden, how's fishing?" The man quickly turned and, taking the stance of a fighter, locked his blazing fish hawk eyes on mine while stolidly remaining silent. Requesting a fishing license, the tightly wound man pulled a wallet from his back pocket seemingly ready to pounce at any moment. This wild cat, indeed formidable warden prey, must be handled with great care.

Stepping back into a defensive position while inspecting his fishing license, I found the physical description in no way described the appearance of the man standing before me. Asking for his date of birth, he tensed and, lips sealed tight as a crawdad's ass, offered no truths or lies. Next, his fiery eyes lasered onto the six gun twenty yards away. Reading his mind like a child's book I, clasping the butt of my holstered Colt barked, "Don't even think about it!" Crossly ordering the man to sit down, he surprisingly complied. Backing to the hefty, .357 magnum, I picked it up, emptied the magazine, pocketed the cartridges and laid the gun back onto the oil cloth. Requesting his driver's license produced his picture and identified one Chaney Hrdnuckle. Recording the information from the 'borrowed' fishing license, I hurriedly scratched a tic for fishing without a license and left. At the trailhead I had the Sheriff's office run Chaney's drivers license and discovered he had been released from prison less than a year ago and now had an active warrant for assault. No surprises here! Requesting backup, I was joined by Sheriff Gary Cure and we intercepted Chaney driving the two-track and arrested him without incident. Handcuffed in the sheriff's vehicle, Chaney remained silent and docile all the way to the Sage Hen jail, perhaps calmed knowing he was no longer a man on the run. The loaded revolver, illegal for a felon to possess, was found wrapped in the oil cloth under the jeep's driver seat.

Wilderness solitude and a formidable weapon could not dispel

Chaney's internal demons. Paranoia, weighing heavily on the mind of this wanted man, coerced him to the edge of criminal behavior. Fishing with a borrowed license to veil his identity was a mistake, but it was his guardedly suspicious demeanor that betrayed Chaney's indiscretions to a wandering warden.

*"No one knows what it's like, to be the bad man..."*

## HOMING PIGEONS

August 1985. Snaking through the rugged, narrow jeep track and passing the trailhead into Two Ledge, I concealed my truck in thick alders near the road's end and stealthily bushwhacked into a favored vantage above the lake. A warming August morning, I celebrated the absence of mosquitoes just before a horsefly rudely drilled deep into my upper forearm. Finding no one there, I moved on to Alder where I spied a young man illegally fishing with three baited rod and lines propped on forked sticks sunk into the lakeshore mud. Once handling all three rods and noting he was armed only with a pocketknife, I made my presence known. Walking the open shoreline, I smilingly observed the lad quickly reel in two poles verifying his first-degree delinquent behavior; he obviously knew the rules. Scratching the tic, the young fisherman expressed remorse and pleasantly accepted his citation with a hint of disbelief of being backwoods bagged by a ghosting warden.

Stalking the Arapaho Lake chain the rest of the morning, I basked in the amazement of finding no one, anywhere! Returning to my truck, I ate lunch on the tailgate watching a pair of black-capped chickadees scurrying through the lower underbrush; the male trilling a testosterone fueled springtime 'hi-lo' mating song, *fee-beee*, to a most unconcerned mate. Suddenly, my tranquility was disturbed by the slow grind of a four-wheel drive vehicle powering its way up the mountain. Hearing slamming doors and loud male voices. I washed down the remaining sardines and crackers with gulps of Mountain Dew, giving my quarry fifteen minutes to stake their claims at the lake. Grabbing my binoculars, I again tracked to my ambuscade overlooking Two Ledge, settling into a pine needle nest behind a log using a sappy lodgepole as a back rest. Focusing my binoculars on five lively young men engrossed in fishermen foreplay, I instantly knew these huckleberries were ripe for picking; brandishing dilapidated, cheap equipment, horrendously tangled lines, amateur fishing skills and, of course, voluminous amounts of beer! One in particular exhibited the epitome of a lowlife outdoor scumbag; chugging a beer with an empty already floating in the lake in front of him. Another pitched an empty Styrofoam worm container into some bank grass behind him; both hitting the bottom of my fishermen scum bucket. Tics for littering were always scratched without remorse, no matter what the circumstances.

Speaking in vulgar tones, their banter resonated across the lake with crystal clarity, chirruping a quintet of warden songs. *Oh, how often the bad tattle their misdeeds!* One, I scribed the Prophet in my notepad, foretold 'rangers' were worthless wannabe figureheads; never wandering far from their vehicles, working only the well-traveled roads of heavily used public waters. The others chorused personal lyrics of warden dearth and idiocy ending with the Prophet's harmonious chant of the ease of eluding the 'crick dicks', even when encountered. I would willingly dispel their myths; the soothsaying Prophet was about to hear the gospel according to Steve. In the course of forty-five minutes, I recorded their behavior plus detailed physical descriptions of each in my notepad. Noting they were 'armed' with only belt knives (no firearms) and displaying no violent tendencies, I elected to noisily approach the lakeshore in plain sight giving them ample time to sense my presence. Breaking their deer in the headlights stares with my signature smile I barked, "Hi guys, how's fishing?" Without hesitation, all five flushed, wildly disappearing like fleas into the doghair pine.

Resisting the instinctive pull of a good chase I noiselessly meandered over to their abandoned equipment. Keeping a detecting eye and ear on the steep hillside, I knew they were close because their crashing departure quickly stopped. Allowing the 'escapees' time to revel in their Icarian flight, I gathered their poles and hiked the short distance to their vehicle, knowing there was only one way out. In less than a half hour I began picking off the singles as, one by one, they cautiously decoyed to their pickup. More fun than singeing ants with a magnifying glass, I focused and burned each one. Netting four of the five, all not having fishing licenses, I 'writed' the wrongs of three and informed the fourth, the owner of the discarded Styrofoam worm container, his tic would be scratched later. The three took their medicine in good character enjoying the blissful feeling of sharing the grief of their misdeeds, while the fourth stood in the haunting wonder of his unknown demise. I held back scratching him because he shared the same littering transgression with the Prophet. The captured four eagerly scanned the terrain for their elusive comrade, enviously hyena chuckling his getaway while boasting I would never find their leader, truly a man of the woods.

In no mood playing 'cat and mouse', I had my own horn to blow and explained I was a very patient man. Sticking my hand through their trucks open window, I honked the horn in several short bursts. Waiting a bit, I honked again and to the amazement of all (including me), like a coyote to a predator call, the proud Prophet appeared laughingly trotting down the road. But his Cheshire cat smile withered rapidly when his eyes focused on the 'worthless, wannabee figurehead.' His driver's license identified one Iam Skel. Admitting not having a fishing license, I scratched out the fourth and fifth tics for no license and littering, repeating my well-rehearsed ass-chewing of those defiling the public domain using their beer can and Styrofoam bait containers as evidence. Speechless, the two long-faced chumps stood silent and forlorn, suffering the embarrassment of wilderness capture.

*Better run through the jungle!*

# TWO BALLS IN THE SIDE POCKET

And there I was, weaving less traveled roads back and forth the 'undistinguishable' Colorado-Wyoming state line. Elk season waning, hunters thinning and a silent radio, I took advantage of the deceptive calm by aimlessly patrolling the outback where unsuspecting miscreants were often flushed from the forested hinterlands. More interested in harvesting a flavorful blue grouse than checking hunters, I 'walked' my 4X4 truck in grandma gear over the rough timber cut roads bordering Damfino Park searching for 'fool hens' before heavy snows pushed them into higher elevations. Rounding a curve and quartering over a water bar, I espied a lone hunter scrutinizing the preponderance of deer and elk tracks zigzagging through the snow covered clear-cut. Detecting my vehicle, the startled hunter paused momentarily before approaching. With a pleasant 'how ya doin' I began my probing dialogue inquiring if he had any luck. Staring at the Bighorn Sheep decal on the door of my truck, the plainly puzzled hunter queried whether he was in Colorado or Wyoming. I replied the state of his state was currently Colorado. Nervously indicating he was hunting with other Wyoming hunters, he admitted to inadvertently wandering into Colorado. Requesting his elk license, I noticed a heavy blood smear above the bulging side pocket of his heavy waist length coat. Eyes locked on hair in the smudge, I curiously questioned the pocket's contents. Ignoring my question, the hunter pulled his license from a buttoned-down shirt pocket and handed it to me. The <u>antlered</u> Wyoming elk license identified one Scrote Toter. Repeating my question, Scrote replied it was a pair of hunting gloves. I asked to see them thinking they may reveal he recently handled a game animal. Imagine my mind-boggling astonishment when Scrote slowly removed the entire sex package of a bull elk! Shaken but not stirred, I shrewdly asked "Why in the wide, wide world of sports would you have those in your pocket?" Scrote's amazingly truthful reply was, "Well, you know!"

I knew indeed! Eager to count coupe on this conspicuously naïve hunter, warden scents steered me to the friendly dumb officer mode (a trait I practiced to perfection). Not wanting to alarm this pod packing poacher with a ticket (illegal possession of elk nuts!) I comforted Scrote by explaining since he was hunting so close to the undefined Wyoming line he was not in trouble. Placing the bull's 'junk' in my pickup bed, Scrote accepted my offer for a ride to his vehicle and haphazardly guided me to a parked U-Haul trailer he said his hunting party used to haul elk to Saratoga, Wyoming. Finding dried blood around the trailer's closed doors and noticing an open padlock hanging from the latch, I asked for a look inside. The metal hinges creaked as daylight revealed a bloodied trailer floor covered with elk hair indicating it had been used to transport elk but now housing, would you believe, only the sacrificed sex packages of two additional bull elk. BLIMEY! Once again clobbered by recurring amazement, I turned to Scrote who simply shrugged his shoulders. Flinging a quiver of sharp-witted arrows piercing Scrote's unwary brain, I casually listened while he innocently divulged his companions' names, who harvested elk and where they were staying. Next, he directed me to a vehicle parked off-road just inside the Wyoming line. With my best poker face, I played into to their game asking this rookie if he wanted to keep the bull's plumbing. Without hesitation, he naively accepted my 'gift'. Bidding him a faux farewell, I memorized the Wyoming license plate, drove to a high point and anxiously made radio contact with my red-shirt compadre, Wyoming Wildlife Officer Biff Burton. Burton, a seasoned 'Har of the Bar' warden, ran the plate number through the Sheriff's Office finding the vehicle belonged to a known leader of game thieves renowned for relentlessly pilfering Wyoming's wild's bounty. Burton chortled he would visit the residence that evening. Colorado and Wyoming require evidence of sex remain attached to all big game carcasses prior to butchering. Licensed to hunt only bulls and cow elk certainly more abundant, these hunters used the sex organs of previously killed bulls to transport illegally killed headless cow elk to their Saratoga residence for processing. If stopped while transporting elk their ploy was to plead ignorance of the law using the unattached bull plumbing as proof of sex, hoping to be charged with the less expensive charge of 'failure to have evidence of sex attached to the carcass' compared to the very costly fines of illegally possessing/transporting the cow elk. Oblivious wardens would believe the carcass was a bull, allow them to keep the elk, adding the (illegal) meat to their larder. Understand, although this may have worked for them in the past, this poaching ruse is easily resolved by wardens utilizing carcass field investigative techniques and/or collecting meat samples for laboratory analysis for determining both species and sex.

Of course, those hunters previously killing elk continued shooting bulls or cows until the season ended or all elk licenses were filled. With my information, a quick hit by Burton could reap a bountiful warden harvest. And it did! Burton, applying my evidence to his investigative skills, uncovered a preponderance of illegal elk hanging in the suspects' garage. Unsurprisingly, while Biff was scratching tics, Scrote and his compadres in crime brought in a 'headless' elk with Scrote's bull tag attached to one leg. And yes, Scrote, pulled out of his pocket the same bull plumbing I discovered earlier that morning as evidence of sex for what proved to be another illegal cow. Needless to say, Officer Burton wrote a plethora of citations carrying phenomenal fines. Interestingly, no mention was made of my previous contact with Scrote, leaving the poaching gang thinking Burton had innocently stumbled into their hunting crimes. Suffering the delirium of working the night from both ends for months, it is these amazing events allowing wardens to keep on, keepin' on. If you are thinking these two wardens teaming up on both sides of the state line were ecstatic:

*You're Bloody Well Right!*

# REIGN ON THE ROARING FORK

July 1978. And there I was! From a vantage above Red Canyon Falls I scoped three men fishing the Roaring Fork, a wild mountain stream intermittently tamed by the incessant labor of beaver. Thundering out of a rugged canyon of sheer, sparsely timbered cliffs into a boulder strewn shrubland valley sprinkled with willow, aspen and pine, it is an eco-geological masterpiece!

At that time this privately held ranchland was leased for hunting and fishing by a Sportsmen Club. It was a balmy, misty still morning capped by low drifting clouds permeated by sporadic outbreaks of warming sunshine, infusing the heavy air with earthy smells of damp sage and pine; it was a good day to take. Driving back down to the property fence, I parked my truck and, under cover of low-growth juniper in aspen and stalked within twenty-five yards of the three anglers.

Walking into plain view, I hesitated momentarily for signs of guilty behavior. Surprisingly, two laid their poles down and rapidly scurried towards me. One, eyes full of anger rudely fired, "game wardens are not welcome here!" We check our own." I ricocheted back, "So do we!" and sternly requested their fishing licenses. Both producing valid fishing licenses, I kept an eye on the third man, no longer fishing, and waved him over. Digging into his wallet he gave me the previous year's license. The smile on my face apparently saying it all, the man shrugged his shoulders and said, "You can't blame a man for trying!" I turned to the other two and said, "Looks like you missed one!" The pair silently watched their humbled comrade sign his citation, becoming a bonified member of my fishing Club.

I continued checking hunters and fishermen on this property, and although my contacts were never sociable, I found all fishermen properly licensed. However, I did make a couple of solid big game poaching cases.

*Opahey! Take charge, Warden!*

# THERE'S A LITTLE PIG IN EVERYONE!

## The Fish Guys

During the 70's and 80's the Bull Pen wardens and the fish biologists were not in the same book, let alone on the same page. Neither buying what each was selling, the hard-headed, badge carrying wardens and the granite minded professional biologists were experiencing the proverbial "failure to communicate"; a mutual intolerance unbecoming to successful wildlife management.

Fortunately for fisheries management, things began changing during the late 80's when a new sheriff and his deputies came to town. Steve Puttman, an owly wise, open minded Regional Fish Biologist, leading a team of field biologists charged to implement a common-sensical approach to science. *Think about that!* Puttman's first rule of management dictated getting along and working closely with the local wardens, or else! *Novel, aye?* Fully aware wardens not only represented the wildlife agency's first line of local biological expertise with direct ties to the community, Puttman also understood they knew the 'lay of the land' like no others. For Puttman, there was no 'division' in the Colorado Division of Wildlife; working with wardens was a no-brainer! *Who is this man?* He did not view, as many resource professionals do, law enforcement as the bastard child of wildlife management. For him it was exactly the opposite; wardens represented the enforcement arm of the laws and regulations essential to the successful implementation of prescribed fisheries management strategies. Over time, Puttman validated his principals by achieving significant advancements for the Bull Pen fisheries. Wildly stubborn, he incessantly challenged the endless politics and bureaucracy in managing wildlife. Right or wrong (mostly right), he took great pride in the thickness of his personnel file documenting what upper staff referred as insubordination (some was!). This rebel with a cause fully supported his skilled field biologists; defensively guarding their backs and providing high-quality equipment and allowing relatively free rein to do their jobs.

Thus, this innovative corps of top gun biologists fervently tackled the unique management challenges of the Bull Pen fisheries. Working side by side, we intensely surveyed the lakes and streams. Data analysis led to proposed management strategies made available to all, with special attention given to the local populace to strengthen support for implementation, including the highly productive but over-harvested 'sage brush' lakes. Sucker populations were reduced significantly with rotenone and experimental wire mesh gravel filtering systems on lake inlets to decrease competition with trout and increase trout growth and survival rates. High elevation lakes were sampled, and stocking schedules adjusted accordingly. Tiger muskies introduced into Big Creek Lakes successfully reduced sucker populations while providing a unique, carnivorous hybrid fish accessible to anglers. Catchable rainbow trout were planted in several heavily fished stream leases (previously never authorized). Diversity for fishermen was achieved by balancing the needs of bait fishermen with the creation of quality gold medal waters managed with fly and lure restrictions, reduced bag limits, and size regulations promoting self-sustaining trout populations. Over time these biologists earned solid community respect due to their tremendous work ethic and unequaled knowledge of the entire Bull Pen fisheries; changes hard to come by in the rural, highly independent, always suspicious community. Their management proposals were supported by the best available data and, if they could not answer a valid question, they collected the essential data to address it. Science integrated with their professional expertise and 'artistic' population and habitat management skills provided the key ingredients for a successful fisheries program.

In less than ten years the Bull Pen evolved into a fishermen's paradise. They were the real meal deal, epitomizing big picture wildlife management. For instance, when their duties expanded to amphibian surveys, I suggested my summer long observations of buffleheads may indicate they were nesting and raising young. The "duck guys" previously made it cynically clear, based on their data, there were no nesting buffleheads in the Bull Pen. But lo and behold the fish guys, sampling for Mountain Wood Frogs and Boreal Toads on the west side kettle ponds, found adult buffleheads <u>with</u> young!

Working as a team, the biologists and wardens generated a knowledgeable, efficient, and professional image of the wildlife agency. We also became very close friends. Warden Kirk Snyder and I referred to our trustworthy comrades as the "fish guys". Their wilderness camps and motel rooms were a sanctuary for wardens needing essential downtime to get away from and temporarily forget the endless business of riding herd over the public mass. Gourmet foods (man could these ugly guys cook!), seasoned with beer and iced spirits provided time to relax and unwind. Kirk provided horses for packing gear into remote wilderness lakes and streams. Gill nets were bushwhacked on our backs to isolated lakes for sampling. Fishermen and women were checked, and tics were scratched. And understand, there was nothing more sacred than our inebriated fireside chatter underneath the massive star-studded wilderness skies.

These wild and imaginative biologists with their mix of seasonal personnel connived endless scenarios of tricks and childish games, making their demanding work even more worthwhile. On one occasion, while mentoring a potential Eagle Scout pursuing a fishing merit badge at Two Ledge Reservoir, I asked the biologists to explain the science behind the lake's special regulations, which they accomplished in an extremely professional manner. While I continued tutoring the lad, the fish guys and their pregnant seasonal employee hiked back to the vehicles, broke out beer, and emptied my service handgun into a tree before leaving. Giving them an ample head start, the boy and I began driving down the steep, narrow jeep road only to discover the biologists, beers in hand, square dancing to a cassette tape. *Yup, square dancing!* Presenting the young scout a non-alcoholic beer brought in by the pregnant seasonal biologist, they left for Sage Hen. As we followed, the boy expressed concern his parents may detect his non-alcoholic beer breath so I provided him a couple sticks of gum while attempting to explain the biologists' peculiar behavior.

The fish guys fall tradition of collecting brown trout eggs from North Delaney Butte Lake became a go to place for wardens, fishermen and the local populace. This highly organized, technical system for catching trout in gill nets, stripping eggs from ripe females, fertilizing them with milt from males, and sending the impregnated eggs to fish hatcheries to hatch, grow, and plant fingerling brown trout statewide became a spectator event attracting tremendous public interest. Naturally, limitless adventures materialized; slinging gill netted suckers from a trap thrower, blasting them with a shotgun and watching them disintegrate into a mist of fins, scales and guts. They also tricked new personnel into believing the sound of eggs being fertilized when stirring in male milt with a goose wing feather was so loud it was necessary to wear hearing protection (large ear muffs) to prevent ear damage. A completely noiseless process creating Kodak moments indeed!

Beginning before daylight and lasting most of the morning, the spawning tasks initially involved long days and several weeks but, as the brown trout population increased in size and numbers with the slot limit and reduced bag regulations, the time necessary to collect eggs from the more mature females was greatly reduced. Their work accomplished around lunchtime provided idle time the industrious fish guys could not tolerate. When their work was done, they found other work. Overlapping with the big game seasons instigated interest to ride shotgun with the wardens. Soon, they became thoroughly entwined in the disorganized chaos of the hunting seasons; mesmerized by the psyche of bad guys captured and number of animals confiscated. Spread thin, warden workloads were far too heavy to effectively resolve the never-ending issues. Predictably, the fish guys stepped up to the plate and filled the gaps by picking up and skinning illegal animals (including moose), talking with witnesses and gathering evidence firsthand at crime scenes.

Initially, the fish guys made clear they were quite uncomfortable actively participating in wildlife law enforcement situations. Understanding the skills, knowledge and expertise necessary for safe and effective law enforcement, they simply did not feel qualified as first on scene wildlife officials. Biologist Ken Kehmeier, a rural, west slope native and avid hunter and fisherman, understood the negative viewpoints many outdoorsmen have towards wildlife law enforcement and 'rogue' wardens. *They must be bad if so many say they are!* Now a state employee realizing the challenges his warden friends were up against, he still experienced uncertainties when confronted with enforcement situations. Kehmeier, always honest and upfront, initially expressed his concerns while accompanying me to learn the vast Bull Pen domain. Repeatedly listening to his issues, I finally replied, *"Kehmeier, there's a little pig in everyone!"* He responded while enforcing wildlife law was not in his nature, he was willing to give it a try. As a result, the fish biologists (including Puttman) joined a Division of Wildlife sanctioned enforcement short course providing knowledge of wildlife statutes, regulations and field techniques, granting them limited enforcement authority. Graduating and declaring themselves (tongue in cheek) 'Junior Beaver Wardens' they began exercising their newly acquired education and soon developed the intuitive catch dog savvy necessary to sniff out and track down wildlife violations. Calling in wardens to mop up messes they uncovered, solid cases were made that would have otherwise gone undetected. They played significant roles the investigations and the recovery of illegal elk in the abhorrent slaughter in the 'Run and Gun' massacre where a gang of notorious Lousiana poachers chased down a herd of elk, killing and wounding the running beasts from their moving vehicles in the open sage below Owl Ridge. They provided essential assistance during the infamous Johnny Moore Mountain Massacre where elk were pushed into open clearcuts and gunned down by a mob of out of control private land poachers. The list went on and on. Soon the eager Junior Beavers became tightly woven throughout the tangled web of wildlife law enforcement. Even their fearless leader Puttman loved riding shotgun, not as a passive sidekick but an active participant providing fresh perspectives and insights while cases were made.

*"Nothing clears up a case so much as stating it to another person."* Sherlock Holmes

And, would you believe, during Kehmeier's first big game season as a Junior Beaver, he found himself in hot pursuit of a vehicle reportedly transporting an illegal elk on a dry gravel road behind Delaney Buttes. Eating dust, Kehmeier radioed and, in his gravelly high-pitched voice shrieked, *"Porter, Is this the Pig coming out of me?"* With a wide grin, I spiritedly responded, *"Yes Kenny, it most certainly is!"* Minutes later, he pulled the vehicle over and was listening to the driver's version of why he was transporting an illegal elk when I joined the party and scratched the tic. Another one of the million warden stories unearthed in the naked woods!

Unfortunately, in a short time this great concept faded into oblivion, a victim of a changing administration expressing legal concerns of personnel not fully trained in law enforcement becoming involved in the field investigations. But this we know, during our watch, it was a very good time to take.


*And that's the way it was!*

# FIELD OSCAR

July 1985. After finding no camps or fishermen on Lone Pine Creek I backtracked to North Delaney Butte Lake, my go-to place for spreading warden wrath. The 'gold medal' regulations restricting trout lengths and limits (at that time, two trout under 12" and/or over 18"were legal to keep), and the 'fly and lure only' designation promoted high catch rates tempting the scheming to illicitly fill their larders. My patience and ability to profile patterns of outdoor misbehavior sluiced abundant prospects for panning nuggets of warden gold.

And there I was, tactically veiled in high sage, scanning the lake's calm waters with my window mounted Redfield scope, the Big Eye, while wolfing down a late lunch. The 'morning shift' timed out, only a single fisherman in a float tube remained providing the rare opportunity of a one-on-one warden game.

Float tubes, increasing in popularity through the 70's and 80's, provide strategic fishing access to the weed beds nourishing the lake's bountiful invertebrate populations. Initially, violations with these 'poor men's boats' seemed non-existent. The 'tubers' embodied a law-abiding corps championing the special regulations by self-policing their ranks utilizing peer pressure and the law. I spent endless hours watching these bobbing boatmen and, up to 1985, nabbed not one law-breaking tuber while, at the same time, incessantly detecting violations of shoreline and hard-bodied boat fishermen. But when the tubers began tattling significant increases in violations within their own ranks, I powered up my undercover surveillance. On the advice of a good friend, I purchased a tube for covertly counting coup on fish poachers while 'out amongst them' – an opportune mix of business and pleasure beneficially scratching my itch as both a fisherman and a warden.

My first float tube case, however, was destined to transpire today. Focusing at 45-power, the tuber was all but in my lap. Stripping in a bead-head, long-shanked marabou nymph pattern *(yes, I could see it all)* along the weed beds, the fisherman was repeatedly rewarded with rod jerking strikes, netting an abundance of brown trout between misses and lost flies. The legendary damsel fly hatch was on!

The fisherman's continuous catch and release of primarily small trout, and surprisingly several broad shouldered 20 plus inch keepers, resulted in me paying more attention to the elaborate top-water courtship 'ballets' of the slick Western Grebes. Nevertheless, a quick peek at the tuber ultimately revealed a behavioral change; his casually carefree demeanor became cautiously vigilant, eyes intensely scanning the shoreline while unhooking a netted trout beneath the water's surface. Up to this point all were released in plain view from the float tube's apron. Long familiar with the mannerisms of a fish poacher, I turned the Big Eye to 60- power and clearly viewed him tuck the fish into his waders before conspicuously raising an empty live bag from the water! *The displacement behavior of a fish filcher!* Once again releasing several small trout in plain view, he warily handled another 'disguised' fish using the same underwater technique. In less than two hours, the fisherman released 25-30 variable sized trout, eliciting his peculiar behavior pattern with five, each emphasized by openly displaying an empty live-bag. Finally, the fisherknave *(Call him Dirk Shamcaster)* foot-paddled backwards to the west shoreline and stepped out of the tube. Awkwardly standing on rubbery legs footed in duck-feet flippers sucked in the lake's mud, he collapsed falling forward into the black goo. Watching tubers beach was one of my favored events, knowing from experience the difficulty of gracefully beaching a tube after marinating one's legs in the cold lake water. Clumsily pushing himself up into a standing position, Shamcaster shuffled backwards onto dry land, removed his flippers and hastily relieved himself in an uncontrolled, spine-shivering surge which, to his obvious dismay, did not clear the inside of his waders.

What happened next was a theatrical performance never equaled during my career. Glaring through the scope until my eyes bled, I watched Shamcaster nonchalantly sit next to a large Coleman water jug at the edge of the shoreline sage, remove its lid and slowly scan the entire perimeter of the lake. Suddenly, hoisting the jug with a vigorous rearward head thrust as if taking a gulp, a trout sailed backwards into the heavy sage! *What the hell?* This incredible melodrama was repeated five times, each trout a 'rabbit trick' pulled from inside his waders and slung behind with another slug of water. Walking into the heavier sage, eyes still searching, Shamcaster casually retrieved each fish and placed them into the jug. Carrying the jug to the parking area and placing it in the back of his jeep, he pulled a black plastic bag from his waders revealing his tactic for screening the illegal trout. While Shamcaster packed his gear, I drove around the lake to bag my 'catch', flagging down the theatrical miscreant as he drove away from the lake. With my signature hair trigger smile, I perplexed Shamcaster with a volley of shots asking for his fishing license, if he had kept any fish, and permission to check his coolers. Shamcaster nervously explained the coolers contained only food and drink and articulated an enchanted fairy tale of honorably releasing every trout caught. Enlightening Shamcaster I had 'scoped' him for several hours, I quickly ended the swindler's fictitious tale by asking about the five trout in the water jug. *The Big Eye doesn't lie!* Gagging with guilt, Shamcaster promptly apologized, his 'deer in the headlights' stare compensating me for the time spent netting this first-degree poacher. Inspection of the cooler revealed the five 'meaty' browns measuring within the illegal-sized slot limit. Scratching the tic, I commended Shamcaster's tremendous acting ability, stating he should receive an Oscar for best man in a slapstick performance of a poacher portraying a sportsman. Shamcaster, clearly devastated, remorsefully accepted the citation thanking me (and the academy) for penalizing his stand-up misbehavior. *A weak man's conscience kicks in after his decisions; a strong man's before.* I scolded him for breaking the very regulations fostering the health and numbers of the trout he caught this afternoon. While Shamcaster signed the ticket, I tested the pilferer's repentance requesting an explanation of his strategy for keeping five 14-16-inch illegal trout and releasing the 'keepers' exceeding the 18-inch legal size.

In a rare declaration of guilt Shamcaster thoroughly detailed his gambit, stating he preferred keeping medium-sized trout for eating, planning to grill two or three trout that night for dinner. His wife was in camp on Grizzly Creek and although licensed she rarely fished, allowing him to (illegally) catch and stockpile two regular limits of trout (16 at that time) on the premise all were caught on the preponderance of public lakes and streams scattered across the Bull Pen. They preferred camping on the National Forest not only because the campgrounds were more aesthetic than Delaney Buttes, but also to avoid suspicious wardens inspecting their coolers; merely fibbing the trout were caught on waters having no restrictions on size or possession limits. He audaciously admitted the ease of deceiving wardens with limits of smaller sized trout rather than weighty fish measuring 18 inches or longer; large trout predominantly inhabit the Bull Pen's productive special regulation lake waters.

Shamcaster acknowledged knowing others utilizing his ploy to disguise their fishing demeanors. He also was aware of significant illegal night activity. Not willing to divulge names, he would provide, in writing, vehicle descriptions. I, familiar with violators repentantly confessing their misdeeds with varying degrees of authenticity, viewed Shamcaster's demeanor to be one of a truly humbled man.

I visited Shamcaster's camp days later finding a bikini clad Mrs. Shamcaster comfortably sunning herself in a hammock. Without being asked, she jumped up and opened the coolers amenably affirming they would never again violate the fishing laws. Comfortable and at ease, she disclosed they learned their lesson and now considered themselves supporters of the Division of Wildlife. She proclaimed her husband was quite impressed with my courteous professionalism. I uncomfortably watched the scantily clothed beauty retrieve her husband's handwritten list describing three vehicles driven by those practicing Shamcaster's poaching techniques. A warden knowing what to look for will find it! And, with this information in hand, I did! A captured man learning from his misdeeds, actively changing his ways and willing to alter the illegal behavior of his peers defines the very essence of successful wardensmanship. Over the years the Shamcasters became personal friends, frequently enjoying our yearly rendezvous at the lakes or their traditional campsite, lightheartedly reminiscing Dirk's float tube capture and how it reformed his perception of wardens and of wildlife law enforcement.

*Private eyes are watching you!*

# RIDIN' HERD ON DEAD HORSE

September 1973. There I was, six months young as a wildlife officer, and today was my first antelope hunting season! I was stoked! Listening to countless war stories articulated by old guard wardens blathering their antelope hunter escapades, I was anxiously prepared to uncover my own adventures. Parking in the inky darkness north of Alkali Lake, I zealously waited for day's first glow over the Rawah mountain range. Much too early, I dawdled over an hour before a volley of rifle shots shattered the morning still, surging me into full alert. 6:15am, well before the required shooting hours of 6:35am. (1/2 hour before sunrise), no one could possibly identify let alone shoot an antelope without using artificial light. A violation occurring within a half mile of my location before I could make out the sagebrush directly in front of my pickup! Driving in the direction of the shots and topping a ridge, I observed a vehicle's taillights disappearing over a ridge a half mile away. Accelerating to the ridge I detected nothing. *DAMN!* Waiting for more daylight, I spotted another truck parked above California Draw but was sidetracked by the dust of another vehicle chasing a herd of antelope. Minutes later, I heard several shots followed by the revving sounds of an accelerating vehicle. Speeding towards the shots again finding nothing, I tracked fresh vehicle tracks along a fence line and found a steaming gut pile with no one around. Who and where are these guys?

More clamor of racing vehicles, more shots, more running antelope and I had yet to contact a single hunter. Changing direction, I finally crossed paths with a man and his son hunting on foot, both extremely irritated by ill-mannered road hunters ruining several of their carefully planned stalks. Properly licensed, these good hunters provided a detailed description of a vehicle chasing antelope (illegal) while shooting from its open window (very illegal), questioning, of course, why I could not catch what they had witnessed all morning!

An hour later, after several unsuccessful attempts to count warden coupe, I was ready to wave the white flag. I was chasing my tail! Fully aware of the long trail of becoming a catch dog, savvy wildlife officer, I was further aggravated by the conspicuous absence of fate, chance and luck. As the saying goes, even a blind squirrel finds a nut once in a while! Not today! However, I had one other field technique in the warden toolbox needing attention, PATIENCE! Taking a deep breath, I bushwhacked to a ridge above Dead Horse Hill, where a commanding view of open sage, a well-traveled county road below, and a good antelope population offered key ingredients for detecting illicit hunting behavior. Build it and maybe, under my patient eyes, they would come.

Parked high on the ridge, glassing the rolling sagebrush draws and ridges with binoculars, I spotted a hunter working downhill towards Placer Draw. Mounting the Big Eye on the side door window, I zoomed in and discovered he was stalking two buck antelope in a draw below my location. Using the ridge as cover, he prowled to within 150 yards of the bucks, knelt into a shooting position and, in two consecutive shots, expertly dropped both, killing one in its tracks and mortally wounding the other. Licensed hunters permitted to harvest only one buck; the game was afoot!

Slowly driving a rough two track into the draw, I found the hunter searching for his antelope. Exiting my vehicle, I pointed out the location of the bucks and he feigned amazement discovering both bucks lying fifteen yards apart. Asking for his license, I watched him nervously thumb through his wallet, exposing two antelope licenses and handing over one. Insisting on inspecting both, I listened to him anxiously explain the second belonged to a hunting companion who could not make the trip. *HMMM!* His buck license and military I.D identified Dr. Iam Lyon, a veterinarian for the U.S. Air Force. Inspecting the second license I stated it was obvious why he purposely killed two buck antelope. Adamantly denying shooting the second buck for his military friend, he insisted not knowing the first buck dropped, he shot again.

Instructing him to field dress both animals, I watched in awe as he surgically gutted both in less than twenty minutes, a fraction of the time it would have taken me to gut one! I made clear his story was corrupt, because the adjacent bucks were in sight during his entire twenty-minute stalk. I emphasized shooting two buck antelope and carrying the illegally transferred license of his hunting partner exhibited both culpability and irresponsibility. I scratched out the tic for illegally killing the second buck and Dr. Lyon demanded a court appearance. He was later found guilty by Judge Price for negligence in shooting the second antelope.

PLAY IT AGAIN SAM! Patience on my side, I returned to the ridge above Dead Horse. Quick as snakebite, I glassed a fast-moving vehicle attempting to intercept a herd of antelope running parallel to the county road. Slamming on the breaks, three men jumped out and fired a barrage of shots from the road. The antelope promptly changed direction and disappeared, all escaping unharmed! Two of the men fired standing using the vehicle for support while the third man fired several shots from a prone position from the middle of the road. Shooting from a public road is illegal. Like a hawk on finches, I flew off the ridge and captured the trio, picking up their empty brass. Long story short, the two men carrying valid licenses were cited for shooting from a public road. The third man, the one shooting while lying prone, stated he was along for the ride and not hunting. He folded, however, as I helped pick up his brass and explained what I observed through my spotting scope. Scratching his tic for both the public road shooting violation and hunting antelope without a license, he responded, "My wife warned me to leave my gun at home!"

Lady Patience on my side and traveling with sisters Chance and Luck, I returned to the ridge and sealed the Fate of yet another hunter, watching him kill and abandon an antelope fawn!

*OH, OH, OH I'M ON FIRE! Bruce Springstein*

# BEARLY TRAPPED

May 1983. And there I was, driving to Twist Meyring's mountain home for yet another spring bear trapping event. Located on an aspen cloaked bench overlooking the Coyote Creek meadows and the timbered foothills of Arapaho Ridge, their home was a mecca for wild mountain birds. It was also a magnet for the local bear population, encouraging those spring beasts emerging from winter dens seeking any and all food sources below the snow line. Bear territories in close proximity to summer homes and cabins like the Meyring's were prime targets. Twist and his wife Ruth epitomized the Bull Pen's authentic pioneer stock I so admired. Their seemingly conflicting personalities melded perfectly; good men have even greater wives. God rest their souls! I consider myself a far better man for knowing both!

Twist, a crusty, hardworking stockman, successfully built a cattle and hay empire spanning several large ranches. Branded by his grizzly gruff demeanor, I learned underneath his gritty exterior was the heart of a very kind and sentimental family man extremely loyal to sustaining the agricultural industry. For example, Twist adamantly opposed the Wildlife Agency's mid-1970's proposal to introduce moose into the Bull Pen because of perceived damages to private land fences, forage and crops. However, once moose were well established, I received an interesting early morning call from Twist. His calls usually began with the gravelly reference to my last name, followed by expressing his latest complaint normally contrary to policies of the wildlife agency. However, this morning's conversation significantly diverged from the norm:

Twist: *"Porter! There's a moose hanging around my home!*

Me: *(Lightheartedly)" I supposed you want it hazed away."*

Twist: *"Hell no! If you chased it away my wife would kill us both! I just wanted to report we had a moose!"*

Ruth, a retired schoolteacher, was described as one of the best in the rich history of the Bull Pen's early education system. She neutralized Twist's cold exterior with her warm personality fueled by a heart of gold. Her devotion to feeding wild birds in 'bottomless' grain and/or sugar water hummingbird feeders invited a mountain aviary where one could observe a plethora of species in one stop. I often visited just to enjoy and identify her birds. Of course, bird feeders and bears go together like ducks take to water and setting live bear traps at Meyring's became one of many spring/summer rituals. The traps consist of a 3-foot diameter, 8-foot long culvert (those round drainage tubes under roads and highways), trailer mounted for vehicle transport, one end plugged with holes for ventilation, the other end equipped with a sliding release door, and an internal baiting mechanism for releasing the trap door

The previous spring, a trainee and I set a live trap for a renegade bear after a barrage of calls from Twist. Finding no one there, we set the trap near the house and ate lunch before moving on. Unbelievingly, a medium-sized brown colored black bear appeared and began ambling back and forth on top of the backyard rail fence, finally clumsily falling off. Without hesitation it ripped laundry from the clothesline, demolished the bird feeders while wolfing down the grain, licked the sugar water from the hummingbird feeders, and shredded a previously damaged snowmobile seat (looking for rodents?). Nose in the air, the bear cautiously approached the trap, crawled on top pacing back and forth and forcefully pushing down with its front feet as if trying to spring it! (No ear tag so it had not been previously caught). Amazingly the trap door was not released. The bear slid down rear end first and devoured the molasses soaked twinkies in front of and just inside the trap. Waiting as long as forever, we watched the bear nervously back in and out of the trap before its stomach lured it to the hambone. The trap door loudly slammed, and the bear hit it with a loud thud. Gotchya! Bear are Nature's clowns and for the recruit, today's show was as good as bear performances and trap training gets.

Today's adventure one year later, essentially mimicked the previous spring's self-inflicted bear crimes. Ruth ignored my warnings to temporarily cease feeding her winged cohorts, electing to suffer the beast's wrath until it crossed the line. The plea for assistance came after the bear repeatedly trashed the feeders, attempted accessing their home and vehicles, and greeted them after dark with a huffing, blowing, tooth chomping, tongue clicking performance while glaring through their glass patio door. The early morning call came when the bear resumed ransacking while they ate breakfast. On the line, Twist growled that last night's wind nearly blew off his cow's horns keeping both wide-awake imagining any and all noises were made by the "phantom' bear. He thoroughly explained the rogue's destructive antics and made crystal clear the bear had to go. Ahh, the divine comedy of humans suffering the wrath of a delinquent bear!

A revitalizing mountain spring morning, I truly needed a little quiet time setting a trap. Pulling off the county road into Twist's uphill driveway, culvert live trap in tow, I was pleasurably welcomed by a bear ambling towards their home. Bear sightings are treasured no matter what the circumstances; these ghosting beasts espying on humans far more than we are given the great pleasure of observing them!

Stopping at the house to inform Ruth I would set the trap on the jeep track behind the house, close enough for them to check if the sliding trap door was down yet far enough away to avoid its foul smell. Surveying the bear's latest war zone, I reiterated the necessity of briefly removing her bird feeders and the dog and cat food dishes. Ruth knew the drill, but would no doubt refuse to march. She said Twist would be home for lunch and would like to talk to me after the trap was set. Winding through the grass covered, aspen choked two-track, I backed the trap into a relatively level spot between two large trees. Unhitching, I dug wheel 'ditches' to hold the trap in place and low enough for easy bear access. Leveling the trap with a cement block under the tongue, all was routinely going well. Then, for reasons unknown, I disregarded crucial live trap protocol meticulously instructed by my elder mentor, Sir Don Gore; mistakes ending with a tenaciously guarded secret not revealed until these writings.

My blunders included:

1. Paying no attention to the difficulty I encountered when opening the trap door.
2. Failing to immediately clean and liberally oil the edges and associated slide channels and the inside and outside door release mechanisms.
3. Failing to wedge a stout branch or 2X4 at the base of the open door. A commonsensical, critical mistake!

The last one using the trap the previous fall was me, neglecting the necessity of preparing it for winter storage. *Mea culpa!* Crawling into the trap to attach a hambone wrapped in maple syrup-soaked burlap to the release mechanism, I discovered last year's extremely rank ham still there. Naturally, wiring the new bait to the old resulted in springing the trap door. *DAMN!* No problem, right? All I needed to do was release the locking cam, pull up the door and crawl out. With some effort I pulled the cam back but no matter how hard I lifted the door would not budge. My uncomfortable crouching position could not produce enough torque to dislodge the neglected door. The morning was quickly heating up and so was I.

Resting on my knees assessing my woes I soon realized I was not alone. My wrenching motions dislodged a preponderance of maggots; the diminutive lucid creatures squirmed across the entire trap floor. Add the greasy coating of last year's baiting wastes mixed with sludgy, aged bear crap, I was imprisoned in an extremely putrid sty. Bears vent their trapping anger with a whole house evacuation of everything consumed during the past 24 hours. EVERYTHING! The trap smelled louder than a dead skunk. *Just another day in paradise!*

But wait, there's more. Given the stench permeating the surrounding atmosphere, the odds were high the bear could show anytime. Even worse, if I did not escape, Twist could come down to see what was going on and if he discovered me in the trap, there would be no end to the angst I would bare. *No pun intended!* Every Bull Pen resident would hear of my self-perpetrated bungle. After all, I was a professional! *Yeah, right!* Blunderbuss awards from colleagues, notoriety at Stockgrowers meetings, and street side backslaps would haunt me the rest of my career. Prompt escape mandatory, I opted the manly solution of exercising wild rage. Mad as buzzing hornets from a shaken nest, I pressed my back against the trap door, put my fingers into the door's air holes and, from a squatting position, powerfully lunged upwards. Lo and behold, on my second attempt, the door broke free allowing me to awkwardly roll out. Scanning for witnesses or bear, I found neither. A grey jay head-cocking from an aspen branch above seemed to be enjoying the entire event. Clothes soiled with sweat and bear excrement, I was in much better condition than minutes ago. After cleaning and oiling the trap mechanisms, propping open the door with an aspen log, I crept into the trap and finished wiring on the new bait. Spreading maple syrup soaked twinkies in front of and in the trap, I removed the log and set the release mechanism.

Finding Twist at home, Ruth invited me in for lunch, but I lied saying I had been called out on a reported trespass. Asked why it took so long, I admitted the trap needed some routine maintenance. Twist commenting on my unusual disheveled appearance and, of course, smelling like the back end of a bear, I worked up my signature smile and asserted it was a job hazard. *The answer my friend, is blowing in the wind!* I could not return home fast enough to take a shower!

Very early the next morning Twist called enthusiastically stating the rogue bear was in the trap.

*Sometimes you catch the bear, and sometimes the bear catches you!*

# CHUMBUMS

C humming, illegal in most states, is defined in Colorado as the "placement of fish, parts of fish, or other material which fish might feed in the waters of the state for the purpose of attracting fish to a particular area in order they might be taken." The law is designed to promote a sporting sense of order and fairness for fishermen and fish alike. Chumming persists as a common violation amongst the ranks of pesky piscators, especially ice fishermen, overcome by craving temptations to increase their success. For wardens, detecting chumming violations requires tenacity using high power spotting scopes from strategically veiled locations. Not considered the wildlife crime of the century, active enforcement serves as warnings that wardens are paying close attention to fishermen behavior. But understand, capturing 'chummers' ranks high as a warden spectator sport. Conversely, chumming provides a high degree of deviousness for fishermen risking capture (like stealing pumpkins on Halloween).

Working my variable power Big Eye, I captured miscreants chumming with granola cereal, salmon eggs, maggots, and chunked up fish parts. I once watched in awe as a local youth, under the direction of his father, poured a gallon can of corn down several ice holes (when I looked down the holes the lake bottom resembled a grain bin). Experienced chummers acquire great skill avoiding detection including nonchalantly piling chum next to ice holes or onto their boot, followed by a slow 360 degree scan of one's surroundings before footing the bait into the hole; pouring bait onto aluminum dipping spoons, waiting a bite and then pretending to scoop ice from the hole; or simply standing above the ice hole dribbling bait down ones leg. My favorite catch by far was the man storing live maggots in his mouth and spitting them into the ice-hole while tending his line.

Sig 'Slick' Palm, a Colorado's warden legend, told the tale of a very successful fly fisherman casting a section of river restricted to the use of flies and lures, fluidly releasing salmon eggs from his pole hand with each forward cast while drifting his baited salmon egg hook through the 'seeded' water. On another occasion, while checking licenses of several early spring bank fishermen during ice off at Lake John, I gasped with delight when one of the men's young grandson pitched several handfuls of corn kernels towards the edge of the ice where their fishing lines entered the water. I and the startled men burst into laughter while the naïve lad pondered their humor. When I explained to the boy the illegality of chumming, the boy blurted, "Grandpa does it all the time!" *Warden Gold!*

So there I was, running an early morning trapline on the Bighorn Ranch after setting three bit 4 1/2 beaver traps on Shafer Creek the previous evening. Stopping in the ranch headquarters (a ranch rule) to advise I was checking traps, the foreman's mother asked me in for coffee. Failing to rouse her comatose son from his previous day's inebriation, she apologized avowing he had been working hard and was really tired. I regarded the man's alcoholism a classic human tragedy quite common amongst the ranching community where too many cowboys lost their life's message in the bottom of a bottle. I honestly liked the man, but it became increasingly rare finding him in a temperate state of mind.

Today, after a pleasant chat with his mother, a tried and true Bull Pen pioneer, I pulled two beaver and would you believe, one coyote out of three drowning sets. Midsummer, the pelts not prime, I threw the carcasses into the ranch's bone pile on my way out. Leaving the ranch, I elected working the public fishing leases along the North Fork and 'back door' into Lake John through a chunk of private land. No fishermen on the leases, I veiled my truck behind the berm of the lakeshore road behind a row of tall sage. While a song sparrow incessantly serenaded its summer song, I scanned the lake and immediately recognized Maximus, a proud retired Filipino, fishing fifty yards away from a rock jetty. Maximus was an honorable, philosophical man who spent the entire summer fishing the Bull Pen's lakes. Well known and highly respected, he was legendary throughout the community as a professional bait fisherman. I often chatted with him for updates on current fishing conditions, frequently finding a couple of large, pink-meated trout in his cooler and nothing in his camper's freezer. Knowing Maximus legally donated much of his catch to friends, I did not rate him high on my most wanted list. However, Maximus was often turned in for fishing law violations. Many were simply jealous of his fishing expertise and success, some whom the wardens knew as first-degree poachers themselves. But even the legal side of the grapevine repeatedly described Maximus as an obsessive/compulsive chummer stockpiling hordes of trout in an accomplice's freezer. If Maximus was breaking the law as reported, he had a sixth sense or a guardian angel warning him of a warden's presence. I had focused the Big Eye on Maximus many times, not once observing him violate fishing law.

Persistence kissed by kismet often results in snaring the wiliest violators. Today, I was on good ground for counting coupe on the unsuspecting Maximus. Watching him cast two power baited lines and cautiously hunker into the rocks while slowly scanning the lakeshore, I wondered, *"Is he looking for me!"* Luckily, when the fisherman's eyes washed over my location, the heavy sage effectively camouflaged my vehicle. Detecting Maximus' left wrist jerk forward I intensified my surveillance and, thinking it was nothing, noticed his hand lurch forward a second time. Turning up the Big Eye, I concentrated on a box of Velveeta cheese sitting on a flat boulder. Maximus repeatedly pinched off a piece, rolled it into a little ball, and set them on the rock.

Finished, Maximus picked up a cheese ball, placed it into the pouch of a slingshot and accurately shot the projectile towards the visible floats attached to his fishing lines. Every time he cast his newly baited rods into the lake he would 'refresh' the area by slinging additional cheese balls! Maximus immediately began catching trout, releasing the small ones, and eventually keeping a limit of two large rainbows. *Cowabunga!* Forewarning my presence, I fired up my pickup, spun my tires onto the road and paused to watch Maximus vigilantly slide his slingshot back into his tackle box and clean up the flat rock. Through my scope I recognized the glaring eyes of a man anticipating capture by a warden bear.

Maximus was well known for his flash temper, experiencing great anger when boats trolled too close to the bank over his lines. I was once called out to take care of the 'mad Oriental' waving a machete, threatening every boat cruising by. Upon contact I found Maximus 'chi' sodden in saki. The old fisherman readily admitted 'waving his sword' to prevent boats from invading 'his' domain.

I knew the principled man presented no threat to my pending warden wrath. Walking down the jetty, I smiled as the seasoned fishing warrior waved a warm greeting. Small talking the nice weather, I wasted little time informing Maximus of his chumming misdeeds. Switching gears, I solicited Maximus' opinion on what I should do. Avoiding eye contact, Maximus unflinchingly stared over the lake and nobly replied, "I do not need to chum to catch fish. I deserve a ticket." A tic was scratched to the humbled yet starkly stoic man, who resolutely requested me not reveal his capture to anyone. In return, he promised to never disobey fishing law again. I, all too familiar with false promises of those sharing my pen, considered Maximus' testament an absolute truth. The wounds of capture stung not because of the ticket, but because he feared he would lose the respect of his friends and gain the ridicule of his enemies.

Maximus, long 'gone under', is no doubt fishing exalted waters with friends in the Great Beyond. So, if the old adage declaring a person is not truly dead until all knowing them have taken their final breath, Maximus remains very much alive! As long as this warden breathes, he will honor Maximus as one of the Bull Pen's finest fishers of men.

*"Justice is Truth in action"*
   Benjamin Disraeli

# THE ROGUES OF ROSEBUD

*"He escapes who is not pursued."* Sophocles

For those unacquainted wayfarers 'on their way to somewhere,' the scanty highway town of Rosebud may seem nothing more than a mere spot on the highway for purchasing gas, food and beer from the convenience store, or a place to dine and imbibe in the town's lively bar. They otherwise regard this southern Bull Pen village as merely a hodgepodge of randomly scattered log cabins, ranch houses, outhouses, barns and sheds in various stages of disrepair. *Oh, what they miss!* Chronicles featuring the Bull Pen would fall far short of the mark without detailing its settlements and the people who decorate them. Rosebud is a landmark western town exemplifying the Bull Pen's rich cultural heritage. Defined by its gRAND inhabitants; a quilt-work of colorful, scrappy personalities bound in the cultural sinew of dependence upon the areas natural resources - loggers, landowners, ranch managers, hunters, fishermen, trappers, snowmobilers, poachers, drunks, whores, thieves, writers, philosophers and business people. If you do not know the people, you miss the unique social fabric these small mountain communities tender.

During my watch, Rosebud's gas station and convenience store was owned and operated by a vibrant husband and wife 'team,' Don and Sandy, whose hard work and imagination carved a first rate living from the wide-ranging visitors and inhabitants of the Bull Pen. This well-organized supply depot, providing the necessary wares for recreational public, was creatively adorned with western relics, a soul warming pot-bellied stove, a variety of antiques, and an awesome collection of western books; a warming atmosphere to coffee up and gossip! Don and Sandy sold hunting and fishing licenses affording me opportunity to chat, inspect licenses sold, snack and kid around with Sandy's parents, especially her father 'Grumps', relentlessly joking about his make-believe wildlife crimes and my inability to catch him.

The village was also blessed with an outstanding five-star western flavored saloon and steak house owned and hosted by the retired 'mile high' produce broker, Cecil Biggerstaff. The Liar's Lair attracted locals and folks far and wide seeking its scrumptious table fare and highly spirited bar offering a savoring ambiance for those needing comfort from everyday routines. Cecil, the 'Old Man of the Mountain', was as solid and stoic as the granite peaks corralling the Bull Pen. His free-spirited independence and common sense, seasoned with a dash of humility, a spicy sense of humor and the sagacity of an owl, earned him tremendous community respect as their leader and mentor. An avid hunter (bears were his passion), fisherman, and beaver trapper, Cecil was THE information source on current local conditions. This highly revered icon served with pride and passion as Rosebud's informal mayor, chief of police, spokesperson and confidante. I too (cautiously) held Cecil in high esteem, often utilizing him as a steadfast sounding board on everything from the current activities of local outdoor miscreants to wildlife biology and management. Cecil, however, maintained a guarded distance from me, purposely shielding pertinent incriminating facts to protect friends and maintain his honored community status. Thus, a close friendship was denied due to a measure of mutual distrust; relationships very common in the warden world. Predictable as a fox killing chickens, I captured the man in a stone faced, eye to eye lie concealing the wildlife violations of two friends. That, of course, is another story. Suffice to say, following this incident my ribeyes grew significantly smaller when dining at his restaurant. Unfortunately, Cecil turned sour as time flaked away his flinty vigor, seemingly haunted by youthful memories of what he could do no longer. Wearing his age like a ball and chain, he unremittingly criticized me and the wildlife agency, partially due to the embarrassment of having been captured as well as the rocky trails the aging process tracks. But this I know, Cecil long since down under, is sadly missed.

Rosebud remains a favored hangout for hunters, fishermen, and game wardens. The grapevine, overly ripened with gossiping fruits of truths, half-truths, and embellished tales, produces an abundance of wittingly camouflaged innuendos regarding whose doing what, to whom, where and why; cultivating endless fodder for a warden reaper to make hay. Just south of Rosebud is the Old Homestead, another drinking establishment with a boar's nest of rental cabins, and a pugilistic owner who went out of his way to protect his clientele, adding more stock to the warden poaching pot. We were routinely requested by the owner to vacate the premises for harassing his patrons.

During the fall hunting seasons the population of the Rosebud community more than doubles in size. The drinking establishments host a horde of famished and thirsty outdoorsmen, sloshing down drinks while embellishing spirited stories of their day's events; modern day mountain man raconteurs spinning gaudy lies. Such lairs for liars provided a prodigious place for a warden mole to sit and listen. I crafted a poaching case while dining at the Lair with fellow officer Larry Budde. Dining with our wives we overheard a boisterous drunk divulge his story of illegally shooting a deer, providing detailed directions allowing us to locate and sit on the deer that very night, and capture the sozzled chap and his sidekicks at the kill site. The Rosebud community provides wardens hunters to chase, information to sort, knowledge for making wildlife management decisions, reliable friendships, undependable relationships and stark enemies, some having shared my pen. I gratefully accepted my role as 'their' warden, knowing I was liked by some and tolerated, talked about, criticized, hated and avoided by others; a good place to be for any warden.

Over time, I became proficient deciphering my wide-ranging conversations with community members, understanding many discreetly provided worthy information in their own subtle way. For the locals, there was a fine line between 'ratting out' one of their own, and 'weeding out' bad behavior. What some perceived as unworthy outdoor behavior often far exceeded my standards for illicit conduct. Of course, any illegal information regarding 'pilgrims', those distrusted outsiders, would be reported in an efficient and detailed manner. Local intolerance of unwelcome newbies was a touchstone followed by most, no matter which side of the law they were on. Throughout my conversations with the populace in and around Rosebud one name, Rueben 'Rue' Pilfer, was regularly mentioned as one needing warden attention. I soon discovered Rue, and the family patriarch Earnest, commanded a clan of Yooper confederates well known for plundering the areas game and fish populations. I routinely crossed paths with Rue hunting both as a lone wolf and with a pack of wily relatives, friends and paying clients (Rue was a state licensed outfitter and guide) reveling in boundless freedom to violate wildlife law; exactly the human game a warden preys for. Their devish jaunts were well planned, fast paced, quick hitting forays often concealed under the cloak of darkness. Seldom returning to the same haunts in successive days, their outdoor crimes were always one fork in the trail ahead of the wardens. Locating these game maggots committing wildlife violations in the field was like finding fly shit in a pepper mill. Their tracks covered, stories synchronized and no witnesses willing to take the steps necessary for scratching tics, the Pack maintained a barrier impenetrable to wardens restricted by the legal guidelines of wildlife law. However, as my grapevine matured, the number of valid reports from the disapproving public increased, revealing a critical flaw in the Pilfer's game plan. As opportunistic, spontaneous and secretive they were, they carelessly tittle-tattled their misdeeds to, unbeknown to them, trustworthy warden double agents. Working both sides of the rumor mill, I not only filtered the gossiping grind but also fed it with my own half-truths to community members who telegraphed my furtive lines almost as fast as I snitched them. Once agonizing over these game pirates as much as Noah worried about porcupines and woodpeckers, now I simply needed to relax, knowing patience, persistence, well-planned strategy and a little luck would eventually defeat these wild rogues. *Maggiore fretta, minore atto – the more haste, the less action.*

*"Time wounds many a heel."*

Rue was a real piece of work. Well known for overtly bragging fabulous fables of his outdoor misdeeds, he considered himself a legendary, seasoned hunter and woodsman. At thirty years of age I measured Rue as the disillusionment of two fifteen-year olds; a self-indulgent poacher filling an empty space in his soul by deceiving himself as a highly revered outdoorsman. Having the skills, fortitude and chutzpah to kill game, he lacked the moral turpitude necessary to make the grade as a modern-day sportsman; Elmer Fudd acting as a Capstick imposter. Not a master of his errant ways, but a slave to them, Rue had several character flaws any seasoned warden would exploit; mental playthings in a warden's toy box. First, Rue was always eager to talk. Second, if his lips were moving, he was lying. Lies hanging like crap from a dung beetle's mouth, Rue fibbed even when the truth was on his side. Third, when pushed hard he would weep; emotionally whining out real crocodile tears! Now game thieves are one thing, but a crying game thief is all I could take. *There is no crying in poaching!* The wolf, only as strong as his pack, when interrogated alone, howled. Rue and I experienced many one-sided discussions covering everything from outright truths to dancing around hearsay. These deliberations often drove Rue into a bawling stupor. *Rosebud's town crier!* Lastly, Rue was extremely paranoid. Obsessive mistrust, blending with his vivid imagination, began creeping into his wicked heart, leading him to believe his beloved community was after him. *Some were!* My probable cause for suspecting Rue, was probably because he was somehow involved in the wildlife crime.

*To him who is in fear, everything rustles. Sophocles*

The bold scent of capture intensifying; harvest was soon at hand. Tics were scratched covering the entire span of the law books. The Pilfer women, rarely in the field, typically 'filled' their licenses first. Party hunting, illegal in Colorado, was a favored ploy of the Pilfer gang. We often found a big game animal tagged by a clan member who, when hastily contacted, was yet aware his or her license had been filled. *Imagine that!* I once contacted Rue in the field with a deer in the back of his jeep tagged with a license belonging to their camp cook who, less than an hour earlier, stated he had not yet hunted. Rue took the hit for killing two deer. Licenses were illegally bartered, traded and transferred at will. Nonresident clan members illegally purchased resident licenses. Reports of trespass, spotlighting, over bags of fish and game, (poaching in so many ways) increased exponentially as the community jointly began cooperating, creating a warden feeding frenzy. Evidence was seized from their campers (one license retrieved from a camper septic system), outbuildings, vehicles, illegally tagged game, billfolds, and license records. Once caught, they normally paid their fines without squawking. Gradually, the thrill of being chased was replaced with the phobic trepidation of capture. The now paranoid clan grew arrogant; spreading the word they were being harassed and persecuted. *True!* The family consistently stood firm on their innocence, even when mired up to their armpits in guilt. One clan member, after losing a pricey license violation in court, suggested "I may want to consider wearing body armor."

Predictably, one radiant September morning midway into the 1988 archery season, there we were; Wildlife Officer Kirk Snyder and I driving through Rosebud following an anonymously dull tip of a Ruefully illegal doe deer hanging 'somewhere' in a private shed hidden in a wooded glade near the Old Homestead. Now it is well known timing has a lot to do with the success of a rain dance. Driving through Rosebud, our plan changed quick as a snake's tongue upon spotting Rue and two of his confederates standing in his front yard.

Like bobcat on hare, I could not resist the sight of the very prey we were stalking and announced, "We're going in!" Weal or woe, it was time to make something happen and not wasting time tracking false scents on old tracks to dead end roads; today would be spent glaring into the eyes of **THE WOLF** in **HIS** den. Exiting our vehicle, two noticeably nervous leatherneck clients decked in full military camo, began whispering with Rue. *Warden spoor!* Rue approached with his normal lab puppy happiness, complaining he had not seen us for quite some time. *No one misses a warden!* I began the wild game stating we were working a poaching case *(the Truth!)* and asked if he heard anything about anything. Rue replied he heard nothing about anything, snap firing he had been away for a while. Kirk explained we had a reliable tip from a local sportsman, providing detailed information on a poaching incident. Suspicious, Rue shamefacedly reacted as if Kirk was referring to him, affirming his integrity as a former marine and a concerned sportsman spending time working for wildlife and the hunting good. *Kind of like Billy the Kid telling Kirk he was a banker!* Kirk began chatting with the two men in camo, Frag Spitzer and Shard Hornady. They said they were bow hunting for deer and antelope. Small talking over the bed of Rue's pickup, as wardens do, Kirk questioned the blood and hair in the truck bed. Rue fibbed the hair belonged to a buck deer he shot earlier in the week, already cut, wrapped and frozen *(the deer the wardens were looking for?)*. Remembering Rue admitted earlier he had not been around, Kirk explained the hair was antelope, not deer. Rue rapid fired another lie stating they helped a hunter haul out an antelope that very morning. Loading our verbal magazine, we continued cross-firing bulleted questions, noticeably hitting bone on both Frig and Sprag, standing taut as a buffalo's ass during fly season. Although the time train did not stop, it slowed considerably as a lingering silence provided time to penetrate the thick musky scent of illegal spoor. Not surprisingly, Rue reversed directions stating he also killed an antelope the previous day but it too had been cut and wrapped! Eyes locked, Kirk and I winked our next move knowing we had wounded and were tracking a beast yet identified. Stilling the din, Rue's young son Hank exploded from the house, walked up to us and said. "Wait'll you see the buck Frag shot." *The cats* *in the cradle!* Hank, the yet tainted yard ape version of his father, a proud minnow swimming in a pool with the big boys, innocently and unknowingly floated into warden waters. Witnessing the expiring moments of denial as the boy blamelessly spoke naive truths over his father's culpable lies, Kirk and I enjoyed the sudden impact as he made our day. Frag immediately admitted arrowing an antelope with his bow the day before, and it too, of course, had been cut and wrapped. Both hunters, staring with the glazed look of a jacklit deer while Rue, brain 'squirming like a toad', pondered his next exonerating falsehood. Kirk asked the lively informant if we could see the buck and Hank eagerly replied it was hanging behind the house. Ah, the phoenix rose from its ashes, newly born from the truthful words of young Hank pompously marching us to a backyard shed, door partially open, containing not one, but three fresh antelope carcasses hanging as pyres of their misdeeds. Turning to his father, the prodigal son began sensing the chaos triggered by his naively innocent declarations. With Rue's permission, I nosed into the shed while Kirk honored my point and guarded the two military men. Rue, chattering like a squirrel watching a pine marten, shadowed me as I pointed out large, bullet inflicted holes in each carcass. Kirk confirmed the two bucks and one doe were obviously killed with 'loud arrows' (warden terms for rifle shot archery kills). Rue's ashen face smoldering in guilt, the 'jarhead' was having a dishonorable discharge, vomiting words of a man trying to delay the inevitable. Spontaneously combusting in the warden heat, Rue wilted, with the droopy eyed gaze of a man undergoing capture myopathy. The wardens now faced the oxymoron of gaining intelligence from a fool.

No time for yarnin, Kirk and I knifed forward, pushing the proverbial Green River up to the hilt with reminders of his past wildlife crimes and twisting with today's blatant testimonial of his incessant criminal outdoor behavior. Predictably, Rue's demise ended with a conventional, gut wrenching shedding of tears. Like the wounded wolf he was, he bawled out another barrage of lies regarding not knowing the location of the rifle used to kill the antelope and why he failed to tag the doe with his license. The marines' military intelligence kicked in, under the influence of Kirk's threat of notifying their Commanders, and both promptly confessed, providing detailed written statements, including the primary role Rue played as their guide. I flogged Rue's corrupt ego by requesting written documentation of his misdeeds. Realizing his printed words would be scrutinized, criticized and used to bury him, Rue refused taking the pen, demanding to know who turned them in.

*"I bet you wonder how we knew!"*

And so, the game played on. The marines promptly paid their fines. Rue elected duking out his misdeeds in court, hiring a hotshot attorney. After a long series of legal bickering and a suppression hearing, justice prevailed with Rue losing his case and even better, his hunting and fishing license privileges. However, innately destined for failure, the Pack continued working hard on their legacy of illicit outdoor misbehavior.

Surprisingly, the very next fall, Rue helped make a rock-hard illegal moose case. During our discourse, Rue cried for forgiveness and the opportunity to regain a trusting relationship with me and my colleagues. *That would require a conscience!* Knowing Rue's remorse held the shelf life of the neck meat of an abandoned moose carcass, I replied I was willing to bury the proverbial hatchet, but it would take time and effort on Rue's part before I could forget where I concealed it.

Oddly, I will always carry a peculiar fondness for Rue, perhaps because he was a patriotic devil dog, and even more upon learning Hank joined the marines and was killed in combat by a sniper's bullet. Rue was not a bad man, just a bad hunter and fisherman. For wardens, chase provides our challenges, and capture honors the wild beasts and rewards the hunting good. Yes Kirk, the Pilfer gang were ruthless poachers, but they were our poachers.

*OOH RAH!*

# WHETHER OR NOT!

O ne dreadful October night I was working Independence
Mountain, warning hunters of a major snowstorm thundering
across the Rockies predicted to drop two to three feet of snow. Drifting
snow beginning to block the rugged mountain roads, driving was
already difficult. Chained up on all four tires, I pulled into a campsite
where a burly, black-bearded Hispanic man was splitting firewood for
a huge campfire near a small, incredibly old camper. Zipping up my
waist length down coat and pulling down the earflaps on my insulated
Dudley Doolittle cap, I opened the truck door and charged into a
barrage of water drenched, doily sized snowflakes to alert him of the
bleak forecast.

Our conversation went as follows:

Warden: "You may want to pull up camp and get off the mountain"

Brutus: "Glad you are here! I have hunted the entire mountain and
have yet to locate timberline." (the second day of the season, it was
impossible to have hunted the entire mountain).

Warden: "There is no timberline on this mountain because of its
low elevation. You need to be more concerned about this snowstorm."

Brutus: Shining his flashlight skyward through the saucer sized flakes piercing through the dark night: "No need to worry, this is the kind of snow that doesn't accumulate!"

Warden: "It is already extremely difficult to stay on the road!"

Brutus: Pointing to his chained up, large, knobby tired four-wheel drive diesel truck he declared, "I can climb trees with this son of a bitch!"

Warden: Stepping back into his vehicle. "Don't say I didn't warn you!"

The next morning, I found Brutus's truck buried in snow and greasy mud and, with great difficulty, pulled him out.

*Keep on truckin warden!*

**FOOTNOTE!** Late spring the following year Brutus was able to retrieve his badly snow damaged camper.

# GOOSE FLATS

It was the best of farts; it was the worst of farts …

Decември 8, 1975. There I was, sitting in an old truck parked in a barnyard owned by an elderly farmer named Rip Gasser. Chilled to the bone, heater running full blast, Rip and I faced a crimson sunrise on a very cold morning after placing five dozen goose decoys around a goose pit two hundred yards from his farmhouse.

Meeting Rip only this morning, we were awaiting the waves of geese leaving a nearby reservoir to feed in his picked corn field, as they had done the past several days. Compadre Sir Don Gore and I, having worked three successive, twelve-hour days checking pheasant and waterfowl hunters, welcomed today's hunt as a hard-earned break before returning to the Bull Pen. Wildlife Officer Johnny Hobbs, a long-time friend of Rip, graciously coordinated today's hunt as our gift for helping him work hunters in the Fort Collins area. Sir Don, warming in Johnny's truck, would soon join me in the pit while Johnny and Rip drank coffee and watched in what typically developed into a productive goose hunt. Rip kindly allowed friends and family to dig a goose pit and use his cutting-edge facilities for cleaning harvested geese.

Exchanging small talk, I discovered Rip to be a soft spoken, down to earth, hardworking man who spent a lifetime raising a family while farming this land. Enjoying our conversation, I found myself totally unprepared for the foul odor suddenly infiltrating the truck's cab. The inaudible, flatulating stench was intense, a stodgy septic smell sharply penetrating my nasal cavities causing eye fogging, taste bud curdling, lung collapsing, stomach spasming sensations one may experience prior to passing out. Even worse, I had no polite way to escape without offending our charitable host. Soul searching for the fortitude to disregard his toxic anal gas bomb as if it were not there, I could not. Years of field necropsying rotten wild beasts, including moose, the holy grail of malodorous smells, had not prepared me for the fermenting intestinal aroma we presently suffered. Honestly, it put a large cattle feedlot to shame. The moment becoming glacial, my watering eyes focused on Rip as he wrapped his loosely clenched hand over his nose.

Understand, flatulence in no way describes Rip's wind breaking blast of rectal turmoil. Searching for a gracious exit, laughter, often my redeeming involuntary defensive mechanism, overtook my civility. Failing to disguise my hoarse snort as a cough, I entered a period of uncontrollable hysteria. Amazingly, Rip joined in and commanded me to roll down my window while he did the same. Sticking our noses into the cold, fresh air like two blood hounds, Rip conceded he had all but crapped his pants, declaring, "I learned a long time ago not to hold those things in!" I thanked God knowing he would not be joining Sir Don and I in the confined goose pit. Once there, relating the story to an amused Sir Don, I realized Rip and I were forever bonded by his fetid flatulence.

Patiently anticipating unremitting flights of geese flushing from Richard's Lake and landing in our decoys, we were not disappointed. Sir Don and I returned to the Bull Pen with a brace of cleaned and picked Canada Geese.

*There are a million stories in the naked woods. This is one of them.*

# DOROTHY AND THE WIZARD

Dorothy, a handicapped lady from Colorado's front range, was a Bull Pen fisherwoman icon. Spending summers in a camper parked in Sage Hen, she passionately pursued her love for fishing the lower elevation lakes – Lake John, and the three Delaney Butte Lakes. Dorothy's physical disabilities required parking her car near the lakes' shoreline, enabling her to fish out of the driver's side window. Flinging a long rod lobbing a large plastic casting bubble approaching the size of a toilet bowl float, with a long leader bearing a baited hook or a fly, this lady caught a lot of trout.

Dorothy's 'Reba' smile disclosed her mischievous sweetness. Because of her spirited fervor for life capable of reviving a roadkill, I greatly enjoyed conversing with her, always leaving happier and revitalized. Perhaps, due to her handicap, I gave her more leeway than most despite the frequent grumbling she was catching, keeping, and canning more than her legal share of trout. Word on the street was she stored an abundance of trout in a friend's freezer for eating during the winter months. Knowing her fish never went to waste, many legally donated to needy families and the elderly, I essentially left her alone. I did, however, as a means of keeping her on her toes, warn her she was being scrutinized and tattled on by outside sources. And, as so often happens with those violating wildlife law, the grapevine began repetitively whining fruit over and above the normal wrath of the jealous and resentful, driving me to pay more attention to Dorothy's fishing behavior.

And there we were, Wildlife Officer Kirk Snyder and I working a warm June evening scoping the Delaney Butte lakes and formulating a plan to work night fishermen. And there they were, Dorothy parked lakeshore on the northwest bay of the South Lake accompanied by none other than our favorite lawbreaking wizard, a man we had shared pens with multiple times, OZ! An omen, indeed! OZ, a bottom shelf boozer, was not a fan of wardens or the agency we worked for. A back-biting dog and prolific bitcher, he hid his anger whenever facing us, but word on the street snitched his persistent criticism and animosity against all working for the Colorado Division of Wildlife. A repetitive, dues paying member of the wildlife offender club, OZ rated high on our list of village idiots, as did we on his. Nightfall looming, the stars aligning, Kirk and I were eager to test the fishing duo's competence of keeping within the bounds of fishing law. Running our hounds silent, I hid my vehicle in willows south of their location, and we stalked the high sage to where we could clearly hear their conversations.

The South Lake was under new regulations requiring anglers to fish with flies or lures only (no bait allowed), obey length limitations on what could be kept, and a reduced daily bag limit of two trout. Because of the high mortality rate on fish deep hooked by swallowing bait, the less damaging lip hooking fly and lure designation was imperative. These regulations create a corresponding reduction in overall fishing pressure (bait fishermen moving to less restricted waters) and promote higher populations of larger fish, in what previously was a highly overfished lake. Skilled fly and lure anglers were now catching and releasing many trout of all sizes while allowed to keep two meeting the established length limits. Sport fishing had never been better. Of course, changing regulations comes with controversy, especially from bait fishermen, despite the obvious improvement of the fishery.

Dorothy and OZ were highly skilled anglers using bait or flies.

Dorothy could cast her line out further from her driver's side window than most men could from shoreline. Kirk and I chuckled at the click of her open face reel, the whooshing sound of her whipping rod, the purr of line floating above the water, followed by the loud **KERPLUNK** of the oversized casting bubble. Sitting in high sage, we were on good ground, and it quickly became evident OZ and Dorothy were quite dismayed with the new regulations, especially the two fish bag limit. Exercising the adage of the impossibility of teaching old dogs new tricks, they were pillaging the lakes improved bounty by keeping all but the smallest trout caught. OZ, deviously hiding their illicit trout under a spare tire in the back of his pickup, vocally chuckled the incompetent wardens would never look there, *HOKA HEY!*

The night black as pitch, we could barely make out silhouettes of the fishing pair. But there was no need to perceive either. Dorothy kept a large hardwood club on the car's floor, called a priest, to administer the 'last rites' to every fish she caught. Reeling her catch up the driver's side door, she struck a skull smashing blow to the trout's head, signaling another trout meeting its maker, making it simple to tally our head count (literally) of every fish she kept. **WHACK!** Kirk and I recorded OZ's catch by his war whoops and noisy prattling of what he kept.

Adding to our entertainment was their continuous carping about the ridiculousness of the new regulations, despite reaping the rewards of the laws they were so blatantly disregarding. OZ, reeling in trout after trout, keeping the large and releasing the small, laughingly waved an arm over the lake and declared, "You call this fishing pressure?" Of course, he was right, there were less fishermen present due to the new restrictions; an essential component of the lake's management strategies. Making clear the inept wardens and fish biologists did not know what they were doing, he continued catching and bitching, the reason Kirk and I nicknamed this all-knowing wizard, OZ.

Our count recorded each keeping six trout when OZ began gathering up his gear. Kirk and I ghosted out of the night's gloom into the dim light of their shoreline lantern. OZ greeted us like the long-lost friends we were not. Apparently, we were no longer the dimwitted morons he called us earlier. *Imagine that!* Sarcastically, I asked if they noticed the decline in fishing pressure and both agreed the change in regulations had certainly improved the fishing. *Wow! A complete reversal of fish management philosophy!* Scofflaws no longer scoffing the law, OZ and Dorothy remained calm as a team of hearse horses.

Aware both had valid fishing licenses from previous checks, Kirk asked if they had caught any fish. Like carrion on a buzzard's breath, they spewed stinking lies of releasing all trout caught except one for Dorothy's dinner. OZ boasted he heartily enjoyed the sporting opportunity of catching and releasing trout of all sizes. Recording their fibs into our creel census notes, we smiled and pretended to be on our way, a ploy Kirk and I often play acted before adding the last nail to a poacher's coffin. On cue, Kirk turned towards OZ and said, "by the way, we do need to check under your spare tire!" OZ, now on a tight line experiencing the terror of capture myopathy, Kirk slid him into the warden net. Dorothy, visibly embarrassed, immediately apologized expressing having fished here for so many years, it was hard to keep only two trout. OZ, of course, storied this was the first time he ever exceeded his limit. Kirk, in his customary menacing manner, made it clear we were aware of OZ's persistent poaching behavior. Allowing each to keep two of the larger legally sized trout, Dorothy politely admitted giving OZ her catch since he had a family to feed. As for OZ, no one really knows what this panhandler really did with his fish.

As Kirk and I scratched out tics to the steel headed fish poachers, I pondered whether our next encounter would involve breaking the law. For OZ, our answer came swiftly as that very winter he was caught chumming through this ice-covered lake. Dorothy, openly admitting her wrongdoings to all, remained effervescent and friendly whenever we crossed paths. A worthy member of the Bull Pen's fishing elite!

*Dorothy: "How can you talk if you haven't got a brain?" Scarecrow: "I don't know… But some people without brains do an awful lot of talking…*
The Wizard of OZ

# DANCIN' WITH THE DEVIL IN THE PALE MOONLIGHT

Octorber 1977, the moon of the changing seasons, found us swamped in the mire of the hunting seasons. A violent high-country snowstorm drove many hunters homeward, but for those die-hard-headed hunting fanatics nestled in cozy cold weather camps, the inclement weather was a welcome blessing. The stars were aligning for hunters and wardens alike; a time when blood runs hot and heavy as deer and elk, forced out of remote high-country lairs, fast track to wintering grounds where they are more accessible and vulnerable. The season winding down, hunters desperate and elk on the move, violations would increase in direct proportion to increased harvest, generating lively times for all players in the hunting game. And there we were, parked on a craggy ridge overlooking the Bighorn Ranch, Wildlife Officer Larry Budde and I absorbed the serenity of an early evening wilderness panorama. The gun barrel blue timber, capped by snow-cone peaks, afforded a spectacular backdrop for vast hay meadows broken by willowy creeks, aspen, and sage. Two Red-tailed Hawks, my spirit bird, wafting imperceptible thermals under the immeasurable polar sky screeched their freedom and independence to the world below. Most raptors having migrated south, this pair possibly were detained by a robust rodent population actively caching their winter's food supply under the closely cropped, windswept hay meadows.

Larry and I were 'stealin' in through the back door towards a secluded elk camp, purposely avoiding the ranch headquarters. Never genuinely welcome, the ranch manager allowed access provided we 'check in' before entering. Warden presence was tolerated but with strings attached; a home rule familiar to most wardens. Limited hunting was taking place on the ranch allowing our legal entry without permission, but I typically communicated with the ranch manager to maintain good relations. However, the creeping grapevine alleged wardens were consistently hoodwinked by the manager 'Paul Revering' their presence. The outlaws, taking advantage of the ranch manager's passion for ardent spirits, proffered ample distilled bribes for alerting them when the 'wardens were coming.' Today, we would not be checking in!

Focusing on the camp's location, befittingly nestled beneath the wilderness scarps called the 'Devil's Backbone', I maneuvered my vehicle over the mere trace of road in grandma gear, grinding over rocky ridges, winding through mixed aspen and pine, coursing across streams and plowing through the black muck of beaver flooded swamps, finally accessing the puzzle-piece hayfields. My state truck, side scraped by willow, aspen and pine and totally encased in mud, made me wish we were in Larry's vehicle!

Over the years I collected endless information from field contacts, tactically placed undercover officers, and disgruntled sportsmen concerning this camp's illegal hunting activities. The hunters, a deep-rooted clone of meat poaching warriors, rationalized their misdeeds as a means of providing an essential winter's meat supply. A true appetite for killing game, the clan hunted illicitly for generations believing their legally purchased licenses allowed filling them in any way they saw fit. They were highly skilled outdoorsmen capable of harvesting their own elk but mandating, if the opportunity arose, all camp members kill any and all elk possible; first degree poachers implementing their time proven plan of strategically guarding key elk crossings day after day, killing elk until all licenses were filled. When a kill was made the meat was quartered, moved away from the gut piles and illegally hidden untagged in old growth pine away from main trails. Meat was cached in the same places year after year. If a hunter needed to return home, he would retrieve an elk and tag it with his or another's tag. Unfilled licenses were left in camp to be filled by the remaining camp members. In the event more elk were killed than available tags, other licensed friends were solicited. There was never a shortage of licenses to launder illegally killed elk. At the season's end the meat was covertly horsed off the mountain to their camp.

Their rules were simple; there were no rules. All were quite aware killing elk for others was illegal and carried serious consequences but, because they so successfully disguised their misdeeds, game hogging venery remained permanently ingrained into their hunting traditions. Thus, most elk were poached; pilfered from the public's common by cheating the very management system sustaining the bountiful elk population. They played as hard hunting as they did in their vocation pouring mortar in the never-ending world of construction on Colorado's front-range. Hunting elk was their recreational avocation; an essential, sacred, longstanding family ritual no one dare meddle with!

Larry and I paid seasonal visits to this camp, stalking in on horse-back, ATVs, on foot or with quick hits from our vehicle as they were doing today. A favored ploy was recurrently checking hunters in the vicinity of the camp anticipating the grapevine would tattle wardens, like fly shit, were everywhere. Of course, with over 1000 square miles to cover, we were not. Except for an occasional legally tagged elk hanging in camp or hunters transporting tagged elk homeward in their vehicles, filled license were rarely checked until the seasons end. Tics were sometimes scratched but we knew many more violations were crawling in the doghair. We once captured a camp member with a spike bull bearing the tag of his pregnant wife who was not in camp. My unsuspecting phone call indicated that 'yes' she had harvested an elk but 'no' she was unsure if it was a bull or a cow, the location of the kill site, the caliber of rifle she used to kill the elk, how many times she shot or if it had indeed been skinned or quartered. Her husband, Chum Stockpile, after gusting a flurry of obscenities concerning my family lineage, reluctantly admitted his misdeeds. Electing to appear in court he whined to an impatient judge that he had been highly mistreated for such a simple act of misusing an elk tag. The woodswise judge, after listening to my testimony, asked Stockpile if he had given the officer credit for not filing any charges against his pregnant wife; charges that still could be filed! Chum's mind did a woods-wise 180 and he hastily entered a guilty plea.

Tickets written, surprise contacts in peculiar places, loaded warden questions, all resulted in nothing less than a doctorate level education for these poachers. They became increasingly sagacious at veiling their crimes. We were a challenge but regarded as an amusing nuisance to the poaching game they relished. We pissed on their posts and they pissed on ours; rambling palavering's where loaded warden questions were disarmed with blank hunter lies. Tenaciously, we knew this close-knit poaching family could, in time, be unraveled. Miscreants persistently violating wildlife law provide predictable dividends. Such family plots often end by digging their own graves, entombing themselves in critical blunders linked to ego, greed and selfishness. Today, bragging their crimes to several 'trusted' hunters steered us to their camp. Larry and I, weary from weeks of working nights from both ends, were revitalized by the strong scent of interred wrongs hopefully to be exhumed.

Cards dealt to either side varied yearly depending on weather, kills, reports etc. Today we drew 'aces and eights.' Poachers carry the watches, opportunistically committing their misdeeds. But wardens possess the time, increasing odds of miscreant capture. Today's intelligence came from crafty foxes hunting close to the family's den. True huntsmen, they were fed up with the camp members aggressively taking control of the area for the entire season, killing more elk than their fair and legal share, stealing opportunities from the lawfully obedient. This year, they dug up dirt on who had killed and who had not, as well as whose licenses were going where. The informants' alopecoid skills cunningly provided reliable, incriminating information. Readjusting our sights, we zeroed in with the improved accuracy of a late-night phone call from one sly vixen yapping, *"The meat is coming out tomorrow night!"* With a full magazine, we were ready to harvest our illicit prey.

Easing my truck through the narrow paint scraping willow-walled road, I turned into a favored hideaway ánd parked. Suiting up in down jackets, lined elk skin gloves, belt flashlights, and binoculars, we stalked the remaining quarter mile to their campsite. Surveying the camp through thick willow we listened as Hill Creek, revived by recent snows, bubbled with giggling effervescence in a harmony only fall streams can resonate. The camp's living quarters consisted of two large connected wall tents, the front for cooking and dining and the rear for sleeping; both warmed by the kitchen's heat casting wood burning stove used for preparing rib- sticking meals sustaining ravenous appetites. The open fire pit, a time-fired circle of blackened rocks guarding the powdery ashen grey talc of the morning's fire, puffed smoky wisps from dying embers. This wilderness cauldron surrounded by log stump chairs and board benches mesmerized wilderness souls for decades. It was a picture perfect 'Cabelas' style elk camp strategically place to spy the ranch meadows. Occasionally, deer or elk were 'shoplifted' from these private meadows by camp members or other hunters stalking the Forest boundary fence.

Sniffing the sweet and sour aroma of manure and urine originating from the high limbed pines where the horses were staked, I mentally logged the horses were gone. An empty, aged meat pole lashed horizontally between two large standing pines tattled the elk meat remained on the mountain. Both good signs the bark of the fox was trustworthy. Sitting comfortably on a log stump chair staring into the smoky campfire was my treasured 'babe of the woods', Phoebe. The firepit heat and the afternoon sun soaking her back sandwiched her in bone thawing warmth. Smoking a cigarillo, she was wearing red stammel, drop-drawer long johns and cowboy boots. A black cowboy hat capped silver-maple locks thickly braided into a ropelike queue tapering down the back of her neck. Silhouetted in columns of forest light totally defined this western cherub as the woman she was; a mischievous yet fair maiden slightly past her prime wearing the feisty beauty of a bobcat. Phoebe was a classic western wilderness wench; solid, independent pioneer stock born perhaps 150 years too late. Although her temperament towards wardens was hypothermic, I considered her a rare native wildflower; beautiful in bloom but leafed with a touch of poison. Her natural looks did not require the disguise of bottles and jars. There was no need to gild this lily.

Walking out of the willows I cleared my throat causing Phoebe to quickly turn, exposing her tanned face splashed with blotchy freckles resembling the egg of a Sora Rail. The twinkling transparency of her blue flax crystalline eyes and her tight-lipped smile betrayed her thoughts; wardens were undoubtedly as welcome as buzzards on a wolf kill.

Unembarrassed by her attire Phoebe stood and glided past us in a straight-backed august gait to a coffee pot sitting on the campfire grate. Pouring herself a tin cupful and adding a dash of brandy she unflinchingly stirred it with her bird finger. Without asking she filled two additional tins with the thick sedimentary goo asking us if we wanted a shot. Reluctantly, we refused cutting the strong, wood-fired java with spirits. Handing us the hand burning cups, Phoebe stood silently waiting for whatever it was we wanted. Suffering the coffee's thick grainy bite, the awkward silence was broken when Phoebe's preschool grandson Rowdy pranced into camp chortling like a spring blackbird. Where he came from was a mystery. Nose running like an artesian well and dirty as a spring pig, I mused over the boy's matted, badger-coarse hair heavily powdered in camp duff. Happy as a wagon hound, the lad stared at the Wildlife Officers as if they were uniformed gargoyles.

Phoebe and her husband Waynjon were the camp's headsman and woman; pillars setting the standards for the entire camp. Waynjon, a black-hatted, horse-wise, roughriding cowboy wore a face displaying the rugged handsomeness of aged youth; bronzed and sculpted by the sun and wind. His heavily bossed uni-brow, salt and peppered stubble beard prickling a square jaw atop the wide shoulders of a tall, lean, long-armed frame made him a living testament to the Marlboro man. Mated for life, Phoebe was his last first love. They were books one could judge by their cover. You did not hunt with this alpha male-female duo unless you were family or had earned the trust necessary to become a pack member.

While Larry attempted to melt Phoebe's glacial aire, I joined the boy throwing rocks into Hill Creek. Wardens routinely take indecorous advantage of the untarnished honesty of the young. Rowdy, naïve as a teepee dog, listened as I whispered under the gurgling sounds of the creek, "Where are the men?" Without hesitation, Rowdy boldly replied, "They are bringing in the elk!" *Waugh!*

*'When the meat comes to camp, the clouds roll away!'* Sioux proverb

Time's essence searing our senses; we needed to strike like a thunder-clap. Clicking my tongue, I announced we were leaving. Phoebe, over-hearing the boy's tattling words, lasered a feral stare revealing all we needed to know. *I got you, babe!* Crossing the creek and walking up the timbered trail, we were quickly encased in darkness as the wilderness night fell with a draping wallop. Flashing our Maglites where the trail forked revealed fresh horse tracks going both directions. Switching off our lights, we silently waited. Shortly, we were intercepted by none other than Waynjon riding a pin-eared roan and leading a stocky black pack horse loaded with meat.

Waynjon, an expert at covering guilt with confidence, never batted an eye when I stated we would accompany him back to camp. The night's black curtain slowly closed as a ridiculously large full moon ascended over Sheep Ridge. The dazzling white, crimson-ringed cratered mass floating skyward halted us in our tracks, breathlessly spellbound by its cresting rise. In camp, Phoebe stood silhouetted in front of the campfire staring at the infamous 'Bad Moon Risin'. Waynjon and Phoebe silently watched us unload and sort the meat belonging to at least two elk. Surprisingly the meat had not yet been tagged, proving we caught the wolf pack completely off their game. When asked who killed these elk, both remained wide-eyed and silent, obviously not enjoying the night's dance. The devil, disguised as two wardens foxtrotting to the music of an unknown vixen, barked the end of this season's party hunt. Larry informed Waynjon we would follow him back up the trail to retrieve the additional elk meat. Diana, goddess of the tonight's' renegade Comanche moon, wild animals and the hunt, was with us; her presence shown by the white-washed forest and sagen hillsides strobing black bear shadows crafted an atmosphere that something unknown was about to happen! Closely trailing the mounted cowboy the pulseless quiet was momentarily interrupted by a flock of migrating geese and an occasional horseshoe sparking rock. Words cannot express the shocking sensations felt when an ear-piercing whistle followed by a flash of light from the hillside above caught us by surprise. Shouting an unintelligible warning, Waynjon hastily dismounted and scurried up the hill. We easily outran the booted cowboy and, like eagle on lamb, swooped towards the flash-light. A voice from a concealed man caused me to take a boxer's stance and as he stepped out of the shadows, his verbal greeting ended in midsentence when his light flashed onto my badge. I asked if he was armed and he murmured his rifle was in the trees. Larry secured the firearm stating no one else was present and, searching with his light, located an untagged, quartered elk covered by the drooping boughs of a large pine. The presence of old rope ties telegraphed that this tree had been used in the past. Recognizing Waynjon in the shadows, the dumbfounded hunter regained his confidence and gruffly stated he had nothing to say. *Works for us!* And so it was, as the moon coursed across the night sky we retrieved additional illegal elk meat guarded by other camp members lurking in the mountain's gloom.

That night the long arm of the law snatched the wretched poachers pirating elk from the common. Back at camp we scratched the tics, trading our names and badge numbers while listening to the poachers profanely growl their woes of capture. Refusing to admit to anything, all meat was confiscated. That really pissed them off! Their toothy howling increased as they demanded to know who turned them in. *'I bet you wonder how we knew!'* I muzzled the wolves by revealing they were caught in their own trap by thoughtlessly whispering their misdeeds to a preponderance of the hunting good, watching with immeasurable pleasure as the poachers' brains frazzled over debating the identity of their turncoats. The pack barked they were hiring a lawyer and would be filing charges against us. I peeled the bark from their deadwood minds by firmly stating they had no choice but court, adding they should hire a good lawyer.

Months later, the wolf pack bawled in court they were honorable individuals *(except when hunting)* relying on elk meat to survive. They tattled the wardens had treated them unjustly using illegal tactics to frame them, accusing them of entrapment using the words of a young, innocent child as a means to substantiate their false charges. They demanded the right to know who set them up and insisted the elk meat be returned to them. However, Larry and I had spun a perfectly tight web with no dangling ends. The judge announced he was not buying what they were selling and addressed them as flagrant poachers guilty of acts not tolerated by the court. Because the elk had not been tagged, the judge deemed all meat illegal and would remain property of the state. *WARDEN GOLD!*

Severely beaten and meatless, the group slunk from the courtroom catching Larry and I in the stairway talking to the sheriff Gary Cure. With one last Parthenian shot they warned if we ever showed our faces in their camp again, they would kill us. Sheriff Cure dutifully reminded them that the courthouse, crawling with county law enforcement officials and a judge, was a very bad place to threaten the life of anyone and, he would know where to start if anything rash happened to the wardens. Revenge rides a rogue bronc. Violating wildlife law and incessantly beating the system was their unfair game. Taking risks and beating the odds rewarded them with the telltale bragging rights of being, in their eyes, greatly skilled hunters. But being captured red-handed, never in their game plan, stole all pleasure from their thievery. Today they were formally labeled poachers, broken down by the hunting good working with the law. Justice for the elk and for those hunting legally, morally and ethically was served. A bar of warden irony comes with the fact the license dollars of all license buyers, poachers included, are used to pursue and catch the bad.

We paid the pack cordial visits annually, checking some in the field at their established hunting stations and others in camp. My warden smile did little to relieve their historical tensions but, in yet another obscure vein of warden irony, a newly formed relationship gilded by respectful tolerance began to evolve. I found myself identifying them more as hunters than poachers, respecting the fact they were passing on their well-honed hunting skills from generation to generation in an atmosphere found only in a western wilderness elk camp. The camp members as well seemingly began accepting us for what we were as well as our responsibilities; a necessity for maintaining a semblance of order in what is often a very chaotic and disorderly hunting world. To say this relationship was a friendship would be a drastic overstatement, but their shaded past provided them a new perspective of the values of modern-day hunting and law enforcement. We may or may not have reduced their violations, for many turning over a new leaf is not possible. But, for what it's worth, we never again obtained information of wildlife violations coming out of their camp. I even worked a deer case where Phoebe and Waynjon served as witnesses.

The rugged trail of America's hunting heritage, blazed by the honorable deeds of dedicated men and women, must evolve with the changing attitudes of modern society. Hunting and fishing, based on sound science and sustainable management, will continue to forge ahead as the fundamental force of state-of-the-art wildlife conservation. The miscreants of the wild, ever present as natural flaws in human nature, remain an unwarranted liability for the hunting good. Those dishonoring wildlife laws are illicit criminals fouling the ranks of today's hunting and fishing sportsmen; weeds that must be removed.

*The Devil Made Me Do It! FLIP WILSON*

# PISCATORY MATH

**M**ay 1983. And there I was, enjoying a warm spring day from a secreted vantage above Seymour Lake. Peering through the Big Eye over high sage veiling my truck, I profiled eight young men as huckleberries, ripe for picking. Fishing success was outstanding due to the tremendous productivity of the lake, the trout overwintering well, and recent heavy fish plants after ice out. Focusing on the eight verified they were catching a preponderance of heavy 14-16-inch rainbow trout. In less than an hour, I logged no less than twenty trout on stringers, the gang showing no signs of stopping fishing or drinking beer! Logging individual fish numbers for an additional hour, I was relieved when five packed their gear, cleaned everyone's fish, and headed to the parking area. Surprisingly, they picked up all the beer cans strewn in the sage behind them. Today's ploy was to witness where they stashed the fish. Given several exceeded today's daily limits, their behavior would most certainly provide warden entertainment. Sure as sweet on honey, the trout were sorted, bagged and placed into a camp cooler. Several additional bags were carried to a large white cooler hidden in the sage fifty yards away. *Hoka Hey!*

Driving into their camp, I smilingly greeted the fishermen, who stood around a blazing campfire drinking more beer, and stated I was checking licenses and fish. Two of them haughtily produced valid licenses and retrieved zip-loc bags containing their limit of eight trout. The other three claimed they were not fishing. *OOPS!* Pointing into the sage, I stated the need to check the fish in the hidden white cooler. All five denied knowledge of such a cooler. Following me as I walked towards the cooler Bude Light, the not so bright leader, steadfastly affirmed the cooler did not belong to anyone in their camp. Bude was rapidly launched out of his state of denial when I opened the cooler revealing the swindler's full name, address and phone number boldly scribed in permanent ink on the lid's underside. Bude's response, "Damn, I hate it when my wife puts our name on stuff!" *That's the way, uh-huh uh-huh I like it, uh-huh, uh-huh…* While I counted 93 trout in the cooler, the other three arrived carrying limits of eight trout each. Predictably, they also denied knowledge of the cooler, but wilted when Bude made it clear they were busted.

Let the circus begin! I requested each claim their share of the illegal trout; all 93 conveniently bagged trout in the cooler. Without discussion or argument all, including the three unlicensed fishermen, displayed their ego driven pride boldly claiming what was theirs. *Honor among thieves!* Correspondingly, they dutifully accepted their medicine, including Pabst who assumed full responsibility for five illegal fish caught by his thirteen-year-old (licensed) son Colt, even explaining to the lad why their misbehavior was wrong. All found a bit of humor admitting they 'luckily' ate a considerable number of fish the evening before.

Bude, the camp mathematician, diligently counted the illegal trout from the white cooler. Precise limits of licensed fishermen were stored in camp to outwit suspicious wardens. Aware they played this game before, I scolded their gluttonous behavior, emphasizing obeying established limits allowed the fishing mass equal opportunity to harvest the lake's bounty. They appeared to be listening.

Individual fines significant, the final tally of $1,345 summed the true value of their misdemeanors:

Bude Lite-8 legal trout - 6 illegal trout
Schlitz-8 legal trout - 10 illegal trout
Falstaff-8 legal trout - 13 illegal trout
Pabst- 8 legal trout - 13 illegal trout
Colt- 8 legal trout - 5 illegal trout (age 13 with license)
Oly- 14 illegal trout (no fishing license)
Blatz- 14 illegal trout (no fishing license)
Miller- 18 illegal trout (no fishing license)

40 legal 93 illegal133 total trout

Receiving a firm handshake, a smile and the always questionable 'thank you' from everyone, including young Colt, I realized these men were not all bad. They were, however, rogue poachers. Blatz, foolishly neglecting to pay his fine, was picked up on a warrant, jailed, posted bond and later found guilty in court for failure to appear as well as his original charge.

*"Stupid is, as stupid does."*
Forrest Gump

# TWO 'MOOS' FOR BROTHER VICAR

"If you had not committed great sins, God would not have sent a punishment like me upon you." *Genghis Khan*

The 1985 elk season dawned as a living nightmare. Prior to that mid-October weekend, Indian Summer masterfully painted a progression of picture-perfect panoramas charming all who worked and played across the Bull Pen's varying landscapes. Twenty-four hour cycles of mercurial extremes where stone-cold mornings were quickly melded by a warmhearted sun radiating Her brilliance over the valley below. However, one must savor these resplendent days with a high degree of mistrust, understanding through experience the weather gods would, at their will, disrupt this seasonal utopia. Nonetheless, the arrival of a massive winter storm caught most by surprise as it freight-trained over the mountains and across the valley floor. The raging cold front, laden with bulleting, heavy snow, fueled by frigid arctic wind, could bed down Santa's reindeer. Deer and elk 'holed up' in deep cover and hunters remained close to their frozen camps until the storm subsided. Unbeknown to one out-of-state elk hunter, the stage was set for his starring role in a hunting tragedy depicting classic human tomfoolery.

After two grueling days fighting snow and mud checking endless reports of stranded and lost hunters and pulling vehicles out of drifted ditches and snow laden bogs, weary Wildlife Officer Keith Kahler and I returned to Sage Hen to regroup and hopefully rest. Predictably, a radio call from the Sheriff's Office turned us around to investigate a report of a hunter killing cattle west of Mexican Ridge. *Seriously!* Racing westward, tires grinding  over the frozen gravel road along Little Grizzly Creek, I marveled at the flocks of horned larks exploding from the snow-plowed roadside edges; colorful, small songbirds previously scattered far and wide across the vast ocean of open sage before the heavy fall snowstorms,  but  now making a living scavenging windblown weed seeds from the snow packed road.  An amazing tribute to the rugged fragility of the wild, indeed.

Our first stop was a visit with the ranch foreman reporting the incident. The day before he had been contacted by Minnesota hunter Ersatz Vicar, admitting he mistakenly shot **two** Hereford cows carrying the ranches brand. The foreman struck a deal with Vicar to reimburse the ranch based on the current market value of $800 - $1,000 for each cow, allowing him to keep the meat. *Holy hamburger!* After being paid, he gave the situation considerable thought and contacted the Sheriff's Office believing the matter needed further investigation.

Anxious to hear Vicar's tale we quickly located his camp on Upper Crosby Creek and luckily found the cattle slayer facing a blazing campfire. Vicar was upfront and cooperative, his pious admissions defining a very humbled, deeply religious man. I commended him for contacting the rancher and taking responsibility for his mistakes. Asking to see the meat, Vicar steered us to a pile of pine boughs covering a large underground cache of expertly boned, bagged and chilled red meat. As we stared at the massive muscle mass, Vicar rationalized concealing the meat to avoid the embarrassment of having other members of his hunting party discover his errors. Vicar proclaimed the Lord graciously granted forgiveness for his transgressions because he handled the incident as a faithful Christian. He was as eager to tell his story, as we were to hear it. I selfishly permitted Vicar to dig the proverbial hole so many transgressors innocently plunge into. Taking notes, I began loading my wits for the impending ambush I sensed was forthcoming.

Vicar explained his mistakes occurred while hunting elk the opening morning from a tree stand below camp on Crosby Creek. Noticing movement under the low growing boughs of a pine tree at approximately 100 yards, he focused on the head of an animal chewing its cud through his 9-power rifle scope. Visibility was poor due to the blizzard conditions plus the lenses of his scope were incessantly fogged by clinging snowflakes. The animal was apparently bedded as he could see nothing but the animal's neck and head extending a few feet above the ground. Theorizing the animal's head was large enough to be an elk, much too large for a deer and not having the facial features of a moose, Vicar said he gave no thought the beast was a domestic cow because he observed cattle being driven off of the national forest two days before. He further reasoned the 'elk' was antlerless because when it moved its head, he saw neither antlers nor any snow knocked off of the pine branches directly above. Thus, he was "pretty sure" the animal was a cow elk. Possessing an antlerless elk tag, he fired a single shot, apparently killing two Herefords at the same time. *A masterful thought process destined for disaster!*

Needing Paul Harvey's 'rest of the story', I announced the necessity to visit the kill site. Staring in wild-eyed disbelief, Vicar strongly objected stating his admissions were the Gospel Truth. Warden scents required further investigation to confirm or refute the evidence at hand. And, of course, it did! Vicar's 100-yard distance between the tree stand and the Herefords was reduced to no more than thirty yards. Boot tracks in the snow revealed the heads, hides and bones of the Herefords had been carefully hidden well away from the gut piles by two men. Vicar's 'single shot' resounded into four as evidenced by the empty brass casings found below the tree stand.

As I inspected the casings, Vicar conveniently remembered emptying his rifle and reloading while in the tree stand. In a newly revised rendition, he explained the first shot instantly killed the first Hereford in its bed causing another unseen animal to stand up. Thinking it was the same animal, he fired three additional shots until the animal fell. Vicar said he waited an hour and a half until his hunting partner returned, both astounded upon finding two dead Herefords. When asked why he had waited so long for his hunting partner, Vicar replied he needed assistance field dressing the 'elk' but did not want to interrupt his companion's hunt and decided to sit it out. Asked if his hunting partner possessed a cow elk license, Vicar nervously admitted he did. The scent getting stronger, I asked him what he would have done if one of the 'cows' turned out to be a bull elk. Vicar unhesitatingly stated it would not have been a problem as there were bull elk licenses in their hunting party and they could therefore cover any elk. *Wrong answer!* Reminding Vicar party hunting was illegal in Colorado, Vicar confessed he was well aware of Colorado law but the filling of other's licenses was routine in their camp because it was legal in Minnesota. When asked if he had shot both animals intentionally and waited for his hunting partner to tag the additional animal, Vicar, wearing guilt like blood on a cougar's face, became awkwardly silent. Climbing into the tree stand, I took time to thoroughly blend Vicar's meat hungry rationalizations with the information the kill site tendered, concluding not only were Vicar's methods of animal identification extremely flawed but also knowing his blatant disregard for Colorado laws played decisive roles in the killing of the two Herefords. Vicar's statement of feeling 'pretty sure' the beast was a cow elk provided compelling evidence his decision to pull the trigger was criminally imprudent.

Back on the ground, I explained Vicar would be cited for careless hunting and the decision of guilt or innocence would be made in a court of law by an impartial judge or a jury. Knowing Vicar mistakenly identified the cows as elk and the fact his faith driven moral compass led him to making righteous decisions afterwards, I wanted to ensure my definition of careless hunting was shared by the legal system. I suggested revealing the truth in court may or may not rid Vicar of his legal woes but formally presenting his perspectives may ease his mind. Vicar responded by crossly accusing me of violating God's written and unwritten codes and shifted blame to the rancher for not placing signs stating cattle remained on public lands. He also accused Officer Kahler for not including the presence of cattle when visiting their camp before opening day advising there were moose inhabiting the area. These verbal assaults solidified my decision to have the case further reviewed. While Vicar's confessional and tithing for killing the two 'slow elk' (a jesting name often given to the inattentive, sluggishness of mountain cattle) can be considered the moral behavior of a Christian man, I strongly felt the entire situation needed to be heard by an impartial judge. *Vicar may want to say a prayer.*

Praise the lord and pass the ticket book!

I perceived Vicar as a Holy Fox using religious codes to veil his trespasses on hunting law. I was long familiar with the often perplexing hunting and fishing misbehavior patterns of religious men and women, including those 'of the cloth' frequently rationalizing their misdeeds by making peace with their God. Religion often entered my contacts, including everything from being called a 'God-damned' game warden to those thanking the Lord for their successful harvest. Some believed God was responsible for their failure to harvest game, and some law breakers even rationalized HE played a role in their capture.

Days later, at a pre-trial meeting with District Attorney Dan Kaup, Vicar, Bible in hand, began quoting scriptures declaring his faith in God vindicated his hunting mistakes and he therefore should be forgiven, and his case dismissed by the court system. Quoting:

It is better to trust in the LORD than to put confidence in man."
Psalms 118.8 "Often considered the center verse in the Bible
**King James Bible (Cambridge Ed.)**

Pardoned in the eyes of his Lord, he stanchly chastised me and District Attorney Dan Kaup for our unjust persecution. Visibly angered, DA Kaup, eager to filet Vicar's sermonizing soul, sharply interrupted his holy discourse and, waving the Colorado Division of Wildlife Law

Book high in the air, tersely announced it would be this book, and not the Bible, determining Vicar's guilt or innocence! *Warden Gold!*

*"Justice? -- You get justice in the next world. In this one you have the law."*
    William Gaddis

Vicar fell silent as the Deputy Dan read out loud the State Law defining careless hunting and explained why Vicar's 'mistakes' fell well within the criminal codes of endangering personal property. I reminded Vicar hunting carries a tremendous amount of responsibility, including the ability to identify exactly what one is shooting and not taking the shot if not 100% positive of the target. Vicar's conscience, casehardened by his religious rationalizations, was not bullet proof. The two lawmen watched Vicar slowly comprehend his blunders violated hunting law. This one slice of his life, his *tranche de vie*, perhaps defined the entire man. I hoped this incident would help Vicar, probably a good man, become a better hunter. Instead, this religiously impaired heathen made it clear he could not separate God's covenants of righteousness from the laws of man. From my window, Vicar's eagerness to kill elk blended with his rationalizations for (illegally) filling the licenses of others, fueled his current predicament. His methods of purchasing beef, ethically sound as he thought them to be, did not make up for his hunting carelessness.

Vicar was found guilty and fined $350 for careless hunting. Leaving the courtroom, Vicar approached me and said "Why?" Not sure what to say I said the answer fell on his shoulders. While faith can move mountains, it cannot justify violations of the law.

*Laus Deo – Praise be to God*

# RESTLESS NATIVES

*You are about to enter another dimension, a dimension not only of sight and sound but of mind. A journey into a wondrous land of imagination. Next stop, the Twilight Zone!*

I have always been captivated by Native American customs and cultures. As a young lad, I relentlessly studied available literature documenting Indian lore, incorporating what I learned into role playing games with neighborhood friends. Wearing hand crafted feathered headbands, breechcloths, leggings, plastic bear-claw necklaces and, of course, warpaint, our childhood quests evolved into intense competitive tournaments for selecting tribal leaders. When playing cowboys and Indians, I was Indian; physically, mentally, emotionally, and spiritually. My parents and sisters were clearly bewildered by our tribe's obsession for roleplaying Native Americans.

Moving into the northwest Ohio countryside during my teenage years, I discovered the first of many Native American artifacts while walking a plowed field along Eagle Creek. Picking up a strikingly hewn, flawless projectile point, I experienced sensations of curious speculation; Why was it there? Who made it? What was his name? Was the projectile shot at an enemy or wild game? For me, it was much more than a mere piece of flint. A coffee can of artifacts gifted by my maternal grandfather from the old family farm further fueled my fascination of North America's original inhabitants. To this day I consider Native American artifacts fundamental, vintage antiques of our country's all but forgotten cultures.

Following college, temporary employment with Natural Resource Agencies in Wyoming and Utah, and marriage, my Native American fixations were renewed when permanently assigned to the Bull Pen as a wildlife officer. Sir Don Gore, my elderly warden mentor, graciously shared his intellectual and spiritual savvy of local Native American lore. He explained that prior to exploration and settlement, the valley was inhabited primarily by the Ute tribe, who called it the Bull Pen because of its large population of game, especially bison, naturally 'fenced' by the surrounding high mountain ranges. He revealed the Utes rigorously guarded 'their' rich hunting grounds from traditional enemies, the Arapaho, and Cheyenne, and later from early trappers, miners and settlers. White trappers entering the park prior to 1820 called this valley 'New Park' as it had not been actively explored earlier due to its remoteness, long harsh winters, and the aggressive presence of the Utes.

As Sir Don disclosed locations of burial trees, buffalo kill sites, camp sites, teepee rings, battle sites and fire pits, I began developing an 'eye' for detecting veiled traces of Native American presence. My inherent curiosity intensified for this faceless culture erased by the 19th century American belief it was the destiny of the United States to expand its supremacy across the entire North American continent.

Documented historical sites, prominent names of warriors and chieftains, names of creeks, rivers, mountain passes, and ridges, are essentially all that remain of a people whose ridgeline camps, nighttime campfires, laughter, language, songs, customs, culture, and legendary stories are forever gone. Detecting the cultural tracks of an ancient society thriving on the Bull Pen's natural resources for food, clothing, and shelter, I found myself haunted by their absence. Walking ridges peppered with flint chips, discovering undocumented campsites, or eating lunch in a teepee ring overlooking the Bull Pen's lower valley sharing the identical 'room with a view' Natives enjoyed for centuries, captivated me.

NOTE. WHAT FOLLOWS WAS NOT INDUCED BY THE PRESENCE OF DRUGS OR ALCOHOL!

And there I was, aimlessly wandering a mountain bench on a rare, windless, warming day, the air heavy with the earthy sage scent signifying the highly anticipated, erratic, Bull Pen spring. Today's ploy was to mask my real goal of searching for shed antlers under the guise of scientifically documenting deer winterkill. The previous winter a large deer herd subsisted on the south facing slopes of Independence Mountain and the area I now walked showed the impact with old tracks, droppings, heavily browsed shrubs, and a few winterkilled carcasses. Trekking a well-defined sage bench rimmed with windblown hardscrabble, I watched in awe as a swirling dust devil materialized, forcefully picking up debris and funneling its way towards me! Twisting along the bench, it blew through me, sand blasting my eyes and filling my nose with dirt before evaporating into the draw below. *Surreal!* Breathless, my entire being became overwhelmed by intensifying sensations, like the prickly whole-body feelings one experiences when repeatedly sneezing, but without the sneezes. It was accompanied by what I can only describe as a sense of free-falling weightlessness.

These feelings skipped weird and traveled to the inexplicably bizarre, far beyond even my fervid imagination! Glancing downward I spied a beautifully crafted projectile point, camouflaged in fine gravel heavily flecked with flint chips. An overpowering urge beckoned me to walk into the bench's heavy sage where I discovered several distinct teepee rings. Astonished by simultaneously encountering the dust devil, the arrowhead, the teepee rings combined with relentless skin crawling sensations, I stood mystically transfixed in an exhilarating soul trance. If reincarnation is real, there is no doubt I had been here in another life.

As my spellbinding experience gradually subsided, I returned to my truck, baffled and weary by the unfathomable ambiance of the incomprehensible event. Relating my otherworldly encounter to my comrade in arms and close friend Kirk Snyder, a uniquely rare free spirit in his own right, he explained I experienced an out of body experience. Not so! My encounter did not involve perceiving myself from outside of my body. It was a phenomenon originating from an unexplainable external energy source consciously recognized from within my mind, heart, and soul.

Understand, I eventually accepted this unsolvable mystery as a paranormal endowment gifted to me by an unidentified outside force. Justifying it is moot. This I know, it was not an imaginative, whimsical dream. It happened! Yeah, I returned to the familiar bench several times and found it perplexingly void of all sensations.

My tracks made throughout the Bull Pen have disappeared, as have those made by its original inhabitants. I cling to personal memories of trekking the same ground as did they and consider myself blessed to have read some of their long abandoned signs; traces most often overlooked by those who cannot see, hear or feel when the earth speaks. And I truly believe, on that very special spring day, the Natives restlessly spoke, rousing my lifeforce with their spiritual presence I will forever hold sacred!

*"Truth is stranger than fiction, but it is because Fiction is obliged to stick to possibilities; Truth isn't."*Mark Twain

# WILHELM– TELLING OVERTURES OF A PILFERING NIMROD

W hat follows is the tell-taling saga of a hunter imposter donned Wilhelm, who earned the status of being the most obstinate liar I ever encountered. Now mind you, I savored listening to the skels of the wild embellish endless tomes to mask their misdeeds; a lively myriad of distorted cock-and-bull hodgepodge fibbed even when the truth was staring them in the face. Wilhelm, however, stood on the summit of Liar's Mountain, a devious cragsman unsurpassed at scaling the steep scarps of outdoor treachery.

An aged man of European descent, Wilhelm was small but solid in stature with sturdy, long arms, large hands and a sculpted, weathered face. A driven hunter and fishermen assaulting the outdoors as conquests: 'Attila' the HUNter playing his games free of legal, moral or ethical canons. Success was measured in numbers and pounds of game and fish taken, lawful or not, assuming he could outwit all crossing his path. After all, he always had! But success rooted in corruption does not a sportsman make.

Wilhelm had been a former member of the United States Nimrod Club; dues paying sportsmen leasing private ranches for hunting and fishing. These properties were patrolled by 'off duty' lawmen granted hunting and fishing privileges in return for enforcing the Club's rules and regulations. Wildlife Officer John Wagner and I befriended them, often sharing information on the misdeeds of paying members. However, these 'private eyes' were frequently reluctant to actively aid our investigations, exercising a 'code of silence' so commonly encountered in the warden world. Predictably, Wilhelm was dismissed from the Club for blatant disregard of their own rules and his inability to get along with other members. Where there's Will, he was always in someone's way and, stripped of his credentials, he was selectively weeded out of the Club's own weeds.

We frequently encountered Wilhelm in the field carrying fancy rifles, his ever-present bipod shooting sticks and/or expensive fishing equipment. Our contacts were as cold as the man himself with few words exchanged and his unwillingness to look us in the eyes. Wagner treated him with the same iciness Wilhelm tendered, while I tortured the man with a barrage of happy-talk the man so despised. We considered him formidable prey; epitomizing the very reasons the outdoors good demand strict wildlife law enforcement. I disliked Wilhelm with our first clammy handshake, instantly recognizing him as a cunning game thief needing considerable warden attention.

Interestingly, a Wildlife Officer from the 'Fort' knew Wilhelm and his family quite well and considered him one of the nicest individuals and skilled outdoorsman she ever encountered. Perhaps the differences in the behavior of a domesticated married man opposed to the same man in the field, the family wolf versus the alpha hunting male.

Officer Wagner, working an anonymous tip, was the first to count coup, citing Wilhelm for illegally shooting another man's elk. This, of course, only intensified the poacher's adeptness for avoiding detection. But time, always on our side, was enhanced by the ever-increasing number of eyes and ears tracking his incessant field misbehavior. The heavy scent of this rogue wolf remained strong, the warden grapevine recurrently whispering his name. Snares set far and wide, Wilhelm was unknowingly being tracked roaming the perceived sanctuary of his wilderness lairs; doomed for entanglement in his own illicit spoor.

As sure as pitch on pine, Wilhelm's demise began to unfold late one September evening when I, after days of working archery hunters, received a call from the outlaw himself demanding a rendezvous to review Owl Mountain land ownership boundaries. Tired and weary, I almost turned down Wilhelm's ultimatum but the ubiquitous voice of Arvins, the mythological Lord of the Chase, whispered a harping warning Wilhelm was plotting more than fence line boundaries. Meeting with him was the right thing to do. Will O' The Wisp was undoubtedly following the swampy phosphorescence of his delusive goals, and I would be remiss to pass a chance to converse with the man in his own lantern light. We would meet the next day on the Owl Mountain Spring Creek school sections.

I spent the next morning tracing a tip from a hunter overhearing a group of 'out of staters' openly declaring their illegal activities at the Liar's Lair Restaurant in Rosebud. Alcohol, a wardens' truth serum, induced the archery licensed 'riflemen' into slurring tales of shooting deer with 'loud' arrows. Amazingly, the informant was in camp; a dedicated sportsman expressing heartfelt concerns about my incompetence in catching those breaking wildlife laws. Making it crystal clear we shared the same trepidations, I thanked him for providing detailed information and promised I would invest the next few days on a high point listening for shots before visiting the alleged poacher's camp. After a lunch on a favored ridge overlooking a bench of teepee rings on Owl Ridge, I found Wilhelm diligently waiting in the shade of an aspen grove. It was a splendidly warm September afternoon blessed with the sun-beaming rays of a cloudless Aqua Velva sky. Wilhelm's lambent face rhythmically shimmered in the sun's filtered translucence through quaking leaflets wafting in an undetectable baby breaths breeze. Owl Mountain's lush aspen hillsides saluted the afternoon with valiant golds and crimsons boldly announcing summers withering exodus. In sharp contrast, Wilhelm donned his familiar bleak December demeanor, appearing arrogantly distressed like the cornered wolf he always seemed to be.

I greeted him with my open hand and smile Wilhelm so loathed. The skel's handshake was limp, cold and damp, like a slab of elk meat. I continued my torturous verbal assault with talk of "how's the fishing' and the "beauty of the day." Wilhelm automatically fired bulleting complaints of unmarked public and private land boundaries. From his open tail gate, I watched him trace his sausage fingers across an unfolded Forest Service map, deafly listening to his mumbo jumbo blend with the chittering of a red squirrel dropping pinecones from the heights of a nearby lodgepole. Mouthing my standard warning of staying away from the lands leased by the very Club ending his membership, I expressed he should be quite familiar with the boundaries having hunted there for years. Recognizing Wilhelm's lobo stare, Arvins whispered yet another warning to pay attention. With greater focus I scanned the familiar colors of BLM browns, USFS greens, and State Land blues all mixed with the private land whites outlining the boundaries Wilhelm questioned. I explained the private lands were adequately fenced and signed and emphasized the State School Lands leased by the ranch were not open to the public. This sent Wilhelm into a raucous rampage attacking everything from government bureaucracies, the legal system, and the communistic tactics of wardens. My eyes tracing the squirrel scampering across the forest floor caching dropped cones, I sympathized with Wilhelm on most school sections being closed to public access and told him so, but reiterated the law was clear and he must avoid these school lands. On his map, Wilhelm traced a road appearing to be open to the public. Closely studying his map, I began realizing something was amiss. The road incorrectly coursed entirely through BLM lands rather than intersecting the privately gated ranch fence. Retrieving my map (identical to Wilhelm's), I laid them side by side finding the colors differed significantly. The BLM browns and the State Land blues on Wilhelm's map extended into the white colored privately lands on mine. Closer examination revealed the private lands on Wilhelm's map had been childishly 'colored' to appear public. Wilhelm presumed his artistic forgeries would, once sanctioned by me, give him legal hunting access to the private lands he so coveted. *Holy wolf crap, Arvins was twice right.* My demeanor switching directions faster than a canyon wind, I pounced on Wilhelm like bobcat on hare and chastised his Crayola fraud, making it crystal clear I would warn ranchers, hunters and Club members to track him during the big game seasons. Ending with the triple dog dare warning if he trespassed onto privately controlled lands during any hunting season, the law would hunt him down. Absorbing my warden wrath in somber fashion, the scheming scamp stood straight, tall, and expressionless. I haughtily drove away watching Wilhelm disappear in my dust, craving any opportunity to share my pen with this diminutive man. Little did either know that day was riding a fast horse.

Weeks later, the opening day of elk season dawned bright and cold over six inches of fresh snow spread evenly across the entire Bull Pen; a clean slate for recording the tracks of man and beast; traces to be deciphered by hunters and wardens. Neither could ask for anything more. Sure as sharp on fang, I received a late morning radio message from the sheriff's office to contact rancher Pat Riley at his cabin on Owl Creek. Riley had information on a trespass hunter killing a bull elk on property leased by the Club. Names not mentioned, the dispatcher relayed Riley indicated the wardens would be quite pleased with the man in question. Mind racing with my truck, I headed to the ranch contemplating the sculpted image of the very man I met with only weeks before. Today may be the day a feral Wilhelm and a taming warden would cross paths. Pulling up to the cabin, I found a smirking Riley standing next to, believe it or not, the stone-faced nimrod himself. *Hoka Hey!* Riley was obviously feasting off a main course already carved from Wilhelm's hind quarters. As I exited the pickup, Wilhelm wasted no time whining a tome of his son, Walther, wounding a bull elk on public land that jumped a fence and died on the private property. He droned Walther became scared when confronted by the Club's patrolman and returned to his home in the Fort. Riley smilingly interjected if that is what really happened, there would be no trespass charges filed and Wilhelm could keep the elk. Wilhelm, puffed up with an air of confidence, appeared about to make it through yet another of his devious ploys. I wrenched thinking the law's tooth and claw would once again be restrained until Riley's eye caught mine and winked, immediately putting me at ease. Not just a flittering eyelid, but a 'damn betch'ya' flash expressing 'go for it'! Wilhelm noticeably squirmed when I explained the truth would be revealed by two exceptionally reliable witnesses, the fresh snow and the dead stag; a matter of comparing Wilhelm story to what both tattled. *There is nothing like first-hand evidence!* My first clue stood before me; a suspicious Wilhelm who, for reasons unknown, appeared much too dapper for a hunter killing and field dressing an elk that very morning! *Release the hounds!*

Wilhelm rode with me to the kill site where we found a familiar Club patrolman all aglow. Riley tailgated my vehicle having no intention of missing Wilhelm's demise. The patrolman was parked in front of a fine-looking five by six bull elk lying in the snow. Now take note, it was a bull with five points on one antler and six on the other, properly field dressed and tagged with Wilhelm's son's license tied to the top time of the bull's rack. The gut pile, already visited by a pair of camp robbers, gleamed like a red diamond in the sunlit fresh snow. The patrolman stated he did not observe the actual shooting but arrived moments after hearing the shots discovering Wilhelm and an unidentified hunter standing over the carcass. The patrolman provided a detailed description of Wilhelm when contacted, commenting he obviously had changed clothes and the fancy rifle now in his hands was not the one carried earlier. The patrolman stated the other hunter was noticeably nervous, anxious to leave and not Wilhelm's son. I was quite pleased with the patrolman's attention to the details. The patrolman further specified Wilhelm immediately declared his son wounded the bull on BLM land, followed it onto the private property, killed it and left because he needed to get back to his job in the Fort. He instructed Wilhelm to field dress the bull and he would contact ranch owner Riley for permission to retrieve it. Riley promptly called the sheriff's office requesting a game warden. The patrolman clarified he chased Wilhelm off the property the previous year near this very spot and was not happy with him. Walking over to the bull I found a 30-06 shell casing melted into the snow; perhaps the killing shot evident high in the bull's neck. Checking Wilhelm's rifle, a custom made .308, I removed the shells from the magazine and placed them into an evidence envelope. Entering my 'Columbo' mode, I hounded Wilhelm with ankle biting questions asking if his son shot the elk with an 'aught-six'. Wilhelm predictably answered the shell in my hand was fired from his son's rifle. Two sets of boot tracks around the bull, one matching Wilhelm's and the other described as belonging to his son. Back-tracking, I followed Wilhelm's and found the familiar set of ski pole shooting sticks and several additional 30-06 brass casings. Marks in the snow detailed where Wilhelm knelt using the sticks to steady his rifle, roughly 60 yards from the dead bull. Returning to the kill site, I separately followed both tracks leading away from the carcass and, after crossing the fence onto the school section, they parted toward two separate vehicle, clearly outlined in the snow. Yes, both vehicles were parked next to the school section, the very lands I previously warned Wilhelm to avoid. *The game is afoot!* I escorted Wilhem back to my pickup sitting him down in the passenger side seat. I read his constitutional rights using 'Miranda' to caution the pilfering land pirate his bad day was getting worse. Constitutional Rights normally illicit a certain amount of distress but Wilhelm, not ready to remain silent, calmly contradicted all evidence facing him. I emphasized there was no indication the bull had been wounded on public land as its tracks and blood were entirely on privately controlled land. Making it crystal clear both hunters had illegally parked and walked from the properly posted school section onto the posted private land, Wilhelm insisted the bull was wounded on public lands, and jumped a fence onto private lands and died.

Holding a high card discovering Wilhelm's license was for antlerless elk only, I questioned the shooting sticks and spent cartridges. Wilhelm explained he lost the poles last year when still a Club member. Reiterating the poles were on **top** of the snow, Wilhelm offered a mere shoulder shrug. Asking for an explanation of why the tracks at the ski poles were his, Wilhelm said I was misinterpreting the tracks explaining his son wore shoes exactly like his. *What one man can invent; another can discern!* I reiterated the patrolman stated the other hunter at the kill site was not his son, meaning there should be an additional set of tracks, two of them the same. *Elementary!* Wilhelm emphatically stated it was his son at the kill site and that there was no other hunter. *If his lips were moving, he was lying.* Offering a tactical change, I tendered one last chance to come clean; now was the time to either tell the truth or face the full consequences of his misdeeds. Wilhelm vigorously defended his nonsensical fabrication. Releasing another hound, I repeated the starkly clear warnings given a few weeks before. Wilhelm, perhaps comprehending he was digging his own grave, became silent. I began flogging the lying scoundrel's ego with whipping truths of the escalating evidence, proclaiming he was undoubtedly the most unethical, irresponsible, immoral poacher I ever encountered. Wilhelm's bushy brows rose like the wings of a great eagle as I fired a barrage of leaden threats, truths and inquiries. Suddenly, Wilhelm seemingly entered a soundproof kef, staring skyward in a drug-like stupor. Familiar with the body language and displacement behavior antics of a captured miscreant, I was thoroughly thunderstruck by what happened next. Wilhelm coolly reached into his shirt pocket, pulled out a pack of waxed dental floss and began dislodging chunks of food particles from his rear molars. For God's sake the scoundrel was flossing his teeth!

On exceptionally good ground, I could easily end this war by scratching out a wad of tics. Seasoned wardensmanship and my love of the game advised me to continue battling Wilhelm's self-inflicted, inevitable doom. In this case, a bird in the hand was worth far less than watching this wounded wretch struggle in the bush. There was certainly more warden gold to be sluiced from the backwash of this poacher's eroding outdoor treachery.

Leaving Wilhelm to his oral hygiene, I returned to the crime scene to take photos and review my notes. I radioed Wildlife Officer Steve Steinert for assistance in transporting the bull to Sage Hen and would you believe Steinert showed up with the very man Wilhelm hunted with that morning: a man Steinert knew well and of course, not Wilhelm's son. This man made it crystal clear Wilhelm's son had not been with them and he himself witnessed Wilhelm shoot the bull. He was extremely upset with Wilhelm for taking him hunting on land they had no right to be on, for shooting an elk he was not licensed to harvest, and tagging it with his son's license. He left Wilhelm at the kill site stating he would never hunt with him again and was going to turn him in. Wispy Will had mistakenly chosen an honorable hunter as this year's ally. While these events were transpiring, Wildlife Officer Kirk Snyder was interviewing the owner of the Powder Horn cabins, who specified Wilhelm returned from hunting mid-morning and made a call from the office phone speaking softly to someone in a foreign language. Obviously, this was when Wilhelm switched rifles, cleaned up and changed clothes; his not so well-planned plot to throw the wardens off his trail. *Stupid is, stupid does! Warden Gump.*

However, the coup de grace for this tragic comedy of errors came from two separate interviews with Wilhelm's son, Walther, by wildlife officers in the Fort. During the first interview Walther admitted he harvested a bull elk that morning on Owl Mountain, field dressed it with his dad and another friend, and hastily returned to the Fort because he had to work. He further stated he was unfamiliar with elk hunting and unable to provide other details. *Say what?* I shared our evidence with these officers and concluded Walther was ripe for another interview. Walther, not having Wilhelm's penchant for lying, admitted his father phoned him from the Powder Horn Cabins speaking in his native Turkic tongue, a language Walther acknowledged he was not fluent. And, are you ready, he stated he had shot the bull **"six times on one side and five on the other"**, unknowingly completely misinterpreting the words his father had so carefully articulated; 'the bull's antlers had six points on one side and five on the other'. Now that my friend, is warden gold! At his cabin, Wilhelm was met by the entire battery of officers working the case, all ready to take their evidentiary shots at the vulnerable loser. Aristotle's "Evil that brings men together." Steinert, walking into the cabin with Wilhelm's early morning hunting cohort obviously wounded the feckless poacher while I began wading Will through the evidentiary quagmire he had so proficiently mucked himself into. Wilhelm's eyes glared terror, not anger, his face exposing a worthless coward confronting full disclosure. Scenting his demise, Wilhelm's coal black eyes glared through wrinkled bossy brows, the snaking blue-green veins on his neck enlarged and as his nostrils flared! Breaking his silence, he boldly asserted he was being unjustly treated and asked for an attorney. Not missing a step, I answered with a favored warden line, "If you are guilty, you certainly need a lawyer."

*"What we have here is a failure to communicate"* – Cool Hand Luke

Expounding bluff no longer an option, I revealed Wilhelm's entire hand was face up on the table. "Sometimes nuthin' is a cool hand," but not tonight. Wilhelm's aces and eights were the dead man's hand of a waning liar. Wilhelm sat silently as I vocally played the cards I was dealt, one at a time: the Ace of Spades, an eye witness account of his hunting partner standing in the room; the King of Spades, the entire incident accurately written in the snow; the Queen of Spades, his son's self-confessed misperceptions of the entire incident; the Jack of Spades, Wilhelm's own absurdly erroneous, uncorroborated lies; and the ten of spades, the wild card of having dutifully warned Wilhelm to stay clear of the property only weeks before. We flushed him out in royal fashion, straight out of his own treacherous misdeeds! Opening the law book, I dropped one last dollop of juris imprudence, a fouling blob of field justice essential for a man having no remorse for his errant ways. Uncompromisingly, because Wilhelm indicated he was being prejudicially mistreated, I informed Will I would scratch out tics for all possible charges, requiring a mandatory court appearance with no opportunity to pay his fines through the mail. Prodigal son Walther would also be written into court as an accomplice, where both could explain their perceptions of mistreatment to the judge. The treasured rifle used in the crime would be confiscated lock, stock and barrel. The shadowy Will-O-The-Wisp, in the false light of the lantern guiding him up to now, stared into the dark and cold abyss he had entered. Poor Will was whipped.

Weighing my indecent proposal, Wilhelm began pleading leniency for Walther, stating his son had nothing to do with today's scandalous schemes. Uncasing the classic 30-06 rifle used to shoot the bull, Wilhelm confessed speaking to his son on the phone in his native Turkic language, explaining details to tell the wardens. Lastly, he pleaded for the option of paying the fines through the mail, having no desire to go to court. As the tics were scratched, Wilhelm's cavernous eyes haughtily glared from his weathered stone face; head held high and back stick straight, he resembled a proudly stoic Hun warrior relinquishing his sword in defeat. The ritual continued as I handed him the citations, instructing him to "press hard there are five copies." William, crumbling under the weight of the hefty fines, would be further burdened by the inevitable loss of his license privileges. I and my compatriots glowed inwardly watching Wilhelm join our prestigious club of game slaying poachers.

Quicker than snake bite Wilhelm mailed in his fine, well before I completed my end of the paperwork. Walther was cited for illegally transferring his license to his father. It was the absolute best we could do for the surroyal bull and the good sportsmen who lost their chances of harvesting him.

Within a year, I received a call from a fellow officer who contacted Wilhelm in the field. Wilhelm, scouting a new hunting area for 'friends', told the officer he received a raw deal from wildlife officials when hunting the Bull Pen, and lost his license privileges for three years. Chastising me by name, he barked since his entrapment, wildlife officers have been stalking him and are constantly watching his house.

*"It starts when you're always afraid*
*You step out of line, the man come and take you away."*
*Stephen Stills and the Buffalo Springfield, 1967. For What It's Worth*

My message to this fellow officer was simple warden logic. Time tattles and someone will undoubtedly cross paths and share pens with Wilhelm again. Contacting him adds to his paranoia, a wardens' reward for a man haunted by his own misery. Not able to change his errant ways, he will be increasingly cautious, careful and alert, always believing someone was watching. What happens in the woods does not always stay in the woods and for the law breaking fearful, the rustling in the shadows never cease.

Years later, I ran into Wilhelm in an office supply store at the Fort. He was peering around some shelves ducking every time I looked his way. Much to his displeasure I purposely caught his eye, smiled and waved as Wilhelm disappeared out the door. Reports of Wilhelm's presence in the Bull Pasture faded and the wardens often pondered his whereabouts, knowing he was out there somewhere. Run rabbit, run!

*Carpe caput lupinum – seize the wolf's head*

# CLOTHES LINED

August 1983. There I was, my vehicle veiled in bowing aspen limbs overhanging the gravel road along Slack-Weiss Reservoir, focusing the Big Eye on a woman smoking cigarettes and boy in his late teens, possibly her son, wearing identical black baseball caps. Rarely detected by fishermen but often Paul Revere by a passerby, I frequently 'road killed' angling miscreants from this vantage. Scoping two sunlit lines extending into the water, I watched the woman reel in, re-bait and cast out both poles while the young man sat and watched. Panning the rest of the lake I found only two other fishermen, a man and a boy casting lures.

A grand warm mountain morning, I melded comfortably into my seat to warden spy, my contentment regaled by a drumming Hairy Woodpecker luridly beating his presence, grubbing a meal beneath the bark of a nearby aspen. Trout were gently nibbling the woman's hooks, keeping us both vigilant. With only four individuals to scrutinize, I had time to script outlandishly accurate notes detailing who was fishing, what they were wearing, number of active rods, and number of fish caught. After an hour the woman continued chain smoking while handling both poles, catching and keeping a couple of rainbow trout.

The young man disappeared into a camper parked above soon after I began my watch.

A slow-moving vehicle approached me from behind with the driver wildly turkey necking me as he passed by weaving, almost going off the road. And sure as crap on a dung beetle's mouth, the stoolpigeon Paul Revered my presence to all three fishermen. It was time to come out of hiding. Before making tracks, I sorted the nervous from the calm to prioritize the order of my contacts. The woman received the honors by quickly reeling in both poles and retreating to the camper. The man and the boy, undaunted, continued fishing. Little did I know my personal identification skills were about to be rigorously tested.

Driving the distance, I parked and walked over to the camper, introduced myself to a very unfriendly man, Bass Elder, and stated I was checking fishing licenses. Bass sternly replied neither he nor his wife was fishing but his son was licensed to fish. Making it clear I needed to speak to his wife because I had observed her fishing, Katy Elder exited the camper and announced it was not her but her son John I had observed fishing. John appeared and produced a valid fishing license properly stamped for the use of two poles. He appeared to now be wearing clothing identical to what I remembered his mother wearing, but that couldn't be right. Temporarily giving them the benefit of my doubts, I returned to my truck and reviewed my notes, my rifling mind quickly re-loaded upon hearing a volley of boisterous laughter coming from the campsite. Studying my field notes while carefully eyeing Katy and John, the stars began to align. These duping doppelgangers, similar in stature, facial features and short dark hair donning identical baseball caps, had the wherewithal to swap clothing in their camper after 'Paul' revered my presence?

To Bass' obvious dismay I approached Katy and made it clear it was indeed her I had observed fishing. *The Big Eye doesn't lie!* Requesting her son to accompany me to my vehicle, John readily admitted leaving his mother with the two poles for longer than he planned but was sure she never handled the poles. Waving Katy over I showed my notes clearly scribed the clothing worn by each when I arrived at the lake, pointing out John was now wearing his mother's clothes while Katy donned his. Asking John if he smoked, he laughingly replied only his mother had the filthy habit before realizing, with a noticeable grimace, my question was a smokescreen aiding my case. *OOPS!* I lightheartedly acknowledged the young man's blunder providing a moment of liberty to reveal their dirty laundry. Predictably, neither was ready to come clean of their misdeeds.

Without warning, Bass charged towards me screaming extremely threatening obscenities; launching a burst of f-bombs demanding they get away from my vehicle and ordering me to cease hassling them, or else! He braggingly declared the wardrobe exchange was his idea and I should be talking to him. I tersely hooked Bass into paternal compliance with the double-barbed warning he was facing arrest on charges of complicity and interference with an officer. Bass retreated and muted his large mouth.

Applauding the cleverness of the pairs' clothes exchange, I divulged their ploy had been betrayed by not trading shoes; Katy still wearing her red sockless boat shoes and John donning black untied tennis shoes. Both, noticeably suffering the doping feeling of capture myopathy, displayed no remorse for their misdeeds.

Because this incident was a team effort, good wardensmanship required mandating a court appearance allowing the three to present their side of the story to the local magistrate. However, Katy contacted the court prior to the court date and entered a guilty plea for fishing without a license. *A good choice, indeed!*

*"Just give me something-something I can use*
*People love it when you lose,*
*They love dirty laundry…*
*Kick 'em when they're up, Kick 'em when they're down…."*
Don Henley/Danny Kortchmar 1995

# FOGGY MOUNTAIN BREAKDOWN

Antelope season, a highly anticipated sporting game for hunters and wardens, is played on a field of rolling sagebrush fragmented by ravines, streams, and meadows. Ridge tops provide vantage and draws afford cover for predator and prey; hunters, antelope and espying wardens. Opening day dawns a chaotic flurry of pursuing vehicles, fleeing beasts, and blazing bullets. Most licenses are filled the first day but for the patient nimrod craving solitude and a higher quality fair chase adventure, opening weekend is to endure or avoid. Generally abundant pronghorn populations offer multiple opportunities for stalking these hawk-eyed prairie goats. For wardens the hunt presents a challenging, highly observable spectator sport witnessed through high-powered lenses from isolated lairs. The Bull Pen's antelope season typically occurs under cloudless ice blue Indian Summer skies in its sagen arena when aspen starkly quake crimson reds and gilded golds. Frosty cold daybreaks melding into warm afternoons the rule, it is a very enjoyable time of year to spend with the wilds. Hunters filling their licenses early often hang out to fish, hunt small game, or relax in comfortable campsites.

The late September 1985 antelope season, however, began as an exception when the entire lower basin was cloaked in an extremely dense ground fog. The thick, murky vapor undulated across the ocean sage with a dankness one could not only see, but also feel and smell. And there we were, Wildlife Officer Keith Kahler and I parked at first light on a strangely familiar ridge blanketed by the low hanging miasma. *Rats!* Nothing to do but wait, I killed the engine and rolled down my window. Kahler, slinking into his seat, entered his familiar passenger side stupor. Taking deep nasal breaths, I tasted the ambrosial scent of the water-soaked sage, listening to the creeping stillness sporadically broken by the radio chatter of my front range compatriots 'skipping' the news over the Medicine Bow Range they too were working in dense fog. As the shrouded sun fluoresced over the condensed soup, a resonating rifle shot pierced the hazy drisk, sending my senses into overdrive and rousing Kahler out of his napping coma. *What the hell?* Minds racing, we glared into the misty blend churning like cream in coffee. Incredulously, a fogdog - a nebulous circle of yellowish light - materialized below revealing a man blazing in hunter orange standing over an antelope carcass. *Warden gold at the end of a fogbow!* Mounting the Big Eye to my window, I focused first on the hunter and then on a hard-topped red jeep parked along the county road. Turning up the power, I clearly observed a woman meticulously **knitting** in the passenger side seat! After spending considerable time inspecting the antelope, the hunter backed his jeep up to the carcass and field dressed it. Watching him easily hoist the antelope, obviously a fawn, into the back of the jeep and disappear into the fog's hazy depths, I reminded Kahler the hunter neither voided his license nor attached a tag to the carcass, as required by Colorado law after harvesting any big game animal. Driving down to the gut pile, I mentally logged the boot prints in the wet soil as well as the jeep's tire tracks. Paralleling the vehicle tracks to the gravel county road, we traced them to a nearby hunting camp. No one around, we inspected the campsite and located an untagged buck fawn antelope under a trailer attached to a motor home. Boot tracks matching those of the hunter observed earlier were evident in the sandy ground next to the trailer. *The games afoot!*

The fog quickly burning away by an incessant sun, we spotted the red jeep grinding its way along a nearby fence line before turning our direction onto the county road. Kahler waved the vehicle into the campsite and, recognizing 'our' hunter, I walked to the driver's side window and lit the 'warden grill' with a sparking smile and searing small talk to smoke out the details of his impending tale. The hunter, Mum Sandballs, produced two antelope licenses: a filled buck license and an unfilled additional doe tag. Wordlessly, the older woman remained absorbed in her knitting, seemingly oblivious to our presence. While Kahler checked a legally tagged buck in the back of the jeep I turned up the flames asking Sandballs if he harvested another antelope earlier that morning. He faintly replied he had not. Pointing to the motorhome, I asked if the fawn antelope under the attached trailer was his. Without recoil, Sandballs answered it was not. Igniting a second burner, I pointed out the magpies circling the location of the nearby gut pile and informed Sandballs Kahler and I witnessed him field dress a fawn at that location, adding his boot prints and jeep tracks matched those at the kill site and this campsite. Sandballs sedately denied it all and, while willowing in his quagmire, another vehicle drove into the campsite. I immediately recognized the driver as close friend Gary Marrou, an avid hunter from the 'Fort', and his young son Dave. Gary and his brother Dale embody solid hunting stock and remain trusted friends to this day. A high strung, tenacious pineapple head, Gary contrasted sharply with his laid-back brother. Both, extremely ardent and responsible hunting warriors, take impeccable care of and are experts in the culinary preparation of harvested wild meat. Requesting Sandballs to remain in the jeep and asking Kahler to stay with him, I walked over to Gary who curiously asked, "What's up?" Exchanging handshakes, I praised the well-mannered boy beaming the great joy of being with his father and uncle on the antelope hunt. Dave has since matured into an honorable family man and a highly skilled, ethical hunter. When asked, Gary curiously acknowledged the camp belonged to him and Dale, his furrowing brow and squinting eyes exposing increasing suspicion. When I explained there was an untagged antelope fawn under the trailer, Gary began spinning like a whirligig beetle. Walking to the trailer, Gary's disbelieving face conveyed he knew absolutely nothing about the fawn. Obviously distressed, arms flailing and eyes fluttering, he vainly made clear neither he nor Dale, currently hunting alone east of camp, would make such a mistake. Grimacing in paranoid wonder, he chattered the infamous Festus Hagan line defining him to this day, "If I'm lying, I'm dying!" Trophy hunters, both sought and typically harvested large antlered or horned big game animals in their many and varied big game hunts. In an effort to calm him down, I asked if he recognized the man sitting in the jeep. Gary stated had no idea who he was. I explained it was this man who shot the antelope and placed it under their trailer. Gary's perplexed mind, locked like a sord of decoying mallards, relentlessly continued prattling testimonials they would never kill an antelope fawn.

Sandballs, isolated in his open pit of lies, refused to obey the proverbial 'Law of Holes': when one finds himself in one, quit digging. Remaining calm, I continued my queries, knowing those armed with a quiver full of sharply honed mistruths, often impale themselves. Knowing what happened but not why, I separated the improbable and concentrated on what probably happened. Aware this adventure was neither a party hunting situation (Sandballs' mother did not possess an antelope license) nor the fawn shot was illegally for 'camp meat' (Sandballs and Gary did not know each other), Sandballs' intention must be connected to stubborn pride resulting from poor or misguided judgement. Walking back to the jeep, finding Sandballs conspicuously uncomfortable, I proceeded as a candid friend desiring to help resolve the misguided liar's hunting woes.


*"People are strange when you're a stranger."*
   The Doors


I sympathetically preached the traditional sermon of walking through the open door, taking the right path to justify his fraudulent ways. Sandballs, mindlessly staring into space, made it crystal clear he was not buying what I was selling. My 'good guy' technique failing miserably, it was time to scratch tics. Hanging paper often encourages offenders to vindicate their misbehavior. I curtly introduced Sandballs to Mr. Miranda, reading his Constitutional Rights before outlining the routine of collecting blood, hair and tissue samples from the gut pile and his jeep to verify a DNA match to the antelope fawn; photographing evidence around the gut pile and the camper; charging him with providing false statements to law enforcement officers and disposing illegal evidence; and illegally transporting an untagged antelope. I explained his mother would be subpoenaed as a witness to testify her knowledge of what took place. All evidence would be presented before the Jackson County magistrate, providing Sandballs ample opportunity to tale his side of the story. Still, Sandballs remained quiet as a midnight owl.

Then, as the angels mothers typically are, Sandballs' mom came to his rescue, firmly stating, "Maybe it is time to start telling this young man the truth." Without missing a stitch, her maternal instincts mended what a warden could not. Her nurturing command convinced her wayward son to blend the durable yarns of honesty and veracity and cross-stitch a just solution. Without hesitation, Mommy's boy tucked in his tail and shamefacedly admitted he shot the fawn, misidentifying it as a doe in the thick fog. Discovering the fawn was a buck he panicked. Not wanting to use his buck tag on a fawn and believing he could not tag the fawn with his doe tag, he hoped the hunters associated with the camper were licensed to cover the buck fawn and it would not go to waste! *Incredible!* I explained a fawn antelope, too young to grow the horn length of a buck, has always been considered a doe antelope. Tagging a buck fawn with a doe tag is perfectly legal. I scolded Sandballs' dishonesty, clouded by ignorance of hunting laws, for dragging the Marrou's into his scheming pit. Praising his mother for having the wherewithal to steer him down the proper path, I charged him with a simple 'failure to tag' violation; a real meal deal for all the trouble he caused. Explaining shooting another doe and tagging it would have resulted in additional, very costly charges, I returned the buck fawn to the now humbly embarrassed Sandballs, making it crystal clear his antelope hunt was over. His mother, knitting away, flashed me a warm smile, a possible sign she was hoping maybe, just maybe, her son of over four decades, gainfully advanced up his long road to manhood. As Sandballs drove away

I turned to Gary, still firmly entrenched in baffled disbelief, unable to regain his composure until his cool, calm and collected brother Dale returned and I clearly described the morning's astounding events.

*"Shakedown, breakdown, takedown.....your busted"*
   Bob Seger

# POUNDING SAND

There we were! Wildlife Officers Kirk Snyder, Keith Kahler and I investigating a report of a large family clan poaching trout at Teal Lake. It was Sunday, July 3, 1988 and the campground was overrun with eager vacationers taking advantage of a long Fourth of July weekend. Teal, and her sister lake Tiago, were heavily stocked with catchable rainbows at rates I imagined raised the lake's water levels. Limits would be enjoyed by proficient and amateur fishermen alike. For stalwart wardens, the ease of miscreant ensnarement in such circumstance's skirts entrapment.

Secreting across the lake into a favored lair, we readily located the reported perps; a beehive of activity around a lakeside campsite buzzed by swarming kids. Fishing poles tended by several adults lined the bank while the tykes scampered round in disorderly chaos. After observing a man clean sixteen trout while his companions fished, we elected to invade the encampment rather than spying undercover. The radio would, no doubt, soon direct us to locations near and far to resolve the multitude of inevitable human conflicts arising from the brimming Independence Day mob.

Arriving undetected, Kirk checked the active fishermen while Keith and I cheerfully checked licenses and fish at the campsite. The man observed cleaning fish, Arguido de Liares, a California Filipino with a pronounced choppy accent, produced his license and led Keith to a cooler containing 37 trout. I pointed to a huge cooler chained and padlocked to the back of a motor home and Arguido's wife explained it was filled with chicken. *Yeah right!* When asked to open the cooler Arguido replied he had misplaced the key and pretended to search for it in the pine duff. When I offered to cut the lock with a bolt cutter Arguido dug deep into a pants pocket and *PRESTO*, the key magically appeared. *A miracle often encountered in warden work!* Unlocking the cooler, this camp magician confessed he had purchased a large number of trout from a nameless stranger. There was no mystery, however, to the 89 meticulously iced, headless trout found in the cooler. Adding what Kirk retrieved from the lakeside stringers plus the initial 37, the camp total now numbered a whopping 161 trout! Interestingly, the total minus the 89 trout in the chained cooler equaled 72 trout, precisely the limits of the 6 licensed adults (48) and the 6 young unlicensed children (including one in diapers) (24)! *Imagine that!* It appeared Arguido was ready to head home with the 89 illegal trout.

While I calculated the fines for 89 illegal trout, Arguido's wife fell to her knees venting like a half-cocked lid on a steam cooker. Declaring she was experiencing a heart attack, Keith announced he would call for an ambulance. Hearing this, the fibbing fishwife experienced a mystic recovery of scriptural proportions. The possum faced Arguido, absorbing the magnitude of their debaucheries, posed starkly still staring vacantly skyward, perhaps thinking playing dead would make the wardens go away. His Sunday morning was indeed coming down. Gathering the six adults around the illegal trout, we asked them to divide them according to who caught what. All remained steadfastly silent even when warned we would divide the 89 by six and write tickets to them all. The unusually quiet kids, well-schooled on what to do in a warden presence, stared in naïve curiosity. Kirk reminded them they were turned in by a concerned fisherman who personally witnessed their misdeeds. Repeating his fable of buying the illegal trout, Arguido miserably faltered when pressured on the amount paid and to whom. Kirk asked the location of the fish haggler's camp and Arguido indicated the man was no longer around. My patience exhausted, I rudely blurted, "Quit pounding sand up my ass," warden slang often reiterated when confronting lying poachers. But for the Filipino these were words he genuinely did not comprehend. Profoundly baffled, perhaps visualizing hammering sand into our buttocks with a mallet, Arguido accentuated;

*"What – you – mean – pound – sand – up - ass?"*

I clarified we wanted him to quit lying. The hilarity of Arguido's answer and his facial expressions would be cached for years as warden banter. As Kirk and Keith bagged and iced the illegal trout, I explained the clan could either pay the fine now or post a bond and appear in court later. Arguido firmly accepted responsibility for the illegal trout emphasizing he would not appear in court but needed time to secure the fine. The wardens accompanied the clan to Sage Hen and confiscated a vehicle until the family came up with $1253, which they did on July 5. Arguido vowed he would never fish Colorado again because he had been treated like a malicious criminal. Kirk, in his unique callousness, advised the woeful man not to be so hard on himself, reiterating Colorado welcomes the good fishing public with open arms; scandalous fish poachers, not so much!

*Press hard Arguido, there's five copies!*

# WILLY PEONYA

Wildlife Officer Kirk Snyder and I savored dissecting the behavior of rookies earning their way into the ranks of the warden world. One recruit quickly realized securing his law enforcement credentials in our circle would not come easily. Dubbing him T-Bone was my courteous adaptation of a slandering, meaty moniker coined in the vilifying writings of a demented wildlife employee. Innocently making it crystal clear he disapproved the original tag, T-Bone ignited Snyder's mischievous fire to char the newbie with repetitive use of the insulting brand. Thus, I nicknamed him T-Bone as a compromising middle ground for a delicate subject.

Like most overly eager recruits, T-Bone's misadventures defined him; overlooking miscreant spoor; blunders when making public contacts; and judgmental errors in interpreting wild law, etc. He habitually nodded off at the drop of a hat, passing into a slumbering stupor even when his attentiveness was mandatory. On one occasion while checking a remote fishing campsite, T-Bone failed to recognize the legally protected squirrel and grey jay carcasses hanging from the branches of the surrounding trees. Under the vigilant guns of his warden band of brothers, his idiosyncrasies were often caught in our critiquing crossfire. Kirk, T-Bone's hanging judge, savored heckling T-

Bone (or anyone else) who, in his opinion, erroneously performed their endeavors. He was expressly fond of censuring English language grammatical improprieties (slang, double negatives, dangling participles, absurd statements etc.). As an example, when discussing two sides of an issue T-Bone would habitually respond, "But shit, on one hand", opening the door for Snyder's reply, "Why would anyone shit on one hand?" I, as T-Bone's mentor, attempted to constructively critique the greenhorn's boondoggles during our roundtable discussions. To his credit, he constructively used our pesky criticism to his advantage, gradually learning from his blunders, eventually meriting the title of wildlife law enforcement officer. T-Bone's early career catastrophes of missing fundamental evidentiary signs became entertainingly clear one October 1984 during deer season.

There we were, T-Bone and I staring through our truck's windshield at the infamous Mendenhall Creek crossing on the east side of the Bull Pen. Currently inundated by a downstream beaver dam enhanced the thrill of a potential subaquatic crossing. The broken ice and muddied water from previous hunter traffic and knowing the submerged road had a good base reinforced our mettle to cross. However, the notoriously slick two-track steeply climbing on the other side, tightly bordered in aspens with a snow-packed mud blend, significantly increased the pucker factor for our pending vertical climb. Tire chains, only an afterthought following several failed attempts of uncontrollably pinballing backwards, sometimes sideways, into the creek, were placed on the vehicle's front tires. Without hesitation, I valiantly gunned the truck's engine and plunged through the bumper deep backwater. Once on the other side, I maintained momentum as the truck clambered upwards, all four mud flinging wheels aggressively spinning while the truck's rear end bounced in and out of the gooey ruts. Always an adrenalin rush, T-Bone and I shared a grin once successfully making it to the top!

Persistent October snowfalls, including yesterday's foot of fresh powder, initiated the fall deer migration from the high country. Does, fawns and smaller sized bucks would be followed by the evasive mature bucks as the snow depths increased. Hunting this prime migration route today should be very good. A dark, dreary cold morning, I

WILLY PEONYA • 213

elected spying from the warmth of my mud camouflaged vehicle, parking in a sandy, cattle scarred salt lick. Decked out in blaze orange, we would hopefully be recognized as hunters, not wildlife officers. Several vehicles motoring the ridges east of our location were dropping off hunters to hound deer from the aspen draws. An antlered only season, the hunter's ploy was to chase deer into the open sage and methodically harvest bucks. T-Bone and I would umpire the impending game of hunter versus deer, one-sidedly rooting for the bucks.

Before T-Bone fell into his ritualistic napping trance, I spotted a hunter trekking the deep snow along the edge of an aspen draw. At end of the draw, he dropped to one knee, hid behind a tree and, using his binoculars, focused on our truck before quickly creeping back into the aspens. *Let's take this dog for a run.* Expressing we must track the hunter down, T-Bone, naïvely inquired, "WHY"? I answered, "Think about it!" On the hunter's heels like beagle on rabbit, we fast tracked to where we last observed the hunter. Entering the aspen, I instructed T-Bone to stay on the man's tracks while I paralleled him in the open sage below hoping to observe the hunter's escape plan. Slowly striding forward, I soon noticed T-Bone had stopped, apparently taking a leak. *Seriously!* Impatiently waiting and intently gazing ahead, I detected human voices and focused my binoculars on a man kneeling in the low growth junipers directly in front of T-Bone! *What the hell?* Guardedly walking towards the pair, I overheard the man ask T-Bone if he was with 'Officer Porter'. Closing the distance, I recognized Dupe B. Ware, a longtime acquaintance who annually hunted the Bull Pen.

Now the story really gets interesting. It seems just as T-Bone pulled down his zipper, Dupe sprung upwards, like a jack in the box, out of the thick juniper bramble. T-Bone, not sensing the tracks stopped, all but soiled himself when Dupe seemingly materialized out of nowhere! *Waugh!!!* Dupe began frantically apologizing for hunting deer without a license to aid his buddies fill their tags. This exceptionally honest, very embarrassed hunter demanded a citation for his deliberate illegalities. After scratching the tic, eyes twinkling, I made clear we do not habitually piss on those breaking the law!

While Dupe sheepishly returned to his hunting party, I schooled T-

Bone on the importance of never letting his guard down; total awareness of his surroundings is a critical element of officer survival. T-Bone, 'on the other hand', knowing he added tinder to his legendary flames, swallowed his pride and agreed. Graciously, I permitted T-Bone to divulge his story to Kirk in his own words, with the caveat he must tell it all. Swearing he did not urinate on poor Dupe, Snyder and I ruthlessly embellished his story, christening his third, well-deserved nickname, Willy Peonya.

Dupe paid his fine before I finished the case report, mailing me a sincere handwritten apology for his thoughtless lapse of judgement, backing it up by providing reliable information on illegal hunting behavior, and joining our ranks as a trusted friend.

*BOOK EM', T-BONE!*

# SHAGGY MANED FUNGUS EATER

And you've just had some kind of mushroom
And your mind is moving low
Go ask Alice
I think she'll know…*Jefferson Airplane*

Actually, I smelled him before I saw him: that spicy, earthy sweet smell of Patchouli oil worn by free spirited hippies.

Late June, early in my career, I was making my first trip into Dinosaur Lake south of Buffalo Pass energized by the excitement of discovering new adventures on unfamiliar ground. Most snowfields melted, the crisp, thin air infused with the smell of pine, aspen and wildflowers, I savored the freedom and independence tendered by wild places.

Trekking the relatively flat path, I came across a disorderly tent camp pitched ridiculously close to the trail. No one around and not seeing firearms or fishing gear, I noticed a half dozen reddish orange, white-star studded mushroom caps, thinly sliced on a flat stone next to a burnt-out campfire. Recognizing the wild toadstools as a one of the highly hallucinogenic, potentially poisonous species of the genus Amanitas, not recommended for consumption by fungi experts, I knew this could possibly be a bad sign.

Unexpectedly, detecting slight movement in a ragged sleeping bag covered with an old wool blanket, I stepped back and observed a sunken-eyed, heavily bearded, long-haired head peeking from the covers. Embarrassed by not sensing a potential threat, I was astonished the lightweight bedding could even conceal a body! Watching a semblance of a diminutive man emerge from the sleeping bag, I could hardly believe my eyes. Sitting yoga style on the bedding was the skinniest, hairiest, dirtiest man I have ever encountered. Wearing only cutoff shorts and sandals, he had enough body hair to weave an Indian blanket. The sweet 'hippie" fragrance instilled in the wool blanket, was annihilated by the hippie's foul-smelling body. Protruding ribs, thin arms and legs lacking any muscle mass, I honestly thought this skeletal being may soon be called on by the Grim Reaper!

Whispering in a raspy, sibilant tone, he asked what day it was. When I replied Wednesday, he thought a moment and believed he had been sick for three days, experiencing a mix of hallucinations, loss of consciousness and seizures. He said, on two occasions, standing where I currently stood, he was looking down on his body watching himself die. He also revealed having several conversations with his deceased father. *DAMN!* My best guess would be the timeworn flower child was in his mid to late twenties.

When I asked about the Amanitas, he murmured finding them while searching for Shaggy Manes and Boletus. Knowing the Amanitas offered pleasant psychedelic pleasures from previous experience, he readily admitted consuming far too many this time and would probably avoid them in the future. *PROBABLY?* When asked if he had been fishing, he replied possibly but may have dreamt it. Not having a vehicle, he had no idea how he got here. Offering to radio for medical attention, he said his mind was back in his body and would be OK. Obviously still under the influence of the Amanitas, and possibly lucky to be alive, I advised him to get rid of the toadstools and take care of himself. Continuing my journey, I could not get him off my mind.

Talking with members of several camps at Dinosaur Lake, no one fishing and no fishing gear around, I found a quiet place and ate lunch. Hiking back, would you believe my hippie was gone. Literally finding neither hide nor hair of the withered non-conformist, he had packed his gear, including the Amanitas, and vanished!

*A hookah smoking caterpillar must have given him a call!*

# BAKER'S DOZEN

Thirteen! The precise number of tips recorded in my pocket log, each an explicitly accurate lead on the illegal poaching activities of one man. Thirteen sinewy clues and I had yet braided rope. Time riding a fast horse, the crimes were taking place during a bighorn sheep season ending in four days! Reviewing the reports shimmered my thoughts like the sun's reflection off a disturbed lake. 13, allegedly an omen of dire luck, but also a delightful digit for the proverbial extra pastry in a baker's dozen. Could it be bad luck for the lawbreaker, or my extra cookie breaking the case, or did it mean nothing at all?

1983. Ten years a Wildlife Officer, I enjoyed harvesting our ripe grapevine regularly yielding warden wine. In this case, my fruitless labors fermented bitter whines from those shaking the vine. The thirteenth tip was the last of several reported by Alexander, a relentless wild spy tattling his repeated conversations with the poacher openly divulging his sheep hunting criminalities in the Never Summer Range, hundreds of miles away from his licensed unit and bordering Rocky Mountain National Park where hunting is prohibited. Using his valid statewide muzzleloader deer license as cover, the poacher told Alexander he pitched a concealed camp near Bowen Pass, bragging his uncanny skills and woods wise abilities easily deceived the local, gullible 'brush cop'. **ME!** My informant, an Olive-skinned Greek with a spirited personality and flash-pan temper, portrayed the stubbornness and flamboyance of an Athenian warrior. Voicing great disappointment the sheep rustler persistently evaded capture despite the preponderance of evidence he provided, Alexander's hard-nosed tenacity roused my catch dog fortitude to spend considerable time scenting and flushing out the alleged sheep poacher. A new game plan was afoot.

*"He escapes who is not pursued" – Sophocles*

I would begin my hunt early Thursday morning, reasoning the poacher would try killing a sheep before Saturday, the day muzzle-loader deer season began. The Never Summer Wilderness not only held good populations of sheep but was also known for its trophy antlered timberline mule deer. These gnarly bucks mysteriously disappear into the ruggedly remote high mountain canyons prior to the early October hunting seasons, then reappear on the lower elevation winter ranges in mid-November for the rut. I realized if 'Joe Buck' stepped in front of the land pirate's rifle before deer season opened, the stag would meet his demise. Either beast taken the next two days would be illegal. Also, the alleged poacher would have no problem secreting his hunts within the National Park boundaries. Warden logic must mimic the mind of a poacher. Quite familiar with taking long shots my spirit was locked and loaded with the heavy charge of tracking down a sheep poacher.

My quarry, Chops Lambaster, was a 'dandy' kerchief, big hat cowboy making his living as a ranch manager and big game outfitter. His tanned face masked under a darkly thick, closely cropped beard sharply contrasted with his lighter shoulder length hair. His wild, blond maned appearance blended well with his clean, crisp western attire. An avid hunter and ardent horseman, Chops spent a great deal of time on sturdy, mountain painted pinto ponies, weaving the ridges, passes, hoary snowfields and talus slopes below the Never Summer's cloud shrouded peaks. Continuously searching for wilderness big game wearing large antlers and horns plus his local reputation as a branded poacher, I was always suspicious.

Chops and I frequently shared information on wildlife observations while trekking the Never Summer Range. We shared foot, horseback and aerial big game classification counts, and recorded them in my annual classification reports. We once set up a camp and rode horseback counting and classifying sheep, studying their habitat and discussing sheep management strategies. I acquired a lot of biological and geographical information from Chops and developed a cautious respect despite the steady reports of his alleged misdeeds. No doubt he was ahead of the warden game. I worked several cases where Chops was not the lead character, but somewhere in the shadows. Wildlife Officer Sir Don Gore and I made a solid bighorn sheep case involving two men illegally hunting Bowen Pass carrying the same Lambaster name; kinsmen disavowing Chops had any knowledge of their misdemeanors. While the present accusations of Chops and his outdoor pilfery came as no surprise, I was staggered by the recent number of fervent pleas to catch Chops in his illicit sheep dipping game.

Thursday, dawning in positive optimism, dusked with the negative displeasure of detecting nothing after painstakingly glassing the high country, checking trailheads, and talking with backpackers. My spirit waning with the late afternoon shadows, my tenacity was rewarded when locating an unlicensed horse trailer below a Forest Service gated road closure accessing a trailhead providing key access into the Never Summer high country. I found two separate boot tracks and hoof prints of two horses around it. Nightfall encroaching, I elected returning early the next morning. Daybreak Friday found me following the horse tracks abandoned the evening before. The distinct horseshoe imprints incredibly stopped, leaving no discernible trace whatsoever. *What the hell!* Before driving to the gated closure, I spent considerable time scoping the high mountain peaks discovering nothing. At the gate I focused on the immediate landscape and intently reviewed the facts currently on hand. There was a horse trailer parked below but no vehicle. Two horseback riders were somewhere ahead and an intensive search for tracks was necessary. Obviously, the horsemen spent at least one night on the mountain. Report **13** from Alexander alleged Chops was somewhere near this location illegally hunting his favored lair. These details should blend and guide me to the truth. The day was young, and I was eager to spend it pursuing the game thief.

*Carpe diem*. Seize the day!

Tenaciously searching behind the gated road closure, I detected several small freshly cut small pine stumps. Around the bend, I found freshly cut pine saplings cached behind a rotting log near the road. Disturbed soil and rock caught my eye and close inspection revealed it was caused by a vehicle bushwhacking its way around the gated road closure. *DAMN! HOW MANY TIMES HAD I BEEN WITHIN 50 YARDS OF THE OBVIOUS?* Returning to the road I realized a dusty section of the two-track had been 'broomed'. Someone 'spruced' up their spoor, sweeping away all tracks with cut pine boughs above the gate and to the horse tracks below! Now, fifty yards above the gate, I not only found vehicle tracks but also discovered tracks of two horses. My senses, melded with instinct, forged a sharply honed blade ready to cut deeper into the investigation. I was in my element, doing what I was made for.

*"The games afoot."*

The vehicle tracks led to a pickup truck neatly stashed in heavy pines, Chop's vehicle! Better yet, there was a handwritten note on the windshield to his wife stating camp was in the "usual spot", listing needed supplies and signed, "Love, Chops". *Warden Gold!* Chops played the game very well but now had a worthy opponent. *Little did he know his message was scripted for my eye.*

A mile up the road I found a tidy wall tent camp hidden in verdant pine adjacent to the high-country trailhead. No one around, I searched the camp and surrounding area finding no sign of outdoor transgressions. Fresh horse tracks leading away from the pickets and two sepa-rate boot tracks around the campfire provided additional evidence. I secured a warren overlooking the camp in some low growth pines and ate lunch – a peanut butter and jelly sandwich, an apple, a candy bar rinsed down with a can of Mountain Dew. Deciding to wait them out, I bided time glassing the surrounding peaks, studying a USGS map, and intently listening to the wilderness quiescence. I examined how the logging activities, with corresponding roads and skid trails, negatively impacted the entire area; erosion heavily loading the drainage with silt and severely degrading the stream's ability to sustain life. Not a good thing for anyone except the logging industry. Logging was based on economics, not ecology, with little thought given to the long-term health and sustainability of the mountain or its inhabitants. Plenty of time to reminisce, my thoughts turned to my wife Betsy, son Marc, and daughter Anne. Oh, what a lucky a man I was to be gifted with such family treasures. Typically, these feelings led to the guilt of spending too much time working; I needed to re-prioritize!

Anxious as bobcat on rabbit, I was amazed how fast the day passed. I thought I heard a shot, maybe two. Maybe! Instinctively I thought of chasing the shots, but common sense prevailed knowing 'pigeons' always return to their roosts. The setting sun stealing the day's warmth, replaced by the creeping cold of a dusking cloudless night. As the canyon shed its light, I slowly experienced the dark-ening agony of being alone. The vivid chance of capturing Chops faded into a plot of poor judgement; my anxiety rose with the moon. Under the vaulted ceiling of pending darkness, the night shadows rudely chased away my valor and brevity. My mind voices whis-pering bold warnings to "get the hell out of there", I debated returning to my truck and calling for backup. I should have let the Sheriff's Office know where I was working. My wife knew what I was doing but without any details. Not soliciting the aid of Wildlife Officer John Wagner officer was a real mistake. Wardens, out of necessity, become careless lone wolves, much too independent taking risks they simply should not. Scared? Damn straight! My stark imagi-nation running wild with spiders, rodents, bats, bears and unfamiliar night noises: **OH MY!** But, facing the opportunity of a major warden coupe, I swallowed my cowardice and (bravely?) decided to wait him out.

The day compressed into a thin gold line margining the horizon, my night demons were instantaneously vaporized by the unmistakable metallic sound of steel-clad hooves ringing off granite, chiming over the steady clip-clopping of horses' hooves! I was no longer alone! Crouching low in the waste high pines, coiled like a disturbed rattler, I took a deep breath to regain my personal fortitude. Painting on my warden face, I prepared for an impending tryst with the bad as the encroaching sounds materialized into shadowy apparitions of men on horseback.

*"I looked, and there before me was a pale horse! Its rider was named… Chops!*

My ears rhythmically drumming with the beating of my heart, all semblance of fear adrenalized into cautious anticipation. The horsemen passed within fifteen feet of my lair. Chops first, trailed by an unidentified man holding a coat covering an 'object' over the saddle horn. Chops dismounted and lit a two mantle Coleman lanterns exposing both riders and their cobby mountain steeds. The second man dismounted, removed the coat from his saddle and rewarded me with the head and cape of a fine mountain ram. *Hoka Hey!* The two wretches hid the illicit glaze-eyed trophy in nearby deadfall, neither realizing the warden wrath that was about to fall upon them.

Working as a team, they picketed the horses and completed the camp chores. The tent stove groaned a warming welcome as the campfire danced its glimmering light off the surrounding pines. Chops pitched a very comfortable hunting camp. I watched intently as the tent wall starkly outlined the silhouettes of both disarming themselves of rifle, pistol and knives before washing up. Returning to the campfire, they bleated the days fleecing as their evening meal cooked over the camp stove. Watching their faces flicker in lambent firelight, I planned my next move. The quiescent chrysalis in my stomach erupted into butterfly fury; excitement overwhelming my very core.

*Release the dogs!*

In full warden mode, I stepped into the edge of the campfire light identifying myself as a wildlife officer, followed by a cordial, "Hi Chops,
how ya doin'?" Closely scrutinizing their eyes as my presence pene-
trated deep within their core, a hush enveloped the campsite broken
only by the crackling campfire wisping smoke and spitting sparks into
the night's open sky.

Chops, stepping into the campfire's full glare, greeted me with a
worried smile and an open hand. Well known as a smooth-talking
gentleman, deceiving more people than a padded bra, I tarnished his
silver-tongue asking point blank what they were hunting. Notably
stunned, both recognized my rifling question as loaded. Firing another
wing shot, I mentioned hearing shots that afternoon high on the mountain. Chops countered they were on the mountain all day and heard no
shots. Firing my fatal shot, I affirmed knowing they were in possession
of an illegal ram. Humanely taking them down with my direct
demeanor and carefully chosen words, both folded! Chops unhesitatingly confessed his wild sins while his compatriot, Shep Fleecer,
shamefacedly nodded in agreement. Poised for the worse, I quickly
realized there would be no trouble here. Clouted off their high horse
by a jousting warden, they pluckily accepted defeat under the weight
of their armored misdeeds. Instructing Shep to retrieve the head and
cape from the underbrush, I kept a watchful eye on the lad as he
sheepishly carried the ram into the lantern light. Chops, shedding guilt
like snakeskin, took full responsibility for the illegal ram, expressing
Shep was only along for the ride. When asked about the meat, Chops
said it was on the mountain and they planned to pack it out the next
day. I quickly formulated an indecent proposal to meet them at the
ranch Monday at noon where the meat would be inspected, confiscated and citations issued. I warned compliance was of utmost importance because their case would be heard by the county judge in
Sage Hen.

Astutely ending my surprise attack, I threw the head and cape over
my shoulders, a horn in each hand and, looking straight into Chop's

eyes, declared I was very disappointed by his illegal behavior. Affirming I would see both on Monday, I backed into the darkness with one last glance at their ghosting faces washed in wavering campfire flames. Heart beating like a drumming ruffed grouse, I briskly hiked a quarter mile before stepping into the pines to watch and listen, making certain I was not being followed. My back trail silent, I quickly coursed to my pickup. During the long, rough drive out, I assessed Chop's demise. Like so many miscreants, Chops chose thieving game close to home, using the security of the familiar where he clearly understood the habits and lairs of the game; where he had the opportunity to kill two great beasts, a bighorn sheep and a trophy buck deer, in one hunt. Hunting sheep in a wrong unit, he not only stole opportunity from a legally licensed hunter, he also filched a sheep from the mountain. His lawless game became the law's game, and this time justice prevailed.

Midnight found me very happy to be home. Betsy worriedly waiting, as usual, I feasted on a microwaved supper, and told my tale of bringing justice to the wild. Not letting me off the hook, she openly deliberated my lax of judgement resulting in poor decisions of working alone, late at night taking great risks with no one knowing my whereabouts; politely insinuating I was a fool! Busted, I readily admitted to my mistakes and would do my best correcting them. And, of course, I failed!

I contacted the sheep filchers the following Monday at the ranch. Chops, through tears and a shaky voice, rifled the story of the misguided bullets targeting his illicit, pre-meditated behavior. His guilt seemingly weighing on his soul like a rain drenched buffalo robe, he portrayed a truly remorseful man. As the tics were scratched, Chops uncomfortably asked the age-old questions of the paranoid. How did I know? Who tipped me off? Enhancing Chop's psychosis, I alleged it was Athenian pluck and the number **13** triggering his capture. Having no clue what I meant, Chops stared in stark wonder. After trading signatures on the final legal documents, Shep broke his silence thanking me for my professionalism and politeness; the strange remorseful response of so many sharing my pen. My equally bizarre answer was a simple, "You're welcome!" Loading the illegal meat into a cooler, Chops acknowledged, "He was sorry!" I agreed, thinking not of repentance but of the sorry excuse of the men standing before me. Any admiration of Chop's hunting skills erased, a sportsman he was not; his capture fully exposed the credentials of a first-degree poacher.

Chops and Shep appeared before the county magistrate, pled guilty and paid hefty fines for their misdeeds. Their embarrassment was compounded by a detailed summary of the case appearing in the weekly newspaper followed by the persistent questioning and criticism from their peers. I could only hope this would curtail any future errant behavior, but it did not. News of the case rode a fast horse throughout the Bull Pen, and I received praise from the majority good for capturing the flagrant poacher; most proclaiming "it was about time." The flashing revelation of exposing Chop's malevolence against the wild resulted in my receiving a commendation from the Director of the Division of Wildlife. But for me, it was all about time being on my side, providing justice not only for Chops and Shep, but also for the bighorn ram and the hunting good, making working for the wild extremely worthwhile,

*"So let it be written, so let it be done!"*Rameses II

# SHEPHERD'S PURSE

And there I was, responding to an early morning phone call from the Sheriff's Office regarding an untagged deer hanging in a thick grove of spruce behind a sheepherder's camp below Rabbit Ears Peak. It was late August when a wandering bowman stumbled across the carcass while hunting back to his remote cabin on Wilset Creek. The archer reported a previous conversation with the Basque shepherd indicated a suspiciously quiet, overtly shy young man. *Basque shepherds, inept at speaking English, are always shy!* The sheep camp was located on a bench above Filcher Creek near the end of a rough two-track I often used as a back-door port of entry into the National Forest, surprising both the hunting good and poaching bad.

A splendid late summer afternoon, I relished the chance to stretch my legs, bushwhacking the last half mile into the camp by skirting the aspen/sage interface above Filcher Creek. Today, the beaver pond quagmire and surrounding uplands provided two alluring attractions; a pair of raspingly loud Sandhill Cranes announcing their annoyance, high stepping through a marsh with a young colt in tow; and a flock of Evening Grosbeaks sunning themselves in aspen, the exotically colored males and less glamorous females and juveniles always a pleasant surprise.

Breaking out of the trees into a dazzlingly yellow balsamroot grass-
land, I spotted the rustic rubber-tired, Conestoga-style sheep wagon
sitting in a grassy aspen meadow. With Rabbit Ears guarding boldly
above, it was a picture-perfect pastoral scene indeed. Circling the tidy
camp, I hollered a friendly 'Hello', finding it vacated; no shepherd, no
horse and no 'healer' sheep dogs; and no chance to 'fly the colors'
advertising the existence of wildlife law and order in this secretive,
wild setting. Spotting the heavy stand of spruce/fir described earlier
by the archery hunter, I closed the distance and found a freshly
skinned hogget (yearling sheep) hanging by its hind legs, its wooly
hide draped hair down draped over the trunk of a fallen fir. Case
solved! Nothing to do but return to my vehicle, I curiously walked
through the camp and was scared witless when a peculiarly clean ewe
bolted from the open door of the sheep wagon, romping my way,
bleating a warm welcome. *Damn, she is really glad to see me!* Tethered to
a stake, she perceptively stopped before reaching the end of the rope.
Overly friendly, this recently shorn Suffolk was no doubt the Basque's
favored companion. Could the age-old jests of shepherds hooking up
with their pick of the flock be true? *NNNAAAHHH!* Grinning wildly, I
pondered the thought of a jolly herdsman tupping with this fine-
looking running age ewe; beauty, of course, is in the eyes of the
beholder!

*Do Ya Think?*

# WASSAILOR

**D**RUNK, SOZZLED, INEBRIATED, SLOSHED! Call them what you want, intoxicated outdoorsmen and women routinely cross paths with wildlife officers. Many are sailors motoring their way over lakes and streams, boating and drinking frequently goes hand in hand. For a few, it will be their last boat ride, accidents sending them or a friend into the water's smothering depths.

It is illegal to operate a motor vessel under the influence of alcohol or drugs and I handled each situation on a case by case basis, scratching costly tics to those endangering themselves or others. Otherwise, issuing the driver a written warning giving his deckhands strict notice that driving the boat was prohibited until he or she sobered up typically resolved their inebriated misbehavior. However, an exception took place one August morning on Cowdrey Lake. Topping the ridge overlooking the lake, I eased my truck behind an outhouse utilizing the two-holer as camouflage to spy on fishermen. Strategically angling the driver's side window and mounting the Big Eye, I began scanning the lake with binoculars. Startled by the rumbling thunder and aerated blasts of exploding flatulence resonating from inside the privy (*the price paid for using the public crapper as cover*) I envisioned a Neandertal brute suffering the wrath of yesterday's camp chili. Imagine my astonishment when an attractive, well-proportioned young lady donning a bikini top and short shorts swaggered out, acknowledging my presence with an innocent grin. *DAMN!*

Unpleasantly amused, my eyes tracked back to the lake and focused on the peculiar sight of a man standing knee deep in a half-submerged boat. Switching to the Big Eye, I zoomed in on the animated chap rocking against the rhythm of the unstable vessel. Forcefully flinging his pole and wondering where his bait landed, he was totally unaware the dangling worm wad splashed far to his right. No matter, he placed the pole into a rod holder and patiently waited for a bite. Apparently in his happy place, the blissful drunkard paid no heed to the condition of his condition. Tipping a gallon jug of wine skyward, nearly losing his balance, he ultimately realized the lid was still attached.

Driving to the boat ramp, I hollered for him to bring his boat into shore. The man waved obedience but was unable to pull the anchor up from the weedy lake. Luckily, another boatman volunteered to tow him in; a challenging task providing ample entertainment to an ever-growing shoreline audience. Nearing the ramp, the tugboat captain threw me the tow rope while I enlisted help to pull in the swamped dinghy. Beaching it revealed a ragged splintering gash in the boat's lower front end.

Expecting a dysfunctional drunk, I was amazed when the swig bender awkwardly hurdled into the waste deep water and floundered towards the bank. An empty gallon of Thunderbird was bobbing in the boat next to its half full brother. Curtly admonishing his behavior, I warned him to stay away from the boat until he sobered up. 'Captain Zebedee' nodded his compliance. Weeble-wobbling towards his truck, the sopping Zebedee turned and, using the universal salutary hand gesture, flipped me off! And the crowd roared! Those camped near Zebedee disclosed he drank heavily the night before and resumed early this morning. The hole in his boat occurred mid-morning when he struck the cement boat ramp at a high rate of speed. The spellbound spectators said Zebedee, without inspecting the damage, staggered towards the john and realizing he would not make it, emptied his bladder facing them all. Returning to his boat, he gracelessly boarded and, unable to start the engine, rowed the waterfilled boat in a zig-zag pattern into the lake and began fishing. When I arrived, he had been fishing for about a half hour. All witnesses readily acknowledged Zebedee was having a very good time.

That evening the Sheriff's Office reported Zebedee once again launched and sank the Titanic. Meeting the state patrolman, we drove to Cowdrey Lake and found the nearly submerged vessel not far from the boat ramp. Onlookers detailed they could not prevent Zebedee from launching his boat. Twenty yards from shore, apparently scared the boat would sink completely, he jumped out and all but drowned wallowing through the weedy muck of the shoreline shallows.

Approaching Zebedee's truck, I smelled his obsession before seeing him. Vomit covered the tail gate and the ball hitch. An empty gallon of Thunderbird surrounded by empty beer cans littered the ground.

*"Opening bottles is what makes a drunkard."* Hemingway Nick Adams.

The overhead door of the camper shell open, I flashed light onto a water soaked sleeping bag. Grabbing a foot, the lonesome loser's head, crammed against the wheel well, lifted and immediately fell with a thud. Identifying myself, I sternly informed Zebedee he was under arrest. Twisted in his bag, Zebedee was feverously shaking, obviously entering the final stages of hypothermia. Slurring, Zebedee spilled a vinic message in indiscernible breaths of inebriated delirium. It took both the State Patrolman and I to maneuver him into a sitting position on the passenger side of my truck. Once in Sage Hen, Zebedee regained a semblance of life while undergoing a blood alcohol test by the town's physician, Doctor France. Zebedee passed the exam honorably, scoring a level of alcohol potentially worth distilling.

Running his name through the enforcement database, the 65-year-old man had no criminal record. Contacts with a family member described a cheerful man who loved fishing. I suggested they accompany him on his next fishing trip and share his happiness. Returning to the jailhouse early next morning, I found Zebedee wearing his hangover like a wet moose hide. The frowzy man, suffering the wrath of grapes, managed a smile and an apology as I scratched the tic. Accepting my offer for a ride he slowly detoxed and asked if I would help hitch his trailer and load his boat. Afterwards, Zebedee stuck out his hand and thanked me for nursing him through his inebriation. I respectfully replied, "Your welcome, but let's not do this again." Asked why he continued drinking after our first contact Zebedee answered, "I needed time to even my keel!" Good wardensmanship required not questioning him any further.

*In vino veratis – there is truth in wine*

# ONE PERCENT

'So lovely was the loneliness
Of a wild lake, with black rock bound
And the tall pines that towered around.'
The Lake - *Edgar Allan Poe*

I selfishly allotted time (never enough) stalking the Bull Pen wilds to unravel the knots and snarls of a mind tangled in the 24/7 demands of an unrelenting public hungry for instantaneous reactions to their wildlife issues. Wandering alone where perchance no humans ever tread replenished the mettle necessary to keep on, keepin' on. Youthfully immortal, stalking the backside of nowhere without backup, I now realize in the event of an accident I may have never been found. Understand the allure of wilderness, proffering feral sensations of true aloneness, satiated innate cravings vital to my overall well-being. The ability to work and play trekking the wilds so many would kill for, I often pondered if I could live without it!

As a badged wilderness warrior, I quickly learned the chance of counting criminal coup in the sparsely inhabited backwoods was extremely high. What it lacked in human quantity was made up by the quality of human contacts. I relished stalking cirque to cirque, playing hide and seek over the rock gilded pockets of trout laden ice water. I considered 'flying the warden flag' to the wilderness minority equally important to checking the multitudes fishing the highly accessible 'drive in' lakes and streams. Wilderness contacts provided opportunity to converse and educate a neglected populace; an essential component of good wardensmanship. Many wilderness jaunts were impulsive changes in my daily plan; spur-of-the-moment assaults with no design other than retreating to a place where I could quickly and quietly vanish.

So there I was, early one August morning, the Moon of the Ripening Berries, driving west for a day patrolling the lowland sagebrush lakes. Instantaneously, my eyes locked on the granite starkness of the heaven piercing crags of the Zirkel Wilderness, boldly contrasting with a, crispy azure sky. The lure of this regal view holding my spirit for ransom, commanded the immediate payment of changing plans. Surrendering, my mind tracked the headwaters of Lone Pine Creek into the crystalline, ice waters of Bighorn Lake. So be it! A hidden gemstone securely set in a granite cirque under the Devil's Backbone, Bighorn Lake is an esteemed destination due to its isolation from the main wilderness trails, a healthy population of cutthroat trout, and a tumbling quicksilver falls nourished by a glacial snowfield; my heaven on earth. My maiden voyage into Bighorn occurred my initial year as a Bull Pen warden. Neighbor and good friend, Charlie McCallister, scrupulously provided directions in the skylarking manner befitting his unsystematic personality; "You can't miss it. Just follow the main trail and turn right at the BIG Tree." Long story short, there were a lot of big trees.

Today's ploy was main trailing into Lake Katherine, check fishermen and continue hiking a cross country contour into Bighorn. Several vehicles parked at the trailhead tendered warden worth for investing time contacting wilderness' recreationists. Donning a daypack, I quickly shed the morning's chill trekking the lower bogs through lush aspen glades before climbing skyward over rocky ridges and talus slopes. Stealing off trail below Katherine, I circled wide to a lair overlooking the long, narrow lake. Focusing my binoculars on several young fishermen, I was immediately rewarded discovering they were catching and keeping an abundance of ten to twelve-inch Lake Trout. At that time, Katherine had size (18+inches) and limit (2 lake trout) restrictions in place for growing larger size Lake Trout. These regulations, however, proved unworthy as the sterile, unproductive lake was unable to sustain the brook trout and sucker forage population at levels necessary to grow healthy populations of lake trout exceeding eighteen inches.

Contacting the anglers, I found them properly licensed. The piscators proudly escorted me to their individual stringers totaling thirteen snaky lake trout; seven over the group's legal limit and all under the eighteen-inch requirement. Knowing the rules protected what the lake could not biologically sustain, yet aware the men obviously gave no thought to reviewing the fishing regulations, I refrained from nailing them for every trout. Because they were properly licensed and keeping track of individual catches, a backwoods rarity, good wardensmanship steered me into scratching tics for exceeding the two fish limits, *(my version of a 'Big Mac Attack')* with the bonus of allowing them to keep all 13 trout; a less expensive transaction providing exceptional flavor to their evening dinner's entrée (fresh trout vs freeze dried camp food)! Moreover, carrying the illegal trout the rest of this warm day in my daypack avoided the heady scent of fermenting fish. I provided a copy of the regulations, bid them a good day and faded into the forest. Bighorn was a thirty-five-minute plus jaunt over an unmarked contour ultimately found by echolocating its rushing falls.

Once enveloped in the forest, I found an ancient decaying spruce stump on the edge of a small meadow and took a King's seat to absorb the explicit feeling of wilderness seclusion. Staring skyward, I unexpectedly sensed a slight movement against the trunk of a tall spruce. Focusing my binoculars, the diminutive form of a Boreal Owl materialized! Lord God! This seldom observed banty owl, outwardly ignoring me, lazily scanned its surroundings in a deceptive 360-degree arc. Previously listening to the mysterious night calls of this feathered treasure on Cameron Pass greatly enhanced today's sighting. A good omen indeed! Filled with euphoria, I continued to Bighorn.

Hearing the rush of the falls, I was soon edging its tree lined boulder field to a vantage where I could quietly watch and listen. Removing my pack and appreciating the slight breeze over my sweaty back, I paused to take a leak, marveling how quickly mosquitoes found any exposed skin not painted with Cutter insect repellent. Today's enormous variety resembled miniature helicopters with dangling landing gear legs, incessantly hovering and alighting over my currently exposed body part. Needless to say, relieving myself was without pause. It was the time of the season when the pesky mosquitoes were being replaced by the flesh drilling deer flies, wilderness endowments one pays dearly for if not properly prepared. My guts grumbling for the Mountain Dew, sardines, crackers and candy bars in my pack, I set up a picnic lunch on a flat boulder. The cascading water, calmed by ebbing glacial melts, babbled its happiness to be a waterfall. Add the sky-scraping granites impeccably mirrored in the lakes glassy surface, the colorful Marsh Marigolds and High-country Cowslips blooming along the edges of the falls enhanced the soul soothing ambience of my mountain cathedral setting. With a pulpy mouthful of mustard sauced pilchards and saltines, I toasted the grandeur of my dining room, declaring it my own with a large gulp of Mountain Dew. Predictably two jays appeared, fearlessly eager to share any morsel I may offer.

Tracking a soft breeze riffling a V over the lake's top water and spotting several large cutthroat shadows submarining through the shoreline shallows, I scolded myself for leaving my fly rod behind. Often finding no one there, I fished long and hard for the finicky cutthroats, my departures procrastinated anticipating an evening caddis hatch. The dusking wilderness darkness crashing like a cellar door, I would find myself scrambling down the relentlessly fading trail to my vehicle. I camped here, not enough, with my son Marc and friends, providing down time to marvel the abundance of salamanders in a hidden kettle pond (a place where I never thought the age old amphibians could possibly exist); to taste a blackened, pan-fried trout over an open fire; to perceive inconceivable quietness while mindlessly staring into a dancing campfire, looking skyward at thousands of spangling stars ornamenting unpolluted night sky. There are no words to describe the wonders of wilderness. It must be experienced.

Suddenly, my tranquil thoughts were rudely shattered by the sound of voices. Wilting into a clump of shrubby spruce I observed two hefty men crammed in a dreadfully small yellow rubber raft bob into view. Facing each other, calves crossed with one's feet dangling in the water, they were doing their unleveled best to cast a lure towards the shoreline. Imagine the pleasantry of watchdogging two generously proportioned men in a blow-up vessel spinning, tipping, and taking on water while attempting to fish. Rub-a-dub-dub! Obviously lacking the required life jackets, *(now really, who would backpack life preservers into these remote lakes?)* the pair already earned a dose of warden wrath. Most wilderness raft fishermen were either ignorant of the life jacket laws or willing to take the slight risk of capture. I normally scolded verbal warnings, rarely issuing a citation unless children under supervision of negligent parents were involved. Then, the parents were cited. The law, however, was justifiably sound, as I packed out several water-soaked corpses, lives seized by the icy grasp of mountain waters; wilderness mortalities still sending shivers up and down my spine.

Stalking to lake's edge, I conspicuously took a seat on a lakeshore boulder. The hand paddling pair splashed by without detecting me, so I shadowed their progress until they beached the raft on the opposite shoreline. One began bank fishing while the other tied the raft to a tree. Crossing the log choked outlet in plain sight, I loudly cleared my throat, momentarily hesitating to enjoy their 'warden shock'. Paying close attention to the fisherman, now drifting backwards into the trees, I identified myself, alternately making eye contact with both. The boat man socially introduced himself as Mitch Garcia and his partner as Zeb Coe, stating they were Chicago schoolteachers, this trip to the Bighorn their annual summer ritual. Zeb, cowering like a ditch cat, wore the guilt-ridden face of ensnarement. *Hoka Hey!*

Prolonging their agony, I continued chatting before requesting fishing licenses. Mitch proudly waved his newly purchased non-resident license, obviously as much for Zeb's benefit as for mine. Inspecting the license, I turned to Zeb who chortled through his froggy throat the slimy tale he had not been fishing. I brusquely cast over his lines, displaying my binoculars affirming I observed both fishing for quite some time. Admitting he did not have a license, Zeb rationalized his misdeed as harmless, hardly worth the efforts of a game warden. I tersely countered with my well-rehearsed lesson from Wardensmanship 101; "These waters are stocked annually with fingerling cutthroat trout by a Division of Wildlife airplane funded by fishing license revenues. And as far as warden worth, checking fishermen anywhere is my job, and you have certainly given value to why I am here!"

Zeb, his day darker than crow guts, wrinkled his face into the unmistakable contortion I so abhorred. Huge crocodile tears emerged from squinting eyes as he reviewed his credentials of being a hardworking citizen and an honorable human being. Reducing himself into a nose running beggar, he wailed for leniency testifying he always purchased fishing licenses. This year, against the strong advice of his comrade, he elected not buying one based on they'd never had their licenses checked in Colorado. I informed Zeb the fine was $68, unless I found any trout in camp. The unlicensed bandit tearfully explained they had eaten all their trout the previous night. Carrying traveler's checks and no cash, I explained escorting Zeb to Sage Hen was necessary to either mail in the fine or post bond at the courthouse.

Declaring, "there is no crying in fishing *(I loved this line),"* I clarified it was time to don his big boy pants and reaffirm his manhood by taking responsibility for his misdeeds. Realizing he was not going to talk this fish hawk out of a trout dinner, Zeb launched one last arrow of defiance, "I have fished Colorado a hundred times without ever seeing a warden. What are the odds I would ever get caught?" Math never my strong suit, this calculation was elementary;

Zeb fished Colorado one hundred times (impossible).
Had been caught once $= 1 / 100 = .01$

Without hesitation, I raucously announced:
"ONE PERCENT!"

The humor escaped Zeb, but not Mitch who folded into gut busting laughter teasing Zeb with different versions of "I told you so." I compassionately offered Zeb a graceful exit, stating fishing without a license was not the crime of the century. *Those playing with sharp knives often get cut.* I affirmed perceiving both as good men, describing myself likewise whose job was educating people on the benefits of purchasing a license. Next year, it was my hope today's whines would be tomorrow's song and Zeb would return with a license.

His tear-well dry, Zeb accepted his wrongdoings. Chit-chatting our way back to town, Zeb cashed some travelers checks and mailed in his fine. Without prodding, Zeb purchased a fishing license at the local sporting goods store. I delivered Zeb back to the trailhead with enough daylight to hike back to his camp. With a thanking handshake, I watched the windy city native disappear into the wilderness.

*Another one bites the dust!*

# TOMMIE FOOLERY

**W**hoa! December 1980. There I was, abruptly forced off the road by a fast-moving jeep driving left of center on a sharp curve. Sliding into loose gravel I regained control and eased back onto the road. Paying more attention to my surroundings than the road itself, I was incredibly lucky to have avoided an accident. Knowing the driver, Tommie Deerwhacker, I pondered his haste while backtracking his solitary vehicle tracks in the fresh snow. The hunting season chaos over, the Bull Pen's December quiet allowed time to reexamine cold cases, check migrating big game herds, and search for the late fall violations of poachers filling their winter larders.

Peaking the Owl Mountain road overlooking Deer Creek, I saw where Deerwhacker's jeep pulled off the road. Boot tracks into an aspen patch led to a freshly field dressed buck deer. *Hoka Hey!* One set of vehicle tracks, one set of boot tracks, one illegal deer, the solution was elementary. Inspection of the carcass revealed the buck had been shot in the head with a small caliber weapon. Returning to Sage Hen to meet with trainee Mike Middleton, I reviewed the case with Wildlife Officer John Wagner and his trainee, Gary Berlin. Working an indisputable deer poaching case would offer a valuable training opportunity for the recruits.

Middleton and I guarded the deer carcass the remainder of the day from a secluded lair and were joined by Wagner and Berlin after dark. After10 p.m. with no sign of Deerwhacker, Wagner and Berlin drove by his log home in Rosebud and saw him standing on the porch, possibly recognizing their vehicle. *RATS!* Pulling into the driveway, Middleton and I walked onto the porch and knocked. Markedly distraught with two wardens darkening his doorway made me believe the hangdog man was ready to wave the white flag. After Middleton read Deerwhacker his constitutional rights, I revealed the extent of his poaching wrongs. Glancing over his shoulder at his wife, he flagrantly denied killing the deer, stating he did not even own a .22 rifle. When confronted with his reckless driving, he acknowledged running late for work due to changing a flat tire and needing to drop it off for repair. Nearing midnight, we left the troubled man to simmer in his illicit, gamey sauce.

The next morning, we confirmed Deerwhacker not only lied about having his tire fixed but also recently purchased a .22 rifle at the local market: benefits of small-town living. Returning to his residence, I invited him into my vehicle and reviewed the financial details of his misdeeds. Stating he needed to speak with his wife, I watched the suffering man slink into the cabin. The windows wide open due to the intense heat radiated by their wood stove, I listened as his wife brutally attacked Tommie for poaching a deer followed with scorching desecrations of my pedigree, my lack of intelligence and the fact I could prove nothing. Now understand, I did not know this woman from Adam, or Eve, and was taken aback by her declarations of my inferior brain power!

*"Sometimes you have to be a high riding bitch to survive, sometimes, being a bitch is all a woman has to hang on to."* Stephen King, Dolores Claiborne

Presuming the impact of his wife's thundering declarations propelled him to maintain his innocence, I began preparing for a court appearance. Deerwhacker, walking up to my open truck window, took a deep breath and, staring at the wrathful woman standing on the porch, confessed! *DAMN!*

Understand, the Deerwhackers were a well-respected Bull Pen family. Tommie, a hardworking man, whipsawed with a new baby and sporadic work, was struggling to make a living. They needed meat and he did wrong for all the right reasons, electing to steal off the common rather than drawing from the dole. Too proud to apply for welfare, he poached from a deer herd he frequently drove by on his way to work. Knowing his dilemma and taking his confession into account, I frankly could not file charges costing them money they did not have. Explaining I had a season's worth of confiscated deer, elk, and moose meat available for donation, he should have contacted me. Scratching the tic for the minimum charge, I provided time to raise money by setting a late court date. Deerwhacker, noticeably at ease, said he did not retrieve the deer because he was alarmed by spotting an unfamiliar warden vehicle (the trainees) in town. Stating he was glad the deer would be given to the needy, I reminded him to contact me regarding the wild meat available for his family.

Shaking hands while his wife's eyes shot daggers at us both, I quickly escaped. Aware her defensive conduct was a means of protecting their family, I also knew, for Tommie, there would be no sugar tonight!


*The house does not rest upon the ground, but upon a woman.*
Mexican proverb.

# SHORTY'S WYAKIN

Her phone call caught me completely off guard!

Our acquaintance began when I routinely crossed paths with this lady and her husband Shorty on Independence Mountain during big game seasons. Pleasantly polite, they were an incredibly happy couple enjoying all aspects of hunting the hinterlands; first-rate ambassadors of the majority hunting good I relentlessly worked for. Most often finding them hunting a favored ridge I also stalked during the earlier muzzleloader season, I made a point to search them out and say hello. Attentively chatting with many hunters, they became essential eyes and ears for current mountain events, several times steering me in the right direction when tracking down game thieves.

And, just like that, they were gone. Their traditional lairs soon occupied by other hunters, I sadly heard Shorty had passed. Years later when she called, I conscientiously listened to the emotionally charged lady detail Shorty's death afore asking me for what she described as a huge favor. After making several visits to the mountain after Shorty's death and unable to locate the trail accessing 'their' ridge, she requested my help. I graciously offered to personally drive and walk her into where they enjoyed so much quality time. She was elated.

Soon after, I picked her up in Sage Hen and pleasantly chatted our way to Independence Mountain. Parking my vehicle, she initially did not recognize the terrain until hiking the timbered trail and breaking into an open basin. Smiling the widest of grins, she led me to 'their' ridge, noticeably in a state of relaxed tranquility.

Their narrow, rocky ridge, bordered behind by heavy timber, overlooked a sage meadow of sparse aspen and pine, was a natural game crossing. The timber behind hid an active spring serving as an elk wallow during the fall rut where I once harvested a testosterone laden raghorn bull bugling his lonesomeness to a larger bull herding a harem of cows and calves. Great hunting ground, indeed! Allowing her to trek the ridge alone, I sat and waited. Soon, I heard her crying the sad song of a joyful life past, its chorale notes floating across their sacred hunting place, simultaneously a God awful and God beautiful melody bringing me to tears. Suddenly, a cracking branch and tumbling rocks caught my attention as a heavily antlered buck deer in full velvet, walked into view and stopped. Momentarily nosing the air for scent, eyes lasered and ears perked towards her, the stag searched for the threat his senses warned was nearby. Turning, it pranced away, stopping for one last look over its shoulder before fading into dark timber. It was as mystical as it was weird. Fifteen minutes later, she walked back and asked if I saw the deer. Smiling, I nodded while she expressed believing Shorty was here. I gave her a long hug and whispered the buck was her WYAKIN, her spiritual guardian signifying Shorty's presence. Not understanding what I meant, I told her to investigate wyakin as it pertains to Native American culture. Few words spoken on our way back to Sage Hen, I bid her a warm goodbye and sadly, we never crossed paths or spoke again.

Reminiscing my last conversation with the hunting pair was near their favored ridge, where it should have been, I remember stepping out of my pickup and Shorty asking, "Where's Steve?" Realizing he was serious, I pointed to my nameplate and he replied, "No, Steve is a much taller man!" Laughing, I said I must appear bigger when sitting in my truck. A heartfelt memory saddened because those days are gone, yet applauded because I lived them.

Disturbingly, I cannot remember their actual names, but will forever miss them both!

*Carpe Diem!*

# LUNCH TAKE

Occasionally, wildlife illegalities materialized with little or no effort on my part. And so it was, one sun drenched late summer morning, finding no human activity and to my dismay, no moose in the Illinois River drainages, I chose to grind my vehicle over the rocky Calamity Pass road. Momentarily pausing to absorb the ecstatic view of the appropriately named Lily Lake, I meandered downwards into the Michigan River drainage, flushing a lone blue grouse on the way. Breaking into the South Fork of the Michigan meadows and spotting two individuals a half mile downriver, I pulled off road and mounted the Big Eye on my window. Zooming in I focused on a man and a young girl fishing through the shrubby willow, the man obviously coaching the girl casting a small lure into the meandering runs and riffles.

*To fish with the young, is fishing in good company.*

Hungry, this picturesque panorama set below the towering Never Summer Range, proffered a perfect picnic location. My vehicle hidden in plain sight above the gurgling waters, I spied both anglers catch and release an occasional small trout as they fished upriver towards me. Chomping saltines laden with mustard sauced sardines', and swigging Mountain Dew, I savored my candy bar dessert. Passing within yards of my pickup, the man smilingly waved and continued fishing. Fifteen minutes later they quit and began walking the road towards me. Exiting my truck, the man's eyes locked on my uniform, the guilt-ridden look on his face confessing his misdeeds before I said a word. Readily admitting that although the thought of purchasing licenses for himself and his 18-year-old daughter crossed his mind that morning, he did not. I politely scolded that his decision placed both in violation of fishing law requiring citations. Good wardensmanship, however, steered me to charging only him and not the naively blameless girl. While scratching the tic, I asked if he thought casually fishing in front of me would con me into not checking their licenses, he lightheartedly replied, "No, I waved thinking you were just a Forest Ranger!

*You, who are on the road*
*Must have a code*
*That you can live by*
*And so*
*Become yourself*
*Because the past*
*Is just a good-bye*
*Teach your children well....Graham Nash*

# SUREFIRE BET

And there we were! Deer season in full swing, Wildlife Officer Howard Spear and I were trailing a pickup truck 'grandma gearing' the tight switchbacks on the east side of Sheep Ridge. The steep, rocky road commanded our full attention to avoid the road's eroded hazards. It was dusk, daylight rapidly waning on the dark side of the mountain. Spear, riding shotgun, maintained a close eye on the rear lights of the pickup, flaring like blazing garnets as the driver repetitively hit the brakes. I flipped the cutoff switch to my brake lights and with the advantage of being above and behind our prey there was little chance of being discovered. Twilight fading, deer would be leaving their bedding haunts and lurking in timbered shadows until nightfall. It was a surefire bet the nimrods below were 'road hunting' their way off the mountain. Indeed, a good time and place for stalking wardens.

Suddenly, their pickup veered left and jerked to a complete stop! I followed suit while Spear spied through his binoculars. Opening my door, I quickly mounted the Big Eye to the window and focused on the vehicle. Knowing well the impulsive mindsets of hunters, I wagered five bucks the passenger was going to fire his rifle at a pair of ducks swimming in a stock pond a hundred yards below. Wearing his trademark smile, Spear scoffed and self-assuredly accepted the improbable wager and intensified his focus on the vehicle.

In a matter of seconds, I drew four consecutive aces: a rifle barrel appearing out of the passenger side window; a puff of smoke; the crack of a rifle; and a high rising splash from the pond. The sniping joker bringing my hand to five of a kind, Spear stared in total disbelief as the ducks flushed wildly and flew out of sight. Committing a first degree water foul carrying multiple violations (shooting from a motor vehicle: attempting to take waterfowl with a rifle; having no small game license and duck stamp) merited the errant shooter exclusive membership to the wardens club of captured miscreants. And the crowd roared!

*So let it be written, so let it be done! Ramses II*

# MEXICAN RIDGE TWENTY AUGHT 06

A tic tight gate, posts 'n wire garbed,
Horseback high, unkempt, and sharply barbed,
The arm bitin' entry to our Ridge of rock and clay.
Leavin' twenty-four seven vocation lifestyles,
For this hunting nirvana of one by two miles,
Where time is clocked as night and day.

Twas eve of early rifle deer season,
Kirb and Stan findin' the Mexican pleasin',
Dressed in fall color of blazin' leaf splendor.
Kirb's truck bouncin' and kickin',
Scoutin' for deer while eatin' fried chicken,
Go cups commencin' the night's ritual bender.

Back in camp in a tent once apprehended,
From a guile guide we captured red-handed,
We weave old stories of grand poacher catches.
Relaxed, contented, and joyful,
Two ardent wardens blissfully youthful,
On a ridge of sage quilted aspen patches.

Oh, we talk of stag and horn,
Our wood stove moanin', glowin' warm,
In musical milieu of song dogs and wapiti.
Critiquing land management schemes,
Wishing for changes beyond our means,
Stymied by old school ranching strategy.

Overuse by overgrazing,
Long term abuse stokes our hearts blazin',
Scarring lands we dearly treasure.
But as Maker's makes its mark,
We succumb to the lateness of the dark,
Meltin' into bags of warm downy pleasure.

With dawn ridin' in on her fast horse,
We wake to strong Colubian and of course,
A trip to Kirb's newly remodeled outdoor throne.
Changin' season, changin' gun,
Slingin's long rifles, our backs to the sun,
We part on Munk's ridge for our time alone.

The mornin' still oh so calm,
Broken by gunshots crackin' our balm,
I spy a buck fleeing across open ground.
Chasing hunters on ATVs appear,
My eyes trace the fine antlered deer,
Pausing quite near, I proffer no sound.

The buck tempting my trigger finger,
My eyes on antlers linger,
Fightin' the squeeze of the hunting devil.
But with visions of antlers bigger,
Releasing my finger from the trigger,
I return to a bigger buck level.

Give this stag a year, maybe two,
Let Nature test him tried and true,
I vision crossin' paths in years to come.
The unknowns providin' the magic,
Life's blazin' glory both joyous and tragic,
I know meetin' him again slim to none.

Thoughts stung by bee buzzin' ATVs,
Road riding thugs, hunter wannabes,
Kirb scolds them for chasin', not stalkin'.
Openin' morn near total ruin,
Our tempers steamin' and stewin',
We retreat to the Hole for some mind healin'.

I ridgin' high, Kirb rimmin' below,
A bobcat stalkin' me crouchin' low,
Countless deer spooky and scattered.
Back to camp for bitchin' and nappin',
Sharing concerns in the order they happened,
Blaming Munk's hunters for our chance shattered.

But it all is just a bad dream,
As we settle into daily routines,
Makin' plans wearing our big buck faces.
We let Nature do our healin',
Fillin' our souls with Her fall season feelins',
Huntin' the mountain for buck deer traces.

Pigeon-toed bear tracks cover the mountain,
I detect love moans of porcupines porkin',
A marvel leaving me quite perplexed.
Twas quite a sight to hear and see,
Them makin' love so carefully,
Bringin' meanin' to safe and careful sex.

A midnite deer mouse in tent stealin',
Bette Davis eyes in my light revealin',
Quickly flees when Kirb loudly farts.
Hiding in kindling tinder,
Kirb chasin' right behind her,
Throwin' boots til out the door it darts.

Kirb awakens moanin' every morn,
Lookin' ragged and forlorn,
Combing his hair asking, "Is my part straight?"
Morning hunt in vain, deer fleeing amuck,
After lunch I ponder, Kirk sleeps in hammock.
The rituals of huntin' dawn til dusky late.

Alas, we discover huntin' is livin',
Our mountain keeps on givin',
Days soarin' like bee buzzin' teal.
A lunch with Marous' eatin' their chili,
Colon blow fuel feelin' good in our belly,
We discuss huntin' big bucks with little boy zeal.

We miss ole Tim and young Keenan,
Casualties of switching to rifle deer season,
We discuss next year and getting back together.
Puttin' thought into our huntin' decisions,
Playing odds to increase precison,
Knowin' success also depends on luck and weather.

Fall aspen colors a sight to remember,
High winds cause the trees to surrender,
Their gilded leaves reigning colored sensations.
Stair stepping rocky ridges,
Stalkin' timber and snowberry hedges,
Deer movin' through in hurried migration.

Crisp mornin's of frantic bulls ruttin',
Hormone driven buglin', herdin', and struttin',
Welcome distraction to our huntin' seclusion.
Small bucks, does and fawns abound.
Bone-headed mossbacks nowhere to be found,
The big boys seemingly no more than a delusion.

Oh big stag how close, how distant?
We challenge the mountain's resistance,
Testing our hearts, our soul, our vigor.
Kirb says we must count 999 plus one
Before our searchin' is done,
The joy found lettin' the little guys grow bigger.

Old tracks and scrapes our clues,
Spoor not making big buck stew,
We cannot turn what was into what is.
It is the chase we cherish and savor,
Facing odds not in our favor,
I admit we might as well be hunting griz.

Alas! I spy a heavily racked deer,
On Munk's ridge browsing quite near,
I clearly see the pearls on antler base.
A few inches shy of thirty,
Stout antlers make him purty,
No brows, short tines, I choose to let him pass.

Season ends with fifty plus buck sightings,
Not surrendering but goin' down fighting,
I return to my Idaho home smiling widely.
Even now making plans for returning,
Next year with my big buck face yearning,
For time hunting with my best friend, KIRB SNIDELY!

**SHP 9/16/2007**

# HINDSIGHT

*"A good hunter's way of hunting is a hard job which demands much from man: he must keep himself fit, face extreme fatigues, accept danger. It involves a complete code of ethics of the most distinguishable design: the hunter who accepts the sporting code of ethics keeps his commandments in the greatest solitude, with no witnesses or audience other than the sharp peaks of the mountain, the roaming cloud, the stern oak, the trembling juniper, and the passing animal."*
Josè Ortega y Gasset, Meditations on Hunting (Belgrade, Mont: Wilderness Adventures Press, 1995), 42

Because many of my tales personify those violating wildlife law, the reader may sense the hunting and fishing majority are deviously bad. Nothing could be further from the truth! Playing the hunting and fishing games on both sides of the fence as an avid outdoorsmen and retired wildlife officer, my endorsement of hunting and fishing remains steadfastly strong. As a participant, I personally experience the unquestionable social, mental, emotional, recreational, and spiritual benefits these sports provide. Moral, ethical, and legal hunters and fishermen reign supreme as mainstream members of the time-honored corps of outdoor sportsmen and women. Their positive influence on wildlife law enforcement, scribed throughout my chronicles, details abundant wildlife crimes exposed and finalized because of information provided by the outdoor good. Corrupt human behavior, intertwined throughout most human activities, is the nature of mankind's beast. Misbehavior amongst the hunting and fishing ranks will always be there. The good news is outdoor misbehavior is facing mounting opposition within the ranks of modern-day sportsmen and women, as well as concerned non-participants. Monies generated by license fees of sportsmen and women funds, not general taxes, are utilized for policing their ranks utilizing professionally trained state and federal officers to capture and convict outdoor miscreants. This unselfish demand for vigorous wildlife law enforcement by the majority good energizes wildlife officers to relentlessly pursue and capture the outdoors bad, creating interesting story lines of human beings being human scribed throughout my writings.

But this I know. As sportsmen numbers decline, especially hunters, continued acceptance by an increasing non-hunting public will ultimately determine the sports future. Societal values evolve, and more people are questioning whether hunting has a place in modern day society. (Mis) perceptions of recreational hunting, wildlife biology and management, and deprivation of time spent in the natural world, distorts the overall integrity and validity of the hunting and fishing sports. Modern day hunting is a privilege that can easily be restricted or banished when the nonhunting majority deems it as unethical, unsportsmanlike behavior. Trapping struck out swinging in many states as voters cried foul and eliminated it with emotionally driven voter initiatives despite scientific based strategies for sustainably harvesting furbearing beasts. Nineteenth century North American trappers, utilizing steel leghold traps for beaver and other furbearing animals, essentially carved the way for exploration and settlement of the west. But it should come as no surprise modern-day citizenry declared leg-hold trapping inhumane. While hunting currently remains on relatively solid ground, signs of instability are evident as formally organized and emotionally charged groups against it strive to influence the majority populace who do not hunt.

The answer is rhetorically simple yet influentially complicated. Seasoned hunters must tenaciously prioritize recruiting and mentoring anyone, young or old, expressing interest in hunting and/or fishing. Safeguarding the future of our sports requires publicly promoting our long history of providing immeasurable financial, manpower, and background support for wildlife conservation while actively displaying hunters and fishermen are ethical, law abiding participants carrying a candid intolerance for wildlife crimes both in and out of the field.

Ironically, during these writings, my then eleven-year-old grandson Laner aroused the tremendous importance of effectively conveying my deep-rooted passion and sanction for hunting. Admiring the iridescent plumage of a mixed brace of mallards and pintails his father and I were field dressing after a successful day of duck hunting Laner, out of the blue, inquired, "Why did these ducks have to die?" *What?* We had zealously enjoyed the wrath of a perfect duck day amidst blizzarding cold winds blowing flurries of ducks into our decoys. Heavily leafed with natural predatory instincts from both sides of his family tree, Laner was questioning the whysdom of hunting; the very heartfelt queries I pondered as a boy so many years ago! And now, my link to immortality stood before me appreciating the striking differences between drakes and hens from beak to feet, contemplating how the breath of life made these stunning wild beasts greater than the sum of their lifeless parts; their eyes life glow smitten by death's quashing ire. Striking a heartfelt chord through a looming cloud of responsibility, I stumbled through an answer resembling something like this:

"Yes Lane, these ducks are beautiful! Today we saw hundreds, maybe even thousands of ducks, geese, and swans. We harvested ten leaving plenty to nest and multiply for next year. Such abundance is a by-product of good waterfowl habitat and population management, most of which is paid for by our hunting and fishing license and water-fowl stamp dollars. We had grand time hunting and will take great pleasure in grilling and eating them. *Blah, blah, blah…*"

Understanding the science of available population surplus

supporting sustainable harvest of game species, my son and I were quite aware population biology falls far short of justifying what drives us to hunt and kill the very beasts we greatly treasure. Toiling through the angst of death through the eyes of a young adult, is a perceivable immersion into the heart-rending certainties and uncertainties of life's mortality. During his youthful time of emotional and spiritual development, it was our responsibility to fervently reveal how exercising our natural beast as a predator, experiencing the electrifying exhilaration of harvest in a charge of sensory overload, nurtures our mind, body, and soul while honoring the dignity of the ducks by following established laws and our personal moral codes, a formidable challenge indeed!

Knowing I had grossly undershot the target of defending killing wild ducks, I experienced the hollow realization that I, a lifetime hunter and retired wildlife professional, was unacceptably prepared to answer such a vitally important question. My answer to the lad's words haunt me to this day. Over time, however, his father and I began understanding his questions could not be answered in a few short statements. Our responsibilities required a tremendous amount of persistent mentoring through his formative hunting and fishing years. Luckily 'Grandfather' time was on my side and, as we provided down-to-earth answers to his voluminous questions, we proudly watched Laner evolve into an ethical, law abiding, and skilled huntsman-conservationist. Hunting and fishing, survival instincts mysteriously packaged into his genetic wiring, encompassed not only DNA but also the guidance proffered by his father and I. Effectively blending Nature with Nurture, we successfully taught, by our words and actions, how civilized hunting and fishing, intertwined with written laws and moral codes, maintains a measure of order in the wild chaos of the outdoor sports, decidedly acceptable by the public majority.

And so, once again there I was, on a brusquely cold late fall Idaho day, hunting turkey with Laner's sister, Kylie. After several failed attempts spot and stalking several morning flocks, we took a warming, sundrenched nap against a haystack waiting for the afternoon feeding migration towards their roost tree. Hidden in a small, brushy cottonwood drainage and quietly calling every fifteen minutes, we witnessed a parade of hens, poults, and jakes stagger past our lair less than twenty yards away. Kylie, snugged tightly in my lap, remained cool, picked out a single hen and calmly harvested her first ever wild game. PRICELESS!

My point here is hunters and fishermen must take a stand to ensure we are not the last link in time-honored chain of their outdoor sports. We must pass on our legacy to anyone displaying an interest, especially our youth! I am extremely proud to be a paying member and advocate of this an elite corps of warriors driven to conserve our nations wildlife resources. As one who cannot live without the wild, hunting and fishing fulfills an innate, primal crave where I become one with nature, a top of the food chain predator experiencing an innate completeness only felt a hunter or fisherman. Hunting and fishing strengthen my reverence for the wild by providing a higher level of understanding of and respect for Nature's complex and never to be fully understood way of sustaining life through death.

I will continue purchasing licenses, maintaining my memberships in conservation organizations, and volunteering in wildlife habitat and youth educational projects. I will convey my heartfelt benevolence for the wild as a hunter, a fisherman, a naturalist, and spectator to my grandchildren, whether they or not they hunt or fish, assuming my role as their advisor, educator, and philosopher. I will graciously mentor them in the legalities, moral codes, and skills necessary for successful harvest, preparing meat for the table and becoming a responsible, modern day outdoor conservationist. I have yet found a child who was disinterested in answering the call of the wilds. If cultivated, the wild is a natural part of their being, an innate gift of their evolutionary past and, in my opinion, integral to their overall development and well-being. That, my friend, will serve as my legacy for championing North American hunters and fishermen as indispensable conservationists for our nations' wildlife resources!

*"When a father gives to his son, both laugh. When his son gives to his father, both cry."*
William Shakespeare

IF MY TALES HAVE ENTERTAINED AND STIMULATED YOUR THOUGHTS AND IF YOU ARE INTERESTED IN A CONTINUED BLEND OF ADVENTUROUS INTERACTIONS BETWEEN HUNTERS, FISHERMEN, WILD BEASTS AND WILDLIFE OFFICERS, PLUS AN IN DEPTH VIEW OF HUNTING WISDOM, UNEARTHING MY SECOND CACHE OF THE BULL PEN CHRONICLES MAY PROVE EVEN MORE THOUGHT-PROVOKING.

# ABOUT THE AUTHOR

Throughout his boyhood, Stephen H. Porter, an Ohio native, was instinctively mesmerized by the relatively domesticated wilds of the Buckeye State's farmlands. As a teenager, .22 rifle in hand, Steve spent much of his idle time wandering alone in 'his wilderness' as an explorer, a shooter of pesky woodchucks, a novice naturalist, and a beginning hunter. Fervently reading escapades of western outdoorsmen and, as a high school senior, discovering opportunities for college degrees in wildlife biology, Steve's restless spirit was lured westward, primarily an excuse to get away and explore new territory. Completing his Bachelor of Science degree in Wildlife Biology at Utah State University while working summer jobs with the U.S. Forest Service and the Utah Division of Wildlife as a range inventory techni-cian, Steve realized the vast open space of the Rocky Mountain west offered his opportunity to evolve into what he was meant to be.

Permanent resource management jobs scarce in the early 70's, Steve accepted a permanent job with the U.S. Fish and Wildlife Service in Raleigh, North Carolina. After a year, the overwhelming desire to return west combined with a heavy dose of fate, luck, chance, plus his formidable personal perseverance, Steve chased down his vision quest and secured an incredibly competitive position as a Wildlife Conservation Officer trainee with the Colorado Division of Wildlife in 1972.

Following a year of intensive classroom and field training, Steve was granted a permanent position in North Park, Colorado as a Wildlife Conservation Officer. Purposely selecting this remote, sparsely populated area for its magnificent wildlife resource, it was the uniquely individualistic mountain culture of loggers, miners, ranchers, and an ever-increasing number of outdoor recreationists that held him and his family there for over two decades. With his gracious wife Betsy, they raised their son Marc and daughter Anne while Steve passionately worked for Colorado's wildlife resource in the massive, northern mountain park the Native Americans called the 'Bull Pen'; an avocation defining him to this very day.

Switching gears, Steve accepted wildlife biologist positions to administer and coordinate Colorado's Habitat Partnership and Game Damage Programs, employing his long-term expertise of collaboratively working with landowners, agency representatives and sportsmen; a two-prong approach for resolving statewide big game conflicts; bear and mountain lion livestock predation, damage to agricultural crops, rangeland habitat improvement projects, and specialized hunts directed at reducing big game/livestock competition.

These assorted essays, poems, and personal adventures represent the time stamped adventures of a young lad answering the call of the wild throughout his career in wildlife law enforcement and management and into his retirement. His writings are a product of the 2020 Coronavirus Pandemic, proffering incalculable time to finalize more tales than he ever envisioned.

Written as memoirs for family and friends, his chronicles may also provide reading enjoyment for hunters, fishermen, and all others interested in the interactions of human beasts interacting with those of the wilds.

Retiring from the Colorado Division of Wildlife in 2003, Steve devotes his time to family and friends, hunting, fishing, wandering the wilds and, of course, tell-taling stories of past adventures. That my friend, is the greatest gift any elderly man could hope for.

# ACKNOWLEDGMENTS

I extend a humble gratitude to North America's hunters and fishermen who, beginning in the 1860's, instigated wildlife conservation movements ultimately evolving into what is now regarded as the world's most successful model for safeguarding wildlife populations, The North American Model of Wildlife Conservation. Founded on the principle's wildlife populations belong to all citizens and must be managed at sustainable population levels, the Model dictates wildlife can be harvested only by legal and ethical means for food, fur, in self-defense, or for the protection of property. Hunters and fishermen, the founding fathers of North American conservation, remain the primary funding source for the management of our diverse wildlife heritage. Through purchases of licenses, permits, duck stamps, taxes on firearms, ammunition, archery equipment, and tireless support of conservation organizations dedicated to the restoration and protection of all wildlife species and their habitats, hunters and fishermen continue providing the primary funding, manpower, and background support for wildlife conservation. This time-honored legacy benefits all cherishing our nation's richly diverse wildlife resources, whether they hunt or fish. These truths, largely unknown by the public mass, mandates modern day hunters and fishermen actively promote themselves as the front-line champions for all wildlife. **Thank you, hunters and fishermen!**

Throughout my tales you will discover the quote, "There are a million stories in the naked woods", a spinoff from the late 50's early 60's television crime drama, The Naked City, I engagingly watched so many years ago! Truth be told, this 'million' is a mere fraction of the stories crafted annually by the 47 million plus hunters journeying into their version of the brazenly 'naked' wilds. My dual avocations as a wildlife officer and an active outdoorsman provided a windfall of adventurous tales from both perspectives. Scribbling my encounters with man and beast began during my college days continue to this day. However, (finally) attempting to articulate this overabundance of disorganized hard scrabble into legible stories, clarified my need for a talented editor. Enter Kerrie Flanagan. Longtime friend, successful writer, and writing consultant, Kerrie gently yet professionally sharpened my writing skills to a point where I began crafting rough drafts into coherent tales. While the inconceivable time I expended researching, contemplating, outlining, writing, and re-writing these chronicles boggles my mind, the immense down time provided by the COVID-19 Pandemic generated more material than I ever envisioned. With Kerrie's unrelenting guidance from editing through publication, we made it happen. Far from considering myself a proficient author, Kerrie challenged me to keep on, keepin' on! I am certainly a better writer today than when I began. **Thank you, Kerrie!**

Lyrics of favored songs and quotations of past philosophers and poets scattered throughout my tales highlight critical themes needing emphasis and interpretation. **Thank you masters of the pen!**

I end with a heartfelt thanks to family, **Betsy, Marc, and Anne, and to all my friends** who suffered the wrath of a zealously passionate warden spending too much time stalking the wilds safeguarding the wild beasts for the common good. But as the 19th century mountain men declared,

*"It was a good job to take!"*

www.ingramcontent.com/pod-product-compliance
Lightning Source LLC
Chambersburg PA
CBHW031545260326
41914CB00002B/280